TEACHER'S BOOK

ARSIDE

PRE-INTERMEDIATE

OUTCOMES

Australia • Brazil • Japan • Korea • Mexico • Singapore • Spain • United Kingdom • United States

Outcomes *Pre-Intermediate Teacher's Book*
Barbara Garside

Publisher: Jason Mann
Senior Commissioning Editor: John Waterman
Development Editor: Heidi North
Product Manager: Ruth McAleavey
Content Project Editor: Amy Smith
Manufacturing Team Lead: Paul Herbert
Cover and text designer: Studio April
Compositor: Q2AMedia

ISBN: 978-1-111-05412-0

Heinle, Cengage Learning EMEA
Cheriton House, North Way, Andover, Hampshire
SP10 5BE United Kingdom

Cengage Learning is a leading provider of customised learning solutions with office locations around the globe, including Singapore, the United Kingdom, Australia, Mexico, Brazil and Japan. Locate our local office at **international.cengage.com/region**

Cengage Learning products are represented in Canada by Nelson Education Ltd.

Visit Heinle online at **elt.heinle.com**
Visit our corporate website at **cengage.com**

Printed in Singapore
1 2 3 4 5 6 7 8 9 10 – 15 14 13 12 11

CONTENTS

INTRODUCTION

WHAT'S IN *OUTCOMES* STUDENT'S BOOK?

16 units based round common topics Each unit has three interlinked 'lessons' of 50–90 minutes. The unit contents give clear practical outcomes. The first lesson teaches language leading to *Conversation Practice*. The second and third spreads develop reading or listening and teach more grammar and vocabulary connected with the topic.

8 writing units The two-page writing units on pp. 120–135 teach different types of writing for everyday life and exams. Each has a model text, *Grammar* or *Vocabulary*, *Keywords for writing* and *Practice*.

4 review units Each review has a learner training discussion, two pages of games, tasks and pronunciation exercises to revise language and then a two-page test including a listening exercise.

Grammar Thirty-five points of grammar are covered. Each *Grammar* section links to the previous text. An explanation or guided questions teach meaning. Exercises give controlled and freer practice. There's a link to the grammar reference if you need extra help.

Grammar reference This is on pp. 136–155 at the back of the book. Each section has an expanded explanation, further natural examples of usage and extra controlled practice exercises with a glossary.

Language patterns This is a short translation exercise into the student's own language and back into English. It draws attention to other aspects of syntax and grammar based on a pattern seen in a text.

Vocabulary Vocabulary is carefully chosen to enable students to talk about the topic in the context of English as a lingua franca. Tasks generally move from meaning, to contextualised usage, to personalised practice. Other sections focus on word-building.

***Outcomes* Vocabulary Builder (OVB)** The separate booklet allows students to look up the meaning of new language which is key to learn, offers several examples of collocations and usage plus a page of revision practice.

Native speaker English Draws attention to common words or phrases that fluent speakers use, which students may hear or want to learn.

Keywords Most writing units have a focus on linking words and patterns, which help develop fluent, coherent writing. There's a link to the text, a short explanation and practice exercises.

Developing conversations The sections teach typical questions, responses and patterns common to conversation. An explanation clarifies the focus while exercises give controlled practice.

Conversation practice A task lets students practise social and practical conversations based on their own experience or through role-play.

Speaking These sections give students the chance to exchange ideas. The final speaking task in each unit is a longer task that draws the language and / or the themes of the unit together.

Listening These sections are introduced with a short description of the context. There is usually a pre-listening speaking task to generate interest or predict content, followed by tasks to guide students to understand the text and focus on vocabulary.

Reading These sections are introduced with a short description of the context. There is usually a pre-reading speaking task to generate interest or predict content, followed by tasks to guide students to understand the text and focus on vocabulary.

WHAT'S IN *OUTCOMES* TEACHER'S BOOK?

The Teacher's book is organised into three sections: Teacher's notes, Writing lessons and Communication activities. **TEACHER'S NOTES** provide guidance on how to use the 16 units and four **REVIEWS** in the Student's book. Each unit opens with a brief **UNIT OVERVIEW** that allows you to understand the main elements of the lesson very quickly.

Under the same headings as in the Student's book, the notes give clear aims and simple steps to provide a very easy path through the material. Answer boxes and audioscripts embedded in the notes ensure you have everything you need at your fingertips. Suggestions throughout the notes help you with ways to set up activities, check and clarify meaning, monitor, conduct feedback, etc. The icon indicates where you might want to use a **Communication Activity** (see next page). In addition, there's help through four mini features.

The **TIP** feature offers ideas on things such as:

- other ways to check meaning;
- how to adapt material for different groups such as mono- or multilingual classes;
- bringing extra material into lessons.

The **NOTE** feature gives bite-size information about:
- places and people in the text;
- how cultures can differ.

The **ALTERNATIVELY** feature provides:
- a different way to stage an activity than the one suggested in the Student's book;
- ideas on how to make an activity more or less challenging.

The **OPTIONAL ACTIVITY** suggests:
- ways to extend an activity if students would benefit from more work.

The **WRITING LESSONS** section opens with a two-page introduction on teaching writing. It explains the approach to writing and suggests ways you can provide feedback to students. The introduction is followed by **Teacher's notes** and the answer key for the eight writing lessons.

The **Communication activities** section contains simple instructions on how to use the 32 photocopiable activities. The activities are designed to revise key grammar and vocabulary from the Student's book in a fun and varied way. There are quizzes, word puzzles, questionnaires, games, information gaps and short role-plays. Each unit has two activities calculated to take 10–15 minutes of class time.

Other *Outcomes* components

***Outcomes* Workbook** The ***Outcomes* Workbook** thoroughly revises all the language areas that are in the Student's book. Each unit also has:
- a listening and a reading with tasks based on topics loosely connected to the theme of the unit and providing interest and extra challenges to students
- **Developing writing** that focuses on types of text students might write in their academic, professional and personal lives and further work on relevant language.

The ***Outcomes* Workbook** also comes with:
- **Audio CD** of recordings of the listening and reading texts.
- **Answer key** and **Audioscript** to aid self-study.

***Outcomes* Exam*View*®** Writing tests to check your students' progress takes a lot of time and work but the **Exam*View*®** CD allows you to create tests and exams in as little as five minutes. What's more:
- all the tests are closely based on the Student's book.
- the software also generates the answer key.
- it provides a variety of exercise types (True / False, Multiple Choice, Yes / No, Matching, Short answer, etc.)
- tests can be printed, computer-based, or on the Internet.
- you can easily edit the questions and add your own.
- you can save all tests for another time.
- it's easy to reorder questions to avoid cheating.

MyOutcomes* online resource** Every copy of the *Outcomes* Student's Book has a unique code at the front of the book which provides access to ***MyOutcomes online resource where students will find additional work on all the elements of the Student's book. There are:
- over 230 activities practising the grammar, vocabulary, pronunciation and conversations in the 16 units.
- additional listening, reading and speaking practice.
- reviews every four units to test students' progress.

Teachers can also use the online resource if they apply for an access code. Go to **myelt.heinle.com** and request a MyELT instructor account. This will allow you to set specific work for all your students and then receive their results. You can then store these results through the **Grade book**, so both you and your students have a record of their marks and progress.

OUTCOMES PRE-INTERMEDIATE

In this introduction we try to answer these questions:
What are the goals of language students?
What is key language for students at Pre-Intermediate?
What is key for teachers to help them teach?

Key goals

The Common European Framework of reference (CEF) states that language learning and teaching overall goals should be:
1.1 to deal with the business of everyday life in another country, and to help foreigners staying in their own country to do so;
1.2 to exchange information and ideas with young people and adults who speak a different language and to communicate their thoughts and feelings to them;
1.3 to achieve a wider and deeper understanding of the way of life and forms of thought of other peoples and of their cultural heritage.
(Council of Europe, 2001, p. 3)

These ideas underpin everything we do in the *Outcomes* series. At Pre-Intermediate, we look at can-do statements for A2 level as a guide to what students might want to achieve.

Business of everyday life You can see the communicative areas that are dealt with in the *how to* sections of the contents and title strip that heads each unit. *Outcomes* has a strong practical thread. For example, students at Pre-Intermediate learn the grammar and vocabulary to:
- describe and get information about places to stay pp. 76–77
- understand menus, order and pay in restaurants pp. 24–25

For many students passing exams is also the business of everyday life, which is why *Outcomes* has a **Grammar reference** with exercises on all the grammar you'd expect. Similarly, **Writing** deals with both practical types of writing (postcards pp. 130–131) and exam-type writing (expressing opinions pp. 122–123).

Communicating thoughts and feelings Practicalities are important, but just as important, and perhaps more motivating, is the ability to communicate in a way which reflects your personality, feelings and opinions. That's why most of the **Developing conversations** and **Conversation practice** work towards practising typical conversations we have to establish and maintain friendships:

- making and responding to compliments pp. 14–15
- asking for permission pp. 46–47

This is also why we constantly give students the chance to exchange their ideas, through **Speaking**, practice activities in **Vocabulary** and **Grammar**, the lead-ins to **Reading** and **Listening** and discussions about the texts.

Understanding other cultures Students will best understand other cultures by talking with other students, which the various speaking activities in *Outcomes* always encourage. However, many classrooms may not have people from a large mix of backgrounds, which is why we use texts with international contexts and reflecting other cultures throughout the world – including Britain. Students come to realise they share many of the same desires and concerns! Among other things, you'll read and hear about:

- the film industry in Nigeria pp. 96–97
- sports around the world pp. 38–39

Native speaker notes also draw attention to ways fluent speakers express themselves, which may be different to the neutral international language that we generally present.

Key language

There were five guides to the input at Pre-Intermediate level – the communicative outcomes (outlined in *Outcomes Goals*), the frequency of words, 'naturalness' of usage, student autonomy and teacher-student expectations or interest.

For example, to 'describe people you know' (pp. 8–9) students need to know a number of core adjectives which are presented and practised in **Vocabulary**. The practice gets them to think of language which might go with these words and the **OVB** provides further help in terms of collocations. **Grammar** looks at ways to describe similarities and contrasts and provides a fuller context for the vocabulary. **Language patterns** draws attention to the grammar around the word *from*. **Listening** then gives a model conversation. **Developing conversations** teaches expressions to respond naturally. **Pronunciation** is based on the phrases students have learnt.

This is typical of the way language input is focused on helping students achieve the stated communicative outcome, but not all language learning can be developed in this way. A lot of vocabulary may be very frequent but not specific to any one topic (e.g. issue, unlike, refer). The language highlighted through texts is largely of this nature. The exercises and **OVB** then show a range of natural collocations. Similarly, some grammar may not be fundamental to a conversation in the way we saw with 'describing people you know'. Here, we make the choice based on what students and teachers expect to be covered at this level or have tested in exams. This may be 'exam grammar', but we try to give natural sounding examples.

Input is also decided on the basis that students need to learn outside the classroom as well. The *word families* strand in **Vocabulary**, the **OVB** language boxes and **Reading** shows students how words are formed. This helps them recognise and learn new words in their own studies. The same motives underlie **Language patterns**, but with a focus on grammar.

Finally, students and non-native speaker teachers often express an interest in colloquial language and idioms. The **Native speaker note** provides explanations and examples of this in contrast to the normal input which can be freely used and understood in contexts where English is a lingua franca.

Key to learn

There are many ways to learn but it seems there are a few essentials:

- Students need to notice.
- Students need to understand.
- Students need to practise – spoken, written, receptive.
- Students need to make mistakes.
- Students need to repeat these steps a lot.

Noticing and understanding Obviously the exercises in **Grammar** and **Vocabulary** encourage students to notice and understand. Visuals and clear explanations of vocabulary and examples of collocations in the **OVB** reinforce meaning. The **Language patterns** exercise trains students to notice and consider how English compares with their own language.

Practice Students always have chance to practise language. This goes from very controlled 'remember and test' and gap-fills to freer role-play and personalised speaking. **Communication activities** in this Teacher's book provide more practice.

Making mistakes Not all teaching and input can or should be provided by the coursebook. We all know from experience and research that people learn new language when they are struggling to express something and the 'correct' or better word is given. This is also why we have lots of speaking activities. They are not just opportunities for students to practise what they know; they are chances for them to try to say something new, stretch themselves and make mistakes, which you can then correct.

Repetition Seeing a word once is not enough! Some say you need to see and understand vocabulary ten times before you have learnt to use it! Maybe grammar takes even longer. Recycling and Revision is therefore a key part of the design of *Outcomes*. For example, the **OVB**, **Workbook** and **ExamView®** allow unit-by-unit revision, while **Review** after every four units ensures further revision at a later date.

With grammar, students can revise after the class by using the **Grammar reference** and exercises, the **Workbook** or the ***MyOutcomes***. Grammar structures are often looked at in several contexts over the course and at various levels. **Review** units test grammar and you can also create tests with **Exam*View*®**.

Apart from this revision we try to repeatedly re-use language from **Vocabulary** in **Listening and Reading**; in **Grammar** and **Grammar Reference**; in **Developing conversations**; in workbook texts; in exercises and texts in other units of the Student's book, and even in other levels of the series. And as we have seen, **Speaking** and **Conversation practice** allow students to re-use language they've learnt.

In terms of speaking, research suggests that students can improve performance with repetition. Within the first two pages of each unit there are often several opportunities to have conversations around the same topic, as we saw with 'describing people you know' through **Vocabulary** or **Grammar** practice, **Developing conversations** and **Conversation practice**. The **Review** units also encourage students to look back and repeat speaking tasks. There are also more ideas about revision in the **Teacher's notes**.

Key TO TEACH

Most teachers need or want material that:

- is quick and easy to prepare
- caters for mixed level classes
- motivates students.

Quick and easy to prepare A coursebook is easy to use when the relation between input and outcomes is clear and we hope you already see that is the case with *Outcomes*. However, other aspects of the design should help you just pick up the book and teach:

- a limited number of sections appear in all units
- a regular structure to the units
- a variety of familiar tasks
- double-pages can exist as unique lessons but six-page units allow you to easily continue
- straightforward rubrics in Student's book fully explain tasks
- **Grammar** and **Vocabulary** have clear links to texts
- **OVB** follows the spreads of the book so you and students can easily look up words in class.

Mixed level classes Students often start at different levels within a class and so the input in *Outcomes* Pre-Intermediate revises and extends language encountered at Elementary. However, the exercises and design of *Outcomes* also works for multi-level classes.

- **OVB** The *Outcomes* Vocabulary Builder allows weaker students to easily look up new words, before, during and after class, because it follows the spreads of the book. Stronger students benefit from the **OVB** because it gives extra input through collocation lists, extra language boxes and practice exercises.
- **Grammar** The short explanations help weaker students with exercises in the units. The grammar reference helps weaker students with more examples, but stronger students will like the extra information that is always given.
- **Easy to difficult** Whether it is grammar or vocabulary, reading or listening, we usually move from easier to more difficult tasks in each section. For example, reading texts often allow language to be pre-taught, the first tasks are then based on general understanding, and further tasks are more detailed.
- **Translation** Several exercises including **Language Patterns** encourage students to translate. Translation is particularly important for weaker students who benefit from the support of their mother tongue and bilingual dictionaries. In monolingual classes especially, it allows stronger students to help others in the class by providing the translations.
- **Test and remember** Tasks like this are comforting for weaker students, but you can also make them more challenging for stronger students by asking them to remember more.
- **Native speaker notes** and **Language patterns** These offer extra input for stronger students and classes. You might consider dropping them for weaker classes.
- **Teacher's notes** There are loads more ideas for dealing with multi-level classes in this book – particularly through the **Tip** and **Alternatively** features.

Motivating students As a teacher motivating students will be a major part of your job; however, we know a coursebook can often work against student motivation by having irrelevant or boring content, unclear, unrealistic or unfulfilled outcomes or simply by a dull design. *Outcomes* helps you motivate students by having:

- outcomes matching students' wants and needs
- a clear menu of input and outcomes at the start of each unit
- input and tasks that carefully match those outcomes
- a manageable number of keywords to learn in the **OVB**
- texts based on authentic sources that we think you'll find by turns informative, funny, even moving
- a range of speaking tasks that allow for play, humour and gossip, as well as serious discussion
- a fresh design with bright, interesting illustration

The CEF and Level There is not a direct correlation between publishers' levels and the CEF. Completing Pre-intermediate will not mean a student has reached B1 but is progressing towards that goal. That's because the CEF descriptions of level or the ALTE can-do statements do *not* exactly describe content, but describe someone's *performance* in a language. We have used can-do statements from the B1 level at Pre-intermediate as a guide to what tasks and outcomes students want to progress towards. However, at this level students' performance in *doing* any of the speaking, reading, listening or writing tasks may be assessed using CEF scales as being A2 (+), B1 (–). If students are regularly outside the range of A2 (+), B1 (–), they are probably at the wrong level for this material.

01 FAMILY AND FRIENDS

UNIT OVERVIEW

The main aims of this unit are to learn **how to ask and respond to common questions, describe people** and **talk about how often you do things**. Students are also introduced to the idea of **recognising collocations**. The main grammar aims are the **present simple** tense to talk about habits and permanent states, and expressions of **similarity and contrast**.

Next class Make photocopies of **1A** p. 128.

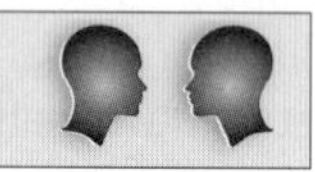

VOCABULARY People you know

Aim

To revise nouns used for people and lead in to *Listening*.

Step 1 Ask students to look at the words in A and put them into three categories: male; female or either. They could do this in pairs or individually, then check in pairs. Check with the whole group. Model, drill and ask concept questions where necessary. With the female / male words, elicit their male / female counterparts.

Answers

Male	Female	Either
brother	actress	cousin
businessman	aunt	colleague
dad	housewife	flatmate
uncle	gran	friend
waiter	sister	teenager
boyfriend		nurse
		lawyer
		retired
		neighbour

Answers for M/F equivalents

Brother–sister; businessman–businesswoman; dad–mum; uncle–aunt; waiter–waitress; boyfriend–girlfriend; actress–actor; housewife–house-husband; gran–gramp (granny–grandad, grandma–grandpa)

Step 2 Put students in pairs and ask them to tell each other about six friends or family members, as in the example in exercise B. Model by telling students about two or three people in your life first. Conduct feedback by asking a few students who their partners told them about.

Step 3 Put students in new pairs or threes and ask them to look at the adjectives in C and try to help each other with meanings. If they have problems, ask them to look at the *Vocabulary Builder* on pp. 2–3. Ask them to discuss the questions in C. Conduct brief feedback.

Step 4 Ask students to choose individually eight words from this part of the unit which were new or not very familiar to them (as in D). Ask them to write them in their vocabulary books with a translation in their own language. Or, if you prefer not to use translation, ask them to write a definition, give an example or draw a picture. Put them in pairs to compare their word lists and help each other with new words.

LISTENING

Aim

To give practice in listening for gist and specific information and to provide a context for the grammar (question formation).

Step 1 Tell students they are going to hear a conversation between two friends, Laura and Maya. Ask them to look at the photo as they listen and try to identify the people in the photo. Play the recording. Check in pairs then check with the whole group.

Answers

Anna from Poland, Maya's brother.

1.1

L = Laura M = Maya

L: Maya
M: Hi Laura. Sorry I'm a bit late.
L: That's OK.
M: How long have you been here?
L: Oh, not long. Ten minutes.
M: Sorry. The traffic was bad.
L: Are you looking for something?
M: Another chair. Oh ... there's one.
L: So who else is coming?
M: My friend Anna from Poland.
L: Oh yeah? How do you know her?
M: I met her on an exchange trip.
L: When did you do that?
M: Year 10 at school. Here. I've got a picture of her on my mobile. She's the girl in the middle.
L: Oh, wow! She's very pretty.

M: Yeah.
L: So is she just visiting?
M: No, she's studying here. She's really clever as well as being pretty and she's good at sport! Some people are so lucky!
L: Yeah. So who's the guy? Is that her boyfriend?
M: No! That's my brother!
L: Really? You don't look very similar.
M: I know. He's quite dark – but look at the nose and mouth.
L: Let me see. Yeah, I guess. So what does he do?
M: He's a nurse. He lives in the States.
L: Really? Why did he go there?
M: He's married and his wife's from there.
L: Really? How old is he?
M: 24.
L: OK. That's quite young.
M: I guess.
L: Do you get on well?
M: Yes, we're quite close. He's very caring – and generous too. Obviously, I don't see him very often now. Actually, the last time I saw him was when I took this photo. It was over a year ago, but we email and talk on the phone quite a lot.
L: Do you have any other brothers or sisters?
M: Yeah – a younger sister.
L: Is that the other girl in the picture?
M: No, she's a friend from my Spanish class.
A: Maya!
M: Anna! How are you? We saved you a seat. Anna – I don't think you know my friend Laura. She's a friend from work. Laura this is Anna.
A: Nice to meet you.
L: Hi – I've heard a lot about you.

Step 2 Put students in pairs. Ask them to look at the questions in B and complete them by putting the correct question word / phrase at the beginning of each one. Then play the recording again for them to check.

Answers
1 How long have you been here?
2 How do you know her?
3 When did you do that?
4 Is she just visiting?
5 What does he do?
6 Why did he go there?
7 How old is he?
8 Do you get on well?

Step 3 Tell students that the answers in exercise B are wrong. In the same pairs, ask them to correct the answers. They can then look at the audioscript on page 162 to check. Check as a class (the answers are underlined in the audioscript 1.1).

LANGUAGE PATTERNS

Aim
To draw students' attention to patterns with *from* to talk about how we know someone.

Step 1 Ask students to look at the sentences in the box and notice the similarities = *from* + place.

Step 2 Ask students to translate these sentences into their own language. In monolingual classes ask students to compare their translations. In multilingual classes ask students to work in pairs and tell each other if the sentences were easy to translate and whether they were able to translate them word for word. Why / Why not?

Step 3 Ask students to cover the English translations and translate the sentences back into English using their translations. Then ask them to compare their translations in pairs against the book.

Alternatively If you prefer not to use translation, ask students to notice the pattern. Concept check any areas of difficulty and elicit a few more examples. If you have time, write the examples on the board and tick them if correct. If the sentences are wrong ask the students to correct them or correct them yourself.

GRAMMAR Question formation

Aim
To present question forms in the present simple and continuous, the past simple and present perfect simple.

Step 1 Ask students to look back at the questions in Listening B. Elicit examples of the four different tenses and check the form/word order for the question in each tense. Or write an example of a question in each tense on the board and use the examples to highlight form and elicit the name of the tense. Either ask students to read the examples in the box or read the examples out to them yourself.

Step 2 Ask students to look at A and put the words in the correct order to form questions. Check in pairs then check with the whole group.

Answers
1 Where do you live?
2 Do you know anyone in the class?
3 How long have you known him?
4 Why are you studying English?
5 Have you studied in this school before?
6 Are you enjoying the class?
7 Did you have a nice weekend?
8 What did you do?

Step 3 Ask students to listen to the next recording and pause so they can repeat each question after they hear it. Model and drill. Then get students to ask and answer the questions in open pairs.

1.2
1: Where do you live?
2: Do you know anyone in this class?
3: How long have you known him?
4: Why are you studying English?
5: Have you studied in this school before?
6: Are you enjoying the class?
7: Did you have a nice weekend?
8: What do you do?

Step 4 Put students in closed pairs and tell them to take turns asking each other the questions in B and answering. They could note down the answers and report back to the rest of the class at the end.
Direct them to the grammar reference on page 136 if they still seem unsure.

1A see Teacher's notes p. 120.

DEVELOPING CONVERSATIONS

Responding naturally

Aim
To show how we respond naturally to questions, and give practice.

Step 1 Read out the box, checking as you read. Then ask students to look at the conversation in A and cross out all the unnecessary words in the answers to make them sound more natural. Do the first example with them.

Step 2 Check in pairs then play the recording for them to check. Check with the whole group.

1.3
A: Where are you from?
B: The Czech Republic.
A: Have you got any brothers or sisters?
B: Yes. Two brothers and six sisters.
A: Are you the oldest?
B: No. I'm in the middle.
A: Do you see your grandparents much?
B: No, not much. They live in a different city.
A: Do you get on with your brother?
B: No, not really. He's quite annoying.
A: Where did you meet your girlfriend?
B: At university. We were in the same class.
A: Do you like sport?
B: No, I hate it, but I walk a lot to keep fit.

CONVERSATION PRACTICE

Aim
To give freer practice of the target language.

Step 1 Tell students they are going to have a similar conversation to the one in *Listening*. Ask them individually to draw simple pictures of three people they know, or use photos of them on their mobile phones if they have them.

Step 2 In pairs ask students to take turns telling each other about their pictures. They should start by asking *Who's that?* and continue with at least four questions about each person. Model one example with a strong student. Monitor and note down errors in target language for a correction slot at the end.

Tip With a weaker class, you might like to direct students to *Listening* B for ideas on the kind of questions to ask. Or elicit some examples of these questions and write them on the board before they start.

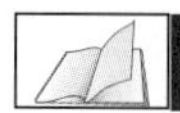
pp. 10–11

Next class Make photocopies of **1B** p. 129.
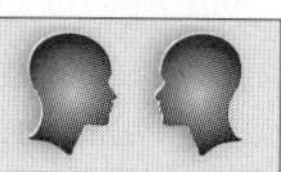

SPEAKING

Aim
To give fluency practice, to personalise and to lead in to the reading.

Step 1 Ask students individually to look at the questions in A and think about how they would answer them. They could make a few notes. Then put students in small groups to discuss their answers to the questions. Conduct brief feedback.

Tip In multilingual groups, try to mix the nationalities as far as possible.

READING

Aim
To introduce the idea of collocations (words which frequently go together to form phrases).

Step 1 Ask students what they know about The Netherlands and Japan. If possible, get students to find the countries on a map. (You could use the world map in File 6 page 157 if you don't have a map in the classroom.) Ask them to look at the pictures, identify the country and describe the pictures.

Note The Netherlands, also called Holland, is in Western Europe and is known for its liberal laws. The capital is Amsterdam and both the nationality and the language are Dutch. Japan, in East Asia, is known for its traditional values and healthy lifestyle. The capital is Tokyo and both the nationality and the language are Japanese.

Step 2 Ask students to read the article quickly, ignoring the words in bold and answer the questions in A. Check in pairs, then with the whole group.

Answers
1 Netherlands: Lots of parks and facilities; most mothers don't go out to work; not much pressure; families open and communicative; Japan: Large number of retired people; healthy diet; exercise; plenty to do
2 he eats well, keeps fit, is a happy patient person and also keeps busy

Step 3 Ask students to read the box, or read it out to them and check they understand. Elicit more examples of different types of collocation about children or home.

Step 4 Ask students to try to complete the phrases in B from memory, then look back at the words in bold in the article to check. Check in pairs then check with the whole group.

Answers
1 a recent report
2 put pressure on someone
3 liberal parents
4 cause arguments
5 spend time with someone
6 a long life
7 fresh fish
8 go swimming

Step 5 Ask students to identify which four phrases are verb + noun and which four are adjective + noun. Check in pairs then check with the whole group.

Answers
verb + noun (2, 4, 5, 8) adjective + noun (1, 3, 6, 7)

Step 6 Put students in pairs to discuss the questions in D. Conduct brief feedback.

GRAMMAR The present simple

Aim
To revise the present simple to talk about regular occurrences / habits and permanent states.

Step 1 Write the examples on the board and ask students which tense this is and how we form the affirmative including third person (*I live / She lives in Madrid*); negative (*I don't / She doesn't live in Madrid*), and questions (*Do you / Does she live in Madrid?*). Elicit some adverbs of frequency by asking students how often they do things. Then ask them to read the box and check their understanding.

Step 2 Ask students to look at the questions in A and complete them using the words in brackets. Check in pairs then with the whole group.

Answers
1 Are any of your brothers and sisters married?
2 Who are you closest to in your family?
3 Where are your parents from originally?
4 Do you get on well with your parents?
5 Do you like studying?
6 Does anyone in your family speak good English?
7 Does anyone you know live abroad?
8 Do you speak any other languages?

Step 3 Put students in pairs and tell them to take turns to ask and answer the questions in A. Monitor and correct mistakes in target language.

Step 4 Ask students to look at the words and phrases in C, then put them in new pairs and tell them to ask each other the questions. They should choose from the words and phrases in the box to answer. Model with a strong student, then in open pairs, before putting students in closed pairs to continue. Monitor and note down errors in target language for a correction slot at the end.
Direct students to the grammar reference on page 137 if they still seem unsure.

Frequency graph
100% always / every day
95% usually / two or three times a week
75% quite often / once or twice a week
50% sometimes / two or three times a month
25% not very often / a few times a year
10% hardly ever
0% never

1B see Teacher's notes p. 120.

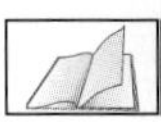
pp. 12–13

Speaking

Aim
To give fluency practice and lead in to the *Listening*.

Step 1 Lead in by writing this question on the board: *What makes us the people we are?* Ask students to discuss this as a class and feed in / check vocabulary: *experiences* = things that have happened to you; *treat* = behave in a certain way to someone; *genes* = parts of cells in animals and humans which control their characteristics; *heart disease* = serious illness of the heart; *criminal behaviour* = acting in an illegal way.

Step 2 Ask students to read the text in A, then in small groups ask them to discuss the questions. Conduct brief feedback.

Listening

Aim
To give practice in listening for gist and specific information.

Step 1 Lead in by asking students to look at the people in the pictures and describe them briefly. Tell them they are going to hear three of them talking about the genes v (*versus*) childhood / upbringing debate. Put them in pairs to discuss why these people might be interested in this subject and what they might say about it.

Step 2 Ask students to listen and decide whether each speaker thinks their character is shaped more by genes or childhood / background. Play the recording. Check in pairs, then with the whole group. Ask students if anything surprises them about the speakers' opinions.

Answers
1 Trent – identical twin, mainly genes (in this case it's genes that makes them different)
2 Angela – adopted, mainly upbringing
3 Justinia – biologist, mainly upbringing

1.4
1 Trent Simons
People think identical twins have the same tastes and personalities, but my brother and I are very different: I'm keen on sport and I'm really fit and active; he hardly ever does anything. I'm confident, I go out, I'm captain of the football team, but he's really quiet. He has friends, but they're a bit strange and they always play video games together. We're probably different because we go to different schools and my parents don't treat us as 'the twins', you know, as one person. Apart from our appearance, I think the only thing that is genetic is having poor sight. But then he wears thick glasses and I wear contact lenses!

2 Angela Martinez
Being adopted, I occasionally wonder where my character comes from. I get good grades at school and people say Chinese are good students and very determined. But then so are my adoptive parents. My dad's clever and mum has a clothes shop in Madrid. I've learnt lots from them. Also I want to be a doctor like my uncle and I know I have to study to do that. I sometimes get frustrated if things go bad and I get really angry. Both my parents are very calm and patient – they never shout. Maybe my anger is because of my genes – but my gran says it's because I have no brothers or sisters and my parents are too liberal!

3 Justinia Lewis
Being a biologist, I obviously think genes are important – it's how evolution works. However, genes are only a small part of who we are: we humans share 30% of our genes with bananas and 98% with chimpanzees. Genes play a part in heart disease and other illnesses, but having a healthy lifestyle is more important and we learn that behaviour from our parents. Now I'm pregnant, I think about my character and my childhood. Neither of my parents are scientists, but they both read a lot and they talked to me about lots of different things. Also, none of us in our family are neat and tidy. I tell my husband it's genetic and that's why I don't put things away, but it's not true.

Step 3 Ask students to look at the questions in C. Put them in pairs and ask them to try to remember whether they are true or false. Then play the recording again for them to check. Check with the whole group.

Answers
1 T 2 T 3 F 4 T 5 T 6 F 7 T 8 T 9 F 10 T

Step 4 Ask students to look at the audioscript on page 162 and choose four new words they want to remember. Ask them to notice which words go with them. Ask them to record their chosen words and any useful collocations in their vocabulary book with a translation or definition. Put them in pairs to compare and help each other.

Step 5 Put students in small groups to discuss the questions in E. Conduct brief feedback at the end.

Native speaker English *Keen on*

Ask students if they remember how Trent says he likes sport = *I'm keen on sport*. Read out the box and check students understand that *keen on* is followed by a noun or *-ing* form. Elicit a few more examples from them on what they are *(not) keen on*.

GRAMMAR Similarities and contrasts

Aim
To introduce ways of talking about similarities and differences between people.

Step 1 Ask students to read the examples from *Listening* in the box. Elicit examples from them about their own families or friends, using *both, neither, all, none, no-one, whereas* and *but*.

Note *None* and *neither* can be followed by either a singular or plural verb. It is considered more standard to use a singular verb, but it often sounds more natural to use a plural one.

Step 2 Ask students to work in pairs and give them five minutes to find as many similarities and differences between them as they can. They should note down their ideas.

Step 3 Ask each pair to join another pair and tell each other about their similarities and differences, using *both, neither, but, whereas*. Monitor and correct where necessary.

Step 4 Ask the groups to report to the class on similarities and differences between their groups, using *all, none* and *no one*. Correct mistakes in target language.
Direct students to the grammar reference on page 137 if they still seem unsure.

VOCABULARY Character and habits

Aim
To introduce vocabulary to talk about personality and behaviour.

Step 1 Ask students to look at sentences 1–8 and a–h and find matching pairs. Do the first one with them. Check in pairs then check with the whole group. Make sure students understand and can pronounce all the adjectives.

Answers
1 d 2 f 3 a 4 e 5 b 6 h 7 c 8 g

Step 2 Put students in pairs and ask them to test each other. They should take turns to close their books, while their partner reads out a sentence from a–h and they try to remember the matching adjectives from 1–8. Then swap and repeat.

PRONUNCIATION *and*

Aim
To draw students' attention to the weak form of *and*, especially in expressions like *neat and tidy*.

Step 1 Read out the box and model and drill some examples, drawing students' attention to the weak form. Ask students to listen and repeat the word pairs. Play the recording.

1.5
1 neat and tidy
2 calm and patient
3 kind and caring
4 open and friendly
5 fit and healthy
6 the cooking and cleaning
7 salt and pepper
8 try and help
9 go and see
10 scream and shout

Step 2 Put students in pairs and ask them to write down all the pairs of words they remember. They could test each other by saying *neat and* ... ? Tell them to look at the audioscript on page 162 to check.

SPEAKING

Aim
To give fluency practice and round off the unit.

Step 1 Ask students to think about how they are similar to and different from people in their family. Ask them to look at the questions and think about how they would answer them. When ready, put students in small groups to discuss. Monitor and note down errors for a correction slot at the end.

02 SHOPS

UNIT OVERVIEW

The main aims of this unit are to learn how to **talk about shops and things you buy**, to **make offers and ask for permission**, and **to make and respond to compliments**. Students also learn how to **understand newspaper headlines**. The main **grammar aims** are **the past simple, comparatives** and **passives**.

Next class Make photocopies of **2A** p. 130.

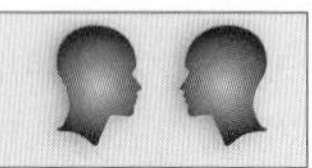

VOCABULARY

Aim

To revise items commonly bought and to practise adjectives to describe them.

Step 1 Ask students what kind of things they enjoy buying. Then ask them to look at the pictures and label them with the words in the box. Check in pairs then check with the whole group. Model and drill the words.

Answers

Picture 1: he's wearing a T-shirt and holding a camera
Picture 2: he's wearing a suit and tie, white shirt, nice watch, with a mobile
Picture 3: she's wearing a skirt, top, coat and hat, she has a laptop

Step 2 Put students in pairs and ask them to discuss the questions in B. Conduct brief feedback.

Step 3 Ask students to read the sentences in C and try to guess the meaning of the words in bold from the context, and then to translate them into their own language. Ask them to look at the *Vocabulary Builder* on page 6 to check. Model and drill for pronunciation and elicit the stress.

Answers

Good quality, last, reliable, wide selection, shut, thick, uncomfortable, complicated, bright, good value, smart, doesn't suit me, neat

Step 4 Ask students to look at the questions in D and think about how they would answer them. Put them in small groups to discuss their answers. Conduct brief feedback.

NATIVE SPEAKER ENGLISH *cool*

Ask students to read the box or read it aloud to them. Elicit a few more examples from them by asking who or what they think is *cool* or *uncool* and why.

LISTENING

Aim

To give practice in listening for specific information and lead in to the grammar (past simple).

Step 1 Tell students they are going to hear a conversation between three friends, Keira, Claire and Dan, about shopping. Ask them to listen and make notes on what each person bought, where they bought it and what each item is like. Check *second-hand* = previously owned by someone else. You could put a table on the board for them to copy and complete. Play the recording. Check in pairs then check with the whole group. Play the recording again if necessary.

Answers

	What	Where	What item is like
Speaker 1	camera	Jessops in town	nice, light, simple
Speaker 2	earrings	second-hand shop	lovely, old
Speaker 3	jacket	same shop	thick and warm, great

2.1

K = Keira, C = Claire, D = Dan

K: Did you have a nice weekend?
C: Yeah, it was good.
K: What did you do?
C: Oh, nothing much. I went for a walk with some friends round Sutton Park yesterday.
K: Oh, nice. It was a lovely clear day.
C: Yeah. It was a bit cold, but it was great. I was taking photos with my new camera.
K: That one? Let's have a look. Wow! That's really neat. Where did you get it?
C: In Jessops in town. I'm really pleased with it. It's really good quality and it's got quite a few different functions.
K: Really? Is it complicated to use?
C: No, not really. There are a few things I don't know yet, but it's OK.
K: Yeah. Well, the pictures look good and it's nice and light as well.
C: Hmm, yeah. It's cool, isn't it? Anyway, what about you two? Did you do anything?
D: Yeah, we went shopping.
C: Oh OK. Did you buy anything nice?
K: Well, I got these earrings.
C: They're lovely! They look quite old.
K: Yeah they are. I got them in a second-hand shop near here. They've got all kinds of things there – books, CDs, clothes. Dan got that jacket there.
C: Really? I love it. It looks really nice and warm.
D: Yeah, it is. It's pure wool and it's nice and thick. And it only cost fifteen pounds.
C: You're joking! That's fantastic. It really suits you as well. It's a great style and colour!
D: Thanks.
C: Did you get any clothes, Keira?
K: No, there were some really nice things, but I didn't find anything that fitted me. Everything was either too big or too small.

Step 2 Put students in pairs and ask them to discuss the questions in B. Conduct brief feedback.

DEVELOPING CONVERSATIONS

Complimenting

Aim

To introduce ways of giving and responding to compliments.

Step 1 Lead in by complimenting some of the students on various accessories and items of clothing, and elicit appropriate replies e.g. *I really like your jacket*. Check *compliment / to pay someone a compliment*. Read out the box and check understanding.

Step 2 Ask students to look at the sentences in A and put the second halves in the correct place. Check in pairs then with the whole group. Model, drill and concept check.

Answers

1 Is it new?
2 It's a really nice design.
3 I'd love one like that.
4 How long have you had it?
5 They look really comfortable.
6 It really suits you.

Step 3 Put students in pairs and ask them to take turns saying a sentence from A and responding appropriately. Model with a strong student, then in open pairs, before continuing in closed pairs. Remind students to use exaggerated intonation (with a wide voice range) to sound more natural and make it more fun. Monitor and correct mistakes in target language.

GRAMMAR The past simple

Aim

To revise and practise the past simple of regular and irregular verbs and the verb *to be*.

Step 1 Lead in by asking one or two students what they did last night or last weekend. Elicit which tense they are using – or should be using.

Step 2 Read out the box or ask students to read it. Or write examples on the board – including *to be*, negative and question forms – and use these to highlight form and meaning, e.g. *I went to the cinema. What did you do? I didn't go to the park. I was / wasn't at home.* Are we talking about the present or past? (Past.) Is this a single or repeated action? (Usually single but could be both.)

Step 3 Ask students to complete the dialogue. Do the first question with them to demonstrate. Then ask them to continue in pairs. Alternatively, you could check in open pairs before checking as a class. Direct students to the grammar reference on page 138 if they still seem unsure.

Answers

A: Did you do anything yesterday?
B: Yes, we went round the market in Rye.
A: Oh, yes. Did you buy anything nice?
B: No, I wanted to get something for my parents, but I didn't see anything I liked. Carol got a nice top, though.
A: Is that the one you're wearing?
C: Yeah, and it wasn't very expensive either. It only cost 20 euros.
A: Really? That's really good value. Did they have any others like that?
C: Not exactly the same, but they had lots of nice things.

2A see Teacher's notes p. 120.

Conversation Practice

Aim
To give freer practice.

Step 1 Tell students they are going to have a conversation similar to the one in *Grammar*. Put students in pairs and ask them to practise conversations, as in the example. Tell them to continue the conversation by asking more questions. Model with a strong student, then in open pairs, before continuing in closed pairs. Monitor and correct mistakes in target language.

Step 2 Put students in small groups and get them to compliment each other on their clothes / accessories, using *I like your ... / That's a nice ... / Those ... are really nice*. They should respond appropriately and also say when / where they bought the item. Monitor and note down errors in target language for a correction slot at the end.

Alternatively Conduct this as a 'mingle'. Get all students to stand up and walk around, paying each other compliments and responding. Monitor and make sure all students always have someone to talk to (they can talk in threes if you have an odd number).

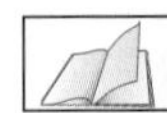 **pp. 16–17**

Listening

Aim
To give practice in listening for specific information and detail.

Step 1 Put students in pairs / threes and ask them to look at the pictures and guess what the people are saying. Tell them they are going to hear five conversations. They should number the pictures in the order in which they hear the conversations that match. Play the recording. Check in pairs, then with the whole group.

Answers

1a	2d	3b	4e	5c

2.2

Conversation 1
A: Is that all you have?
B: Yeah, it is.
A: Well, do you want to go first?
B: Are you sure?
A: Of course. I have lots of things.
B: Great. Thanks.

Conversation 2
C: Would you like it wrapped?
D: Um ... what's the paper like?
C: It's this green paper.
D: Hmm, it's a bit plain. Do you have anything a bit prettier? It's a special present.
C: Well, there's quite a big selection in the stationery department. Do you want to choose something and bring it here and I'll wrap it for you?
D: Really? You don't mind?
C: Of course not.
D: Thanks.

Conversation 3
E: Yes sir. How can I help you?
F: I bought this the other day and it's damaged. When I got it home and took it out of the box, I found the button was loose and it's damaged here. Look, you see?
E: Are you sure you didn't drop it or anything?
F: No, of course not!
E: It's just that this kind of damage doesn't happen unless you do something. It's not a manufacturing fault.
F: Honestly, when I got home I took it out of the box and it was already damaged.
E: Have you got a receipt and the box?
F: I didn't bring the box. I've got the receipt, though.

Conversation 4
G: Is there anyone serving here?
H: Yes, but I don't think you can pay here.
G: That's OK. I just want to find out if they have something in stock.
H: Well, there was a guy here and he said he would be back in a minute, but that was ten minutes ago.
G: Oh right.
H: It's typical! The service is always terrible here.
G: Hmm.
H: Hatton's is better really. Their service is much more reliable and their things are generally better quality.
G: Really? Well, why didn't you go there?
H: Well, I do normally, but I saw in the window they had a sale here.
G: Ah!
H: There he is! About time!
I: Sorry.
H: That's OK.

Conversation 5
J: Excuse me. Do you have one of these in a smaller size? This one's a bit big.
K: I'm afraid not. That's why they're at a reduced price.
J: Never mind, Timmy. You'll grow into it.
L: But I don't like it.
J: Don't be silly. You look lovely. It really suits you.

Step 2 Put students in pairs and ask them to try to identify which conversation the questions in C are from and what the answers were. Play the recording again for them to check.

Answers
a Conversation 3 – No, of course not.
b Conversation 5 – I'm afraid not.
c Conversation 2 – Well, there's quite a big selection in the stationery department.
d Conversation 1 – Are you sure?
e Conversation 4 – Yes, but I don't think you can pay here.

Step 3 Put students in pairs and ask them to answer the questions in D. Then tell them to look at the audioscript on page 163 to check their answers. (Note: change the question for Conversation 4 to *Why is the second customer unhappy?*

Answers
1 he has lots of things
2 to wrap the present
3 a camera
4 The customer thinks the service is terrible.
5 She thinks it suits her son and it's reduced.

Step 4 Ask students to look at the questions in E and think about how they would answer them. Put them in small groups to discuss. Conduct brief feedback.

LANGUAGE PATTERNS

Aim
To draw students' attention to patterns with *the other day / week*.

Step 1 Ask students to look at the sentences in the box and notice the similarities (*the other day / week*). Check they understand that this is fairly informal and refers to recent – but not very specific – time.

Step 2 Ask students to translate these sentences into their own language. In monolingual classes ask students to compare their translations. In multilingual classes ask students to work in pairs and tell each other if the sentences were easy to translate and whether they were able to translate them word for word.

Step 3 Ask students to cover the English translations and translate the sentences back into English using their translations. Then ask them to compare their translations in pairs against the book.

Alternatively If you prefer not to use translation, ask students to notice the patterns. Concept check any areas of difficulty and elicit a few more examples. If time, write the examples on the board and tick them if correct. If the sentences are wrong, ask the students to correct them or correct them yourself.

DEVELOPING CONVERSATIONS
Making offers and checking

Aim
To introduce ways of making offers and checking things are OK and to give practice.

Step 1 Lead in by eliciting examples of offers from *Listening:* e.g. *Do you want to go first?* How does the speaker check this is OK? By asking, *Are you sure?* Then read out the examples in the box or ask students to read them. Model some example four-line conversations with a strong student, then model in open pairs, starting with *Do you want me to open the window?*

Step 2 Put students in pairs and ask them to practise similar conversations, using the sentences in A as starters. Monitor and correct where necessary.

GRAMMAR Comparatives

Aim
To revise and practise basic comparative forms, including short and long adjectives / adverbs and adverbs of degree (*a bit, much*).

Step 1 Elicit some examples of comparatives by showing / drawing pictures or asking two students to stand up and the others to describe differences, e.g. *Juan's taller than Kristina*. Then ask students to read the box, or read it out to them. Write a range of examples on the board and use them to highlight form and meaning.

Step 2 Ask students to complete the sentences in A, using the comparative form of the adjective in brackets. Do the first example with them. Check in pairs then with the whole group.

Answers
1 smaller
2 easier
3 bigger
4 smarter
5 better, longer
6 brighter, more colourful
7 more comfortable, more practical, lighter, more easily

Step 3 In small groups ask students to discuss what they think the speakers are talking about in each of the sentences in A.

Suggested answers
1 shoes
2 computer or camera
3 shirt or jacket
4 scruffy clothes / jeans and T-shirt
5 chair or table
6 anything, could be item of clothing
7 pushchair or pram

Step 4 Ask students to test each other. Give them time to look again at the follow-up questions and try to memorise them. They should then take turns to close their books, while their partner reads out the first sentence in each of the examples 1–7. They should try to say the follow-up question. Then swap. Direct them to the grammar reference on page 138 if they still seem unsure.

Step 5 Elicit ways of making negative comparatives by eliciting the opposite of *more* = *less*. Ask what's another way of saying *smaller?* (*Not as big.*) Then read out the box.

Step 6 Tell students they're going to disagree with the statements in D. Read out the example and then model some answers with a strong student, e.g. 2 *They may be more comfortable but they're not as smart.* Then continue in open pairs. Put students in closed pairs to practise the conversations in D. Monitor and correct mistakes in target language.

SPEAKING

Aim
To give fluency practice of the target language.

Step 1 Put students in small groups and ask them to think of examples of the shops and brands in A. Or elicit these from the whole group and write them on the board.

Step 2 Ask students individually to decide which shops and brands they prefer. Tell them to make a list of reasons using comparatives and their own experience. Tell them to read the example in B. They should make some notes but not write out the whole paragraph.

Step 3 Put students in small groups to discuss. Monitor and note down errors in target language for a correction slot at the end.

pp. 18–19

Next class Make photocopies of **2B** p. 131.

READING

Aim
To give practice in predicting, guessing from context, and reading for gist and detail.

Step 1 Put students in pairs and ask them to look at the headlines and try to guess the meaning of the highlighted words and predict what the articles are about.

Tip Bring along a real newspaper and show students, eliciting *article* and *headline*. Elicit the features of headlines (short, words missing, often in present tense).

Step 2 Put students in groups of four and ask them to form A and B pairs. Pair A should read File 12 on page 158 and pair B should read File 22 on page 161. In pairs, they should try to answer the questions in B as they read and match their article with one of the headlines in A.

Answers
Text 1: **a** Macau **b** tourists **c** because it was part of their tour **d** they wanted to see historic buildings rather than shops e no one was hurt (not stated)

Text 2: **a** London **b** shoppers **c** because a new shop was opening and there were rumours of a sale **d** they were fighting to get in first **e** two people were hurt

Step 3 Ask students, in the same pairs, to discuss and try to help each other with any vocabulary they are not sure about in their article. Tell them to check their ideas in the *Vocabulary Builder* on pp. 7–8.

Step 4 Put students in new AB pairs and ask them to close their books and re-tell their stories. They should then compare them and discuss their reactions.

Step 5 Ask students, in the same pairs, to look at the collocations from both articles and complete each one with the correct word from the box.

Answers

1 crowd	4 injury	7 discount
2 temple	5 coach	8 mixture
3 rumour	6 item	

Step 7 Put students in small groups to discuss the questions in G. Do the first one with them, you might like to prompt them to talk about architectural styles. Conduct brief feedback at the end.

LISTENING

Aim
To give practice in predicting, listening for gist and responding to text.

Step 1 Tell students they are going to listen to a podcast about the two stories they read. Check they understand *podcast* = a digital audio file that can be listened to on a computer or digital music player (e.g. iPod).

Step 2 Put students in pairs and ask them to predict which of the people in the stories they read about the podcaster will have more sympathy with. Play the recording for them to check their ideas.

Answer
More sympathy with people in story two.

2.3
There were two stories about fights connected with shopping this week – one to annoy the anti-shopper and one to make them happy. The first was the riot at the opening of the *Primark* store in London. How stupid can people be? It amazes me that people will wait for hours outside a shop because they think they will get a coat or T-shirt five pounds cheaper. Then they injure each other by pushing and fighting to get a coat or T-shirt that they probably didn't need anyway. Even when the shoppers discovered there were actually no discounts, they still bought things.

The second story was about a group of Chinese tourists in Macau. They started a mini riot because the tour guides were trying to take them to too many shops and they didn't want to buy anything. I can totally understand how the tourists felt. When I go into my city centre, I often think there are too many shops. There are 30 shops that just sell shoes! There are five that just sell socks! Of course, the Chinese group wanted to go and see the sights instead of going shopping – they were on holiday after all! When you go on holiday, you want to relax. You want to do something *different*, like go to the beach or visit beautiful buildings – temples and cathedrals, museums and galleries. Why does anyone want to travel a long way to buy things you can almost certainly buy in your own country anyway?

Step 3 Ask students in the same pairs to talk about whether they agree or disagree with the podcaster and why. Conduct brief feedback at the end.

GRAMMAR Passives

Aim
To introduce / revise passive forms.

Step 1 Ask students to look at the sentences in A, *Who called the police in each sentence?* (1 managers, 2 angry tourists). *Which verb is the passive?* (*were called*). Elicit the information in the box and / or read it out. Check that students understand.

Step 2 Ask students to look back at the articles from *Reading* and find more examples of passive forms and underline them. Check in pairs then with the whole group.

Suggested answers
text 1 (File 12): were paid, were called, were locked, were arrested, text 2 (File 22): were injured, were opened, were taken

Step 3 Ask students to look at the picture and say what they think is happening. Then ask them to read the text quickly, ignoring the grammar practice for the moment. Check overall understanding by asking what they found out about Primark.

Step 4 Ask students to choose the correct verb form – either active or passive – to complete the story. Check in pairs then with the whole group. Direct students to the grammar reference on page 139 if they still seem unsure.

Answers

1 sells
2 was established
3 operates
4 are supplied
5 discovered
6 were paid
7 were used
8 were introduced
9 was accused
10 charges

Step 5 Put students in small groups to discuss the questions in D. Conduct brief feedback.

PRONUNCIATION

Aim
To focus on contractions and weak forms of the verb *to be* in passive forms.

Step 1 Read out the box to students and check they understand. Ask them to look at the sentences in A and say them to each other in pairs, paying attention to weak forms and contractions.

Step 2 Ask them to listen and check the pronunciation. They could repeat after each sentence.

2.4
1 I am not paid very well.
2 It is sold in most shops.
3 They are supplied by a firm in India.
4 We were charged 100 euros for it.
5 Luckily, no-one was injured.

SPEAKING

Aim
To give writing and speaking practice.

Step 1 Ask students to look at the headlines from *Reading*. Is the verb *to be* included? (No.) Why? (Because headlines are short and some words are understood.) Tell them to read the information box or read it out to them.

Step 2 Put students in pairs and ask what each headline in A means and what they think each article is about. Check their ideas.

Suggested answers
1 A man stole 10 kilos of bananas from a supermarket and was arrested by the police.
2 A woman slipped on a wet floor in a changing room and sued the shop for $20,000.
3 A woman called 999 and asked the ambulance service to help her carry her shopping.

Step 3 Ask students individually to choose one of the headlines and write a short news report (60–80 words) about it. Monitor and correct as they write, especially their use of passive forms.

Step 4 If time, put students in small groups to tell each other their stories.

2B see Teacher's notes p. 120.

03 EAT

UNIT OVERVIEW

The main aims of this unit are to learn how to **describe restaurants, meals and food**, to **order and pay in restaurants** and to **make and respond to suggestions**. The main grammar aims are using the **present perfect simple** to talk about past experience, using ***too* and *enough***, and **offers, requests** and **ways of asking for** and **giving permission**.

Next class Make photocopies of **3A** p. 132.

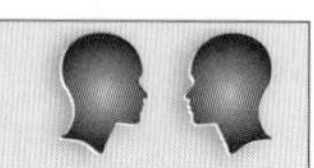

SPEAKING

Aim

To lead in to the topic / unit and give fluency practice.

Step 1 Ask students to look at the pictures and describe the restaurants. Then ask them to look at the questions in A and think about how they would answer them. Check they understand all the vocabulary in the word box.

Step 2 Put students in small groups of three or four, and ask them to discuss the questions in A. Ask them to note any similarities or differences within their group. Conduct brief feedback by asking a member of each group to report back on any similarities.

VOCABULARY Restaurants

Aim

To introduce words and phrases about restaurants and give practice.

Step 1 Lead in by asking students about what kind of restaurants they like. Ask them to look at the words in the box and choose the correct pairs of words to complete sentences 1–8. Do the first example with them. (The first time I went there, the food was *delicious*, but I went there again recently and it was *disgusting*!) Tell them to look in the *Vocabulary Builder* on page 10 if they need help. Check in pairs then check with the whole group.

Answers

1 delicious + disgusting
2 money + portions
3 service + staff
4 busy + seat
5 dishes + choose
6 choice + options
7 place + do
8 terrace + view

Step 2 Ask students individually to look again at the sentences in A and underline any words or expressions that describe two restaurants they know. Then put students in pairs to tell each other about them, using as much of the language as they can, as in the example. Conduct brief feedback.

LISTENING

Aim

To give practice in listening for specific information and taking notes.

Step 1 Tell students they are going to listen to two friends deciding where to eat. Ask them to look at the table in A and make notes on what they hear about each of the places as they listen. Play the recording. Check in pairs then check with the whole group.

Answers

the Thai restaurant	nearby, spicy food
the steak restaurant	near department store
Sofra	Turkish, good selection, delicious food, busy

3.1

A: Are you hungry?
B: Yeah, a bit.
A: Do you want to get something to eat?
B: I'd love to, yeah. Where are you thinking of going?
A: Well, there's a really nice Thai place just down the road. Do you know it?
B: I've seen it, but I've never eaten there. I don't really feel like spicy food today, though, so ...
A: OK. No problem. I'm happy to go somewhere else.
B: There's a great steak restaurant near the big department store in the centre of town. How about that?
A: To be honest, I don't really like red meat.
B: Well, we could go to Sofra instead. Have you been there?
A: No. I've never heard of it. Where is it?
B: It's about fifteen minutes' walk from here. It's just round the corner from the bus station.
A: Oh, OK. And what kind of restaurant is it?
B: It's Turkish. It's really good. I go there almost every week.
A: Really?
B: Yeah, the food's delicious – and they've got a really good selection of dishes, so there's plenty to choose from.
A: Oh, it sounds great.
B: Yeah. The only problem is that it gets really busy. Sometimes you have to wait to get a table, so maybe we should phone and book.
A: Yeah. That's probably a good idea.

Step 2 Ask students to look at the words / phrases in B and decide which conversation each one applies to. Ask them to compare their ideas in pairs then play the recording again for them to check. Check with the whole group.

Answers
spicy food = Thai place
big department store = near steak restaurant
red meat = steak restaurant
the bus station = near Turkish restaurant
dishes = Sofra has a good selection
phone = they should phone to book at Sofra

Step 3 Put students in pairs or threes to discuss the questions in C. Conduct brief feedback.

Developing conversations

Suggestions

Aim

To show how we make and respond to suggestions and give practice.

Step 1 Read out the box, checking understanding as you read. Ask students what phrases are used to make a suggestion (*how about, we could* ...) and to reject a suggestion (*I don't really feel like* ...). Then ask students to practise conversations using the prompts in A. Tell them to suggest somewhere, their partner should reject it, and they should suggest somewhere else. Model with a strong student then in open pairs, before continuing in closed pairs. Monitor and note down errors in target language for a correction slot at the end.

Step 2 Conduct brief feedback.

Grammar

The present perfect simple

Aim

To focus on the present perfect simple to talk about experiences at an unspecified time in the past.

Step 1 Lead in by asking the students *Have you ever...?* questions about food and restaurants. Ask them which tense they are using, or should be using (present perfect simple). Read out the explanation in the box, checking as you read. Or write the examples on the board and use them to highlight form and meaning. *Have you been there? I've seen it , but I've never eaten there.* Subject + *have / has* + (+ *not*) + past participle. Are we talking about the present or the past? (The past.) Do we know / care about when in the past? (No.)

Step 2 Put students in pairs and ask them to say all three forms of each of the verbs. Check with the whole group.

Alternatively Conduct this as a board race. Put students in two teams and shout out one of the infinitives. One student from each team should run up and write the other two parts on the board. The team which gets the most correct answers wins.

Answers
be was been; become became become; break broke broken; bring brought brought; choose chose chosen; eat ate eaten; forget forgot forgotten; find found found; go went gone; have had had; hear heard heard; leave left left; lose lost lost; read read read; see saw seen; think thought thought; try tried tried; win won won.

Note Check students understand the difference between *been* and *gone*. Both can be past participles of *to be*. *Gone* means the person is still there now (i.e. hasn't come back). *Been* means gone and come back.

Step 3 Ask students to complete the sentences in B with the present perfect form of the verb in brackets. Check in pairs then check with the whole group. Ask students which tense B uses in answers 4 and 5 and why (past simple, because he / she is referring to a specific time in the past.)

Answers

1A have, been	4A Have, found
1B have / 've tried	5A Have, complained
2A Have, eaten	6A Have, tried
2B have / 've had	6B have / 've, heard
3A Have, been	

Direct them to the grammar reference on page 140 if they still seem unsure.

Step 4 Put students in pairs. Tell them to take turns asking the questions in B and giving answers which are true for them. Monitor and correct mistakes in target language.

Step 5 Ask students in the same pairs to write five more *Have you ever ... ?* questions. Put them in new pairs to ask and answer their questions. Conduct brief feedback.

Alternatively You could conduct the last stage as a 'mingle'. Ask students to stand up and walk around and ask different students their questions. They should note down their names and their answers. When they're finished, tell them to sit down and ask them a few things they found out about each other.

3A see Teacher's notes p. 121.

Conversation practice

Aim

To extend the topic and give further practice.

Step 1 Give students a few minutes to individually think about three places where they like eating and why.

Step 2 Elicit ways of suggesting a restaurant from *Listening* and *Developing conversations*. *How about...? Well, we could go to... Well, there's a really nice...*, etc. Put students in pairs and ask them to have similar conversations, using their own ideas from Step 1. They should reject the first one or two suggestions, giving reasons, before reaching an agreement. They should take turns asking, *Are you hungry?* Model with a strong student then in open pairs. Monitor and correct mistakes in target language.

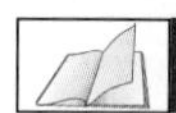

pp. 22–23

Speaking

Aim

To give fluency practice and lead in to the *Reading*.

Step 1 Ask students to look at the questions in A and think about how they would answer them.

Step 2 Put students in small groups and ask them to discuss the questions. Conduct brief feedback.

Reading

Aim

To give practice in predicting and reading for specific information.

Step 1 Lead in by asking students what they usually have for breakfast. Then ask them to look at the pictures and label them with the words from the box. Check in pairs then check with the whole group. Model and drill for stress / pronunciation.

Answers

1 olives
2 flat bread
3 boiled egg
4 grilled fish
5 toast
6 honey
7 fried egg
8 onion
9 yoghurt

Step 2 Put students in pairs / threes and ask them to answer the questions in B. Do not check their answers, as they'll be doing this in the next exercise.

Step 3 Direct students to the questions in C. Ask them to read the text and try to answer the questions. Check in pairs, then check with the whole group.

Answers

1 South Korea = toast, cereal; Bulgaria = boiled eggs, olives, honey, yoghurt; Costa Rica = rice, fried eggs, Egypt = flat bread, onions; Ireland = fried eggs, toast
2 South Korea = traditional breakfast of rice and soup, grilled fish and vegetables; Bulgaria = tea, strong coffee and kiselo mlyako (local yoghurt); Costa Rice = plantain, strong coffee; Egypt = pickled vegetables, or nothing; Ireland = white / black pudding, fried mushrooms and tea
3 healthy = rice and soup, grilled fish, vegetables, yoghurt, fattening = all fried food; filling = Irish breakfast, fried rice and beans, boiled eggs; spicy = pickled cabbage
4 *kimchi* = pickled cabbage with chillies, *gallo pinto* = fried rice and beans, *auga dulce* = water with cane sugar juice, *kieslo mlyako* = Bulgarian yoghurt, *plantain* = banana-like fruit, *foul medammes* = broad beans cooked with tomatoes and onions

Step 4 Put students in pairs or small groups and ask them to discuss the questions in D. Conduct brief feedback.

Tip If you have students from any of these countries, you could ask them if this is really what they eat for breakfast.

GRAMMAR *too / not ... enough*

Aim
To introduce or revise *too / not ... enough* and give practice.

Step 1 Ask students to read the box or read it out to them. Write the examples on the board and use them to elicit / highlight form and meaning. Elicit a few more examples about food or restaurants.

Step 2 Ask students to complete the sentences in A, using *too* or *not ... enough* and the correct adjective from the box. Check in pairs, then check with the whole group.

Answers
1 It's too hot to eat
2 the portions aren't big enough
3 the service isn't good enough
4 it's too expensive
5 it's too fattening
6 my steak wasn't cooked enough

Step 3 Put students in pairs / threes and ask them to discuss possible problems with the items in B, using *too / not enough* + adjective. Monitor and correct mistakes in target language and conduct brief feedback at the end.

NATIVE SPEAKER ENGLISH *Grab*

Ask students to look back at the South Korea section of the reading and ask them what they think *grab* means here (= to have something quickly, often on the go). Read out the box, then elicit a few more examples.

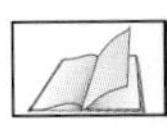

pp. 24–25

Next class Make photocopies of **3B** p. 133.

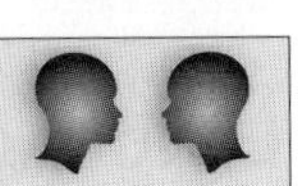

SPEAKING

Aim
To extend the topic of restaurants and give fluency practice.

Step 1 Ask students to look at the questions in A and think about how they would answer them.

Step 2 Put students in small groups to discuss the questions. Conduct brief feedback.

VOCABULARY Describing food

Aim
To extend students' vocabulary about food and help them to describe it in more detail.

Step 1 Tell students to look at the table in A. Check they understand that *part of the body* refers to meat here. Ask them to put the words from the box in the correct column. Check in pairs then check with the whole group. Model and drill for pronunciation / stress and concept check by asking for examples.

Answers

kind of food	part of body / vegetable	taste / texture	how cooked / eaten
meat	leg	strong	fried
fish	seed	sweet	boiled
vegetable	skin	hard	roasted
fruit	shell	thick	raw
seafood	stone	soft	grilled
herb		mild	
sauce		bitter	
		salty	

Step 2 Ask students to look at the pictures and match them with the descriptions. Elicit what each one is (1 = scallop, 2 = avocado). Ask students if they like them and how they cook / eat them.

Step 3 Ask students to think of four more kinds of food and ways to describe them. Put them in pairs and ask them to take turns to describe their items and guess their partner's. Conduct brief feedback at the end.

LISTENING

Aim
To give practice in predicting, listening for gist and detail.

Step 1 Ask students to look at the menu and tick [√] the items that look good, put a cross [×] by items that don't look good and a question mark [?] by items they don't understand.

Step 2 Put students in small groups to discuss their ideas about the menu. Get them to try to explain dishes to each other, and say what they would order and why. Tell them to check any unknown items in the *Vocabulary Builder* on pp. 11–12.

Step 3 Ask students to look at the questions in C and number them in order for a visit to a restaurant. Ask them to check in pairs. Then ask them to think about who would say each one – a waiter / waitress or a customer.

Step 4 Tell students they are going to hear six short conversations in a restaurant. They should listen and check their numbering from Step 3. Check in pairs then check with the whole group.

Answers
7, 8, 6, 3, 5, 2, 1, 10, 9, 4

3.2
C1 = male diner, C2 = female diner, W = waiter

Conversation 1
W: How many people is it?
C1: There are three of us.
W: And have you booked?
C1: No. Is that a problem?
W: No, but do you mind waiting?
C1: How long?
W: Maybe ten or fifteen minutes.
C2: OK. That's fine.
C1: Could I change the baby somewhere?
W: I'm afraid we don't have any special facilities. You can use the toilet. It's not very big, though.
C1: That's OK.
W: It's just at the end there, down the stairs.

Conversation 2
W: Is this table here OK?
C1: Yeah, this is fine. Thank you.
W: Would you like a high chair for the little girl?
C1: That'd be great. Thanks. He's actually a boy, though!
W: Oh, I'm so sorry! Anyway, here are your menus. I'll get the chair.

Conversation 3
W: Are you ready to order?
C1: Not quite. Could you just give us two more minutes?
W: Yes, of course.
C2: Right. OK. Could I have the grilled squid for starters, please? And for my main course, I think I'll have the chicken.
W: And what kind of potatoes would you like?
C2: Roast potatoes, please.
W: OK.
C1: I'll go for the aubergines stuffed with rice for my main course, please. And the country stew? Does it contain any meat? I'm vegetarian.
W: Yes, sorry. It's got lamb in it. I could ask them to take it out.
C1: No, it's OK. I'll just have the tomato and avocado salad. And can we get some water as well?
W: Of course. Sparkling or still?
C1: Just tap water, please, if possible.
W: Sure.
C2: And could we have a small plate for our son? We're going to share our dishes with him.

Conversation 4
C1: Oh, dear – what a mess!
C2: I'll get the waiter. Oh, excuse me. I'm really sorry, but could you get us a cloth, please? My son's dropped some water on the floor.
W: Certainly madam. I'll just go and get one.
C2: Thank you.

Conversation 5
W: Would you like to see the dessert menu?
C1: I'm OK, thanks. I'm really full, but if you want something.
C2: No, no. I couldn't eat another thing. It was lovely, though. Could I just have a coffee, please?
C1: Me too. An espresso.

Conversation 6
C1: Could we have the bill, please?
W: Yes, of course.
C1: Great. Thanks.
C2: That's very reasonable, isn't it? Shall we leave a tip?
C1: No, look. Service is included.
C2: Wow. Then that really is good value for money. We should come here again sometime.

Step 5 Put students in pairs and ask them to try to remember the answers to the questions in C. Ask them to work together and note them down. Play the recording again for them to check. Check with the whole group.

Answers (in order they appear on recording)
1 No. Is that a problem?
2 That'd be great.
3 Not quite.
4 Yes, sorry. It's got lamb in it.
5 Of course. Sparkling or still?
6 I'm OK, thanks.
7 Me too. An espresso.
8 Certainly madam.
9 Yes, of course.
10 No, look. Service is included.

LANGUAGE PATTERNS

Aim
To draw students' attention to patterns with *mind*.

Step 1 Ask students to look at the sentences in the box and notice the similarities (all use *mind*). Ask students to translate a few of these sentences into their own language. In monolingual classes ask students to compare their translations. In multilingual classes ask students to work in pairs and tell each other if the sentences were easy to translate and whether they were able to translate them word for word.

Step 2 Ask students to cover the English translations and translate the sentences back into English using their translations. Then ask them to compare their translations in pairs against the book.

Alternatively If you prefer not to use translation, ask students to notice the patterns. Concept check any areas of difficulty and elicit a few more examples from the students. Write their examples on the board and tick them if correct. If the sentences are wrong ask the students to correct them or correct them yourself.

Grammar

Offers, requests, permission, suggestions

Aim

To focus on the use of *would, could* and *shall* in the context of a restaurant and give practice.

Step 1 Read out the explanation in the box, checking they understand the difference between *would* (for offers), *could* (for permission) and *shall* (for suggestions). Then ask students to look at the sentences in A and complete them with *would, could* or *shall*. Do the first one with them. Check in pairs then check with the whole group.

Answers

1A Could (request / asking for permission)
2A Shall (suggestion)
3A Could (request / asking for permission)
4A Would (offer)
4B Could (request / asking for permission)
5A Shall (suggestion)
6A Could (request)
7A Would (offer)
8A Shall (suggestion)

Step 2 Put students in pairs and ask them to practise conversations by using the questions in A and giving their own answers. Model with a strong student, then in open pairs, before continuing in closed pairs. Monitor and correct where necessary.

Step 3 Put students in small groups and get them to think of suitable offers / requests / suggestions for the situations in C. Conduct brief feedback. Direct students to the grammar reference on page 141 if they seem unsure.

Suggested answers

1 You could ask the waiter to translate. Would you like a menu in English?
2 Could I have the sauce without the tomatoes?
3 Shall we do the washing up? Could you pay?
4 Could you stop smoking please? Would you like a different table?
5 Would you like desert? Shall we have a dessert?

Speaking

Aim

To give fluency practice and round off the unit.

Step 1 Tell students they are going to role-play a situation in The Globe Restaurant. Divide them into AB pairs. Ask As to look at the File 2 on page 156 and Bs to look at File 16 on page 159. Give them time to think about what they are going to say. Tell them to look at the rest of the unit and the audioscript on page 164 for ideas and useful expressions. They could make a few notes.

Step 2 When they are ready, ask them to role-play the conversation and try to use as much language from the unit as they can. Monitor and note down errors in target language. Conduct a brief correction slot at the end.

Step 3 If time, ask one or two strong pairs to role-play the situation for the class.

3B see Teacher's notes p. 121.

04 JOBS

UNIT OVERVIEW
The main aims of this unit are to learn how to **talk about jobs** and **what you are doing at the moment** and to **tell stories about your experiences**. The main grammar aims are to contrast **the present simple and present continuous**, and **the past simple and past continuous**, and to **talk about plans and wishes for the future**.

VOCABULARY Talking about jobs

Aim
To lead in to the topic and extend students' vocabulary about jobs.

Step 1 Lead in by asking students about jobs they do or would like to do. Ask students to look at the pictures in File 21 on page 161 and discuss the questions in A in pairs. Conduct brief feedback.

Step 2 Ask students to read sentences 1–6 and to match each phrase in bold with the correct alternative endings in a–f. Do the first one with them. Check in pairs, then check with the whole group. Check concept, model and drill where necessary.

Answers

1 c	2 d	3 b	4 a	5 e	6 f

Step 3 Put students in new pairs to 'test' each other. They should take turns to choose a job from the list in File 21 on page 161 and describe it using phrases from B. Their partner should guess the job. If they get it wrong, the first student should add more phrases until they get it right. Model with a strong student, then in open pairs. Monitor and correct where necessary.

Step 4 Put students in pairs or threes and ask them to look at the phrases in D and talk about which jobs go with each one. Check they understand *negotiate a price* = discuss the price until you reach an agreement, *appointments* = agreed time / date for formal meeting, *arrest* = take someone to the police station for questioning, *sort out* = solve, *someone's rights* = the things they are entitled to do / have. Conduct brief feedback.

Suggested Answers
Negotiate a price = retail or sales; make appointments = business person, secretary; sort out a problem = teacher; arrest somebody = police person; fight for someone's rights = lawyer; install a computer system = IT

Note Make sure students understand the difference between job (countable) and work (uncountable), e.g. *It's a good job; it's hard work.* To ask about someone's profession, we usually say *What's your job?* or *What do you do?* And answer *I'm a / an ... .*

DEVELOPING CONVERSATIONS Questions about jobs

Aim
To introduce common questions about jobs.

Step 1 Ask students what questions you could ask someone about their job. Then read out the box or ask students to read it.

Step 2 Ask students to match questions 1–6 in A with the correct answers a–g. They could do this in pairs, or individually and then check in pairs. Then ask them to try to memorise the questions for two minutes, then close their books and try to recall the questions together.

Answers

1 c	2 e	3 b	4 a	5 g	6 f

Step 3 Put students in pairs. Ask them to take turns asking each other the questions and giving different, invented answers. Monitor and correct where necessary.

LISTENING

Aim
To hear the target language in context and practise listening for specific information.

Step 1 Tell students they are going to hear two people talking about work. They should listen and tick the questions from *Developing conversations* that they hear. Play the recording. Check in pairs, then with the whole group.

Answers
1 What do you do?
2 Where do you work?
3 How long have you worked for them?
4 Do you enjoy it?
5 What are the hours like?
6 How do you get on with the people you work with? (Is it difficult being the boss's daughter?)

4.1
Conversation 1
A: So what you do? You haven't told me.
B: I'm an engineer.
A: Right. Where do you work?
B: Well, the company I work for is based in London, but I travel around quite a lot. I'm actually working in Scotland at the moment – in Glasgow. They're building a new stadium there and I'm working on that.
A: Really? Where do you live, then?
B: In London, but I'm renting a flat in Glasgow while I'm there. I usually come down to London every two weeks, if I can.
A: And do you enjoy it?
B: Yeah, it's great. I don't really mind the travelling and the money's good – and I don't really have much time to spend it!
A: Really? What're the hours like?
B: Oh, I work hard. I often do a 60-hour week.
A: Really? That's a lot.
B: Yeah, but it's OK and I get on really well with the other people I work with.

Conversation 2
C: So what do you do?
D: Well, I work for a small company back in Korea, but I'm actually a student at the moment.
C: Oh OK. What are you studying?
D: I'm doing a Masters in Marketing.
C: Is that what you do in your company? Marketing?
D: Yes, more or less.
C: So how long have you worked for them?
D: About two years.
C: Only two years and they're sending you abroad to study! That's fantastic!
D: Yeah, well, actually my father runs the company and he wants me to become the marketing manager.
C: Oh right. I see. So how do you get on with the other people you work with? Is it difficult being the boss's daughter?
D: Maybe a little bit sometimes.

Step 2 Put students in pairs and ask them to note down the answers to the questions that they remember. Then play the recording again for them to check.

Answers
Conversation 1
1 I'm an engineer.
2 The company I work for is based in London, but I travel around quite a bit.
3 Yeah, it's great.
4 I often do a 60-hour week.

Conversation 2
1 I work for a small company in Korea / I'm a student.
3 About two years.
6 Maybe a little bit sometimes.

Step 3 Put students in small groups to discuss the questions in C. Conduct brief feedback.

NATIVE SPEAKER ENGLISH *money*

Ask students for another word for *salary* as used in *Listening* (*money*). Then ask them to read the box. Elicit a few more examples by asking them about jobs they or people they know have had.

GRAMMAR

Present continuous and present simple

Aim
To contrast the present continuous, to talk about what people are doing now or around now, with the present simple, to talk about what they generally do or permanent states.

Step 1 Lead in by asking students what they and people they know do as jobs and what they think they are doing at the moment. Read out the box and ask checking questions as you read. Or write up the examples on the board and use them to highlight form and meaning. *I'm working in Scotland at the moment*, subject + *be* + verb + *ing* = to talk about a temporary situation, happening around now. *I usually come down to London every two weeks*, subject (+ adverb of frequency) + base form (add -s / -es in third person) = to talk about what people generally do.

Step 2 Ask students to look at the sentences in A and choose the correct form. Do the first example with them. Check in pairs, then with the whole group.

Answers

1A What do you do?	4 I'm looking
2A How's your job going?	5 I'm doing
2B We're working	6A do you start
3 is doing	6B I usually leave, get up

Direct students to the grammar reference on page 142 if they still seem unsure.

Step 3 Ask students to look at the instructions and examples in B and think about possible responses. Then put them in small groups to talk about their ideas. Check students understand *construction work* = building new houses or offices.

Conversation practice

Aim
To extend the topic and give personalised practice.

Step 1 Ask students to think about their own job, their parents' jobs or choose one of the jobs from the list in File 21 page 161. They should look at the questions in *Developing conversations* and think about how to answer them in relation to their chosen job. Remind them to include at least one example of the present continuous in their answers.

Step 2 Put students in small groups and ask them to have conversations, as if the job was their own, starting *So what do you do? You haven't told me ...* Ask them to continue them as long as they can. Monitor for a correction slot at the end.

pp. 28–29

Next class Make photocopies of **4A** p. 134.

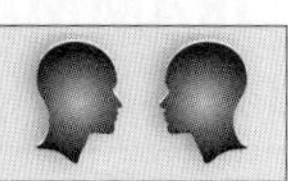

Listening

Aim
To extend the topic and give practice in listening for specific information and detail.

Step 1 Lead in by asking students about unpaid (*voluntary*) work and some reasons for doing it. Put students in pairs and ask them to make a list of different jobs people do for no money. Then ask them to join another pair to compare their lists and discuss the questions in B. Conduct brief feedback.

Step 2 Tell students they are going to hear three people talking about unpaid work. They should listen and make notes on the answers to the questions in C about each one. Play the recording. Check in pairs, then with the whole group.

Answers
Claudia:
1 unpaid work with a public relations company
2 couldn't get a job after university
3 not happy about it
4 to look for a new, paid job
Jerome:
1 a doctor in Sierra Leone
2 he retired but got bored
3 best thing he's ever done
4 to stay another year
Sulochana:
1 an organisation that's fighting for the rights of housewives in Kerala
2 feels it's important
3 want to get paid / recognised for what they do
4 planning to start a website to tell more people about our situation and maybe going on strike

4.2
Claudia
I graduated in Germany two years ago with a degree in Media Studies and after that I applied for jobs in film and television. I know it's a competitive area, but it was depressing, because I didn't get one interview! Everyone wanted me to have work experience, but how can you experience work if nobody gives you a job?

In the end, I took unpaid work with a public relations company. To begin with, I hated it. I only did boring jobs like making coffee for people and photocopying, but recently I've started doing more interesting things. At the moment, I'm helping to advertise a German film.

I'm not happy working for no money, and sometimes I think the company is exploiting me. If they don't offer me a paid job soon, I'm going to start looking for something else!

Jerome
I worked as a doctor in a small town in Switzerland for almost thirty years and I retired five years ago. To begin with, I enjoyed it, but I soon got bored. I saw an advertisement for the Voluntary Service Overseas and applied. I got a job in Sierra Leone and I've been here for nine months. They pay my rent, but basically I'm working for nothing.

It's the best thing I've ever done! People here live in very difficult circumstances, but have a really positive attitude. Now, I'm doing some training with local doctors and advising them how to improve services. My contract ends in three months, but I'm planning to stay here for another year, if I can.

Sulochana
I belong to an organisation that's fighting for the rights of housewives in Kerala, in the south-west of India. We're hoping to make the government pay us a salary and a pension for the work we do in the home. Something similar is already happening in Venezuela. Women play an important part in building the nation. Without mothers and wives at home, how can men work? But men don't appreciate this and that's why we're organising ourselves.

We're planning to start a website to tell more people about our situation and if we don't get what we want, we're thinking of stopping work and going on strike. Let's see how men survive without our help then!

Step 3 Put students in pairs and ask them to look at the phrases in D and try to remember which of the speakers said each one and why. Then play the recording again for them to check.

Answers

1 Sulochana (3)
2 Claudia (1)
3 Jerome (2)
4 Sulochana (3)
5 Jerome (2)
6 Claudia (1)
7 Sulochana (3)
8 Jerome (2)
9 Claudia (1)

LANGUAGE PATTERNS

Aim

To draw students' attention to patterns with *work (-ing) as a / an* to talk about jobs.

Step 1 Ask students to look at the sentences in the box and notice the similarities. Ask students to translate these sentences into their own language. In monolingual classes ask students to compare their translations. In multilingual classes ask students to work in pairs and tell each other if the sentences were easy to translate and whether they were able to translate them word for word.

Step 2 Ask students to cover the English translations and translate the sentences back into English using their translations. Then ask them to compare their translations in pairs against the book.

Alternatively If you prefer not to use translation, ask students to notice the patterns. Concept check any areas of difficulty and if time elicit a few more examples from the students. If time, write these on the board and tick them if correct. If the sentences are wrong ask the students to correct them or correct them yourself.

SPEAKING

Aim

To give fluency practice and encourage students to express their opinions.

Step 1 Ask students to look at the questions in A and think about how they would answer them. Then put them in groups to discuss the questions. Conduct brief feedback.

VOCABULARY Activities at work

Aim

To introduce words and phrases commonly used in association with work and give practice of these with the present continuous.

Step 1 Ask students to read the box or read it out to them. Ask students whether these sentences describe what people are doing around this time or what they generally do (around this time) and which tense is used here (present continuous). Then ask them to complete the sentences in A using the correct verb from the box in the present continuous. Check in pairs, then with the whole group. Model, drill and concept check where necessary. Elicit other nouns / noun phrases that could go with the verbs.

Answers

1 I'm currently advising
2 I'm doing, I'm teaching
3 I'm organising
4 We're negotiating
5 I'm doing
6 I'm working on
7 I'm installing
8 I'm attending. We're learning

Step 2 Put students in pairs and ask them to discuss the questions in B. Conduct brief feedback.

GRAMMAR Plans and wishes for the future

Aim

To introduce / revise ways of talking about the future in relation to jobs.

Step 1 Lead in by asking students what they plan / hope to do in the future in relation to work and study. Elicit some forms they used. Then ask them to read out the box or read it out to them, or write the examples on the board and use them to highlight form and meaning. *I'm going to start looking for another job soon*, subject + *be* + going to + base form = to talk about a definite future plan or intention. *I'd like to work here full-time*, subject + *would like to* + base form. *We're hoping to make them pay us a fixed salary*, subject + *be* + *hoping to* + base form = to talk about things we want to do or to happen in the future. *I'm planning to stay here for another year*, subject + be + *planning to* + base form = to talk about something you have thought about and have a plan to do. *We're thinking of*, subject + verb + *-ing* = to talk about future plans that are not yet certain.

Step 2 Ask students to look at the sentences in A and correct the mistakes. Do the first example together. Check in pairs, then with the whole group. Direct them to the grammar reference on page 142 if they still seem unsure.

Answers
1 I'm hoping **to** become a photographer.
2 My parents **are going** to give me a job.
3 **I'd like** to run my own business in the future.
4 I'm thinking **of** negotiating a new contract.
5 I'm planning **to apply** for a new job next year.
6 I **wouldn't** like to work for myself.

Step 3 Ask students to look at the sentences in B and to complete them using their own ideas. Give them an example to start. Remind them to use *to* + base form with all of them except *thinking of*. Monitor and help as necessary. Then put them in pairs to compare and correct what they have written.

Step 4 Ask students to look at the instructions in C and think about how to respond. Then put them in small groups to discuss their ideas.

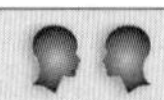
4A see Teacher's notes p. 121.

PRONUNCIATION *going to*

Aim
To focus on different ways of pronouncing *going to*.

Step 1 Read out the box. Then tell students they are going to hear six sentences, each pronounced in two different ways and that the first time will be faster. They should write down each of the sentences once. Play the recording.

4.3
1 I'm going to sort it out tomorrow.
2 They're going to do an English course.
3 He's going to rent a small flat.
4 I'm going to talk to my boss about it.
5 What're you going to do?
6 She's not going to go to university.

Step 2 Put students in pairs to compare what they have written. Then play the recording again for them to check. Ask them to discuss which is easier to understand / say. Then ask them to say the sentences to each other in the way they find easier.

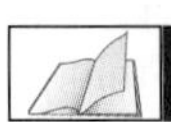
pp. 30–31

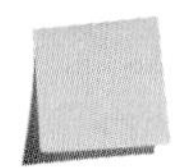
Next class Make photocopies of **4B** p. 135.

SPEAKING

Aim
To give speaking practice and to lead in to *Reading*.

Step 1 Ask students to look at the comments in A and think about whether they agree or disagree and why. Then put them in pairs or threes to discuss their ideas.

READING

Aim
To read for gist and detail and to focus on collocations.

Step 1 Ask students to look at the picture and say what is happening. Then ask them to read the text quickly, ignoring the words in bold and try to identify the people in the picture. Point out that the glossary is there to help them. Check in pairs, then with the whole group.

Answers
1 Rick 2 Marian 3 Harry 4 Ugly Boss 5 Jilly

Step 2 Put students in pairs and ask them to discuss the questions in B. Check their answers as a class.

Answers
1 She is awful and looked happy when Annie was caught out for not paying attention in the meeting.
2 He is angry because he had to ask her a question two or three times.
3 She put his papers in the shredder instead of copying them.

Step 3 Ask students to look at the words in bold in the text and find the verbs that go with them. Then try to think of more verbs that could go with each noun. Tell them to check in the *Vocabulary Builder*, compare in pairs, then check with the whole group.

Answers
skills: improve; also develop, demonstrate, learn;
figures: present; also show, work out, calculate;
link: check out; also go to, click on, find;
button: press; also push;
desk: leave on; also put on, move, sit at

Step 4 Put students in small groups and ask them to discuss the questions in D. Conduct brief feedback.

VOCABULARY Forming words

Aim
To look at common suffixes used to form nouns.

Step 1 Lead in by eliciting the nouns from *communicate (communication)* and *improve* (*improvement*). Then read out the box, eliciting more examples as you read, e.g. *educate-education, locate-location, manage-management, govern-government*.

Step 2 Put students in pairs and ask them to identify the verbs in the list that can also be nouns. Check with the whole group. Elicit the noun forms from the other verbs.

Answers
Interview, plan, repair, experience, produce (stress changes), arrest, research, return, offer, proposal, organisation, negotiation

Step 3 Ask students to write the verbs from the nouns in B. Check in pairs, then check with the whole group. Concept check, model and drill focusing on word stress.

Answers

1 impress	5 manage
2 present	6 advertise
3 exploit	7 apply
4 contribute	

GRAMMAR
The past continuous and past simple

Aim
To contrast the past continuous to talk about a background situation / unfinished action in the past, with the past simple to talk about a single action / event.

Step 1 Read out the box or put the example and timeline on the board and use to highlight form and meaning. E.g. *I met Harry when I was working for a public relations company*. Are we talking about the present or the past? (the past). Which action started first? (*was working*). Which is the longer action? (*was working*). Which is a short action? (*met*). After I met Harry, did I continue to work for the public relations company? (yes).

Step 2 Ask students to match the sentence in A with the correct picture. Ask them what they think Rick meant about the coffee. Check in pairs then with the whole group.

Answers
He probably meant the office coffee was of poor quality.

Step 3 Ask students if they remember what each person in exercise B was doing when Annie's boss asked her a question at the meeting. Ask them to look back at the text to check. Check with the whole group.

Answers
1 Marian was presenting some figures.
2 Annie was looking at Harry and thinking about him.
3 Harry was wearing a nice suit.

Step 4 Ask students to complete the sentences, using the correct form (past simple or continuous) of the verb in brackets. Check in pairs, then check with the whole group.

Answers
1 we were working
2 were you doing
3 came
4 was not feeling
5 was talking, walked
6 did not know
7 crashed, as driving
8 was not looking, was going

Direct students to the grammar reference on pp 143 if they still seem unsure.

SPEAKING

Aim
To give personalised writing and speaking practice of the past simple and continuous.

Step 1 Ask students to look at the topics in A and choose one to write a short story about (100-120 words). Monitor and help as they write.

Step 2 Put students in small groups and ask them to re-tell their stories – from memory as far as possible. Monitor and note down mistakes in target language for a correction slot at the end.

Tip They could write their stories for homework and bring as a starter for the next class.

4B see Teacher's notes p. 121.

01 REVIEW

OVERALL AIMS

It is rarely enough for students to meet 'new' language and skills once. In reality, people learn things by being exposed to them and activating them again and again. Therefore, each of the four review units are designed to revise material covered in the previous four units. They also introduce a *Learner training* section (helping students to become more aware of their learning style / strategies and enabling them to learn more effectively). The first two pages are designed to revise the material in a fun, interactive way. The second two pages are more traditional listening, grammar and vocabulary exercises, which could be given as a progress test. In addition, these test pages expose students to exam-type questions they are likely to meet in common English exams.

LEARNER TRAINING

Overview

Research has shown that effective language learners develop strategies for dealing with a range of situations, from making sense of unknown language to recording and reviewing grammar and vocabulary. The *Learner training* feature encourages students to review their own strategies, whether implicit or explicit, as well as developing new strategies so they become more effective language learners.

Aim

To help students think about what steps they can take to help themselves learn and remember new vocabulary.

Step 1 Lead in by asking students what they do when they meet a new word / phrase, how they remember it etc. Then read out the introduction, asking checking questions as you read, e.g. *Where is the Vocabulary Builder?*

Step 2 Ask students to read out the strategies and think about them. Then put them in threes to discuss which ones they already do, which ones are a good idea / not a good idea, etc. They could make a few notes.

Step 3 Ask students to report back to the rest of the class. Tell them to try out one new strategy each and see if it helps them to remember new words / phrases.

GAME

Overview

Games are valuable for language learners because as they become involved in the activity they become less self-conscious about speaking in a foreign language and less worried about making mistakes. In addition, games help develop classroom dynamics and they are fun – it's important to enjoy learning!

Aim

To recycle some of the language covered in the units in a fun, student-centred way.

Step 1 Put students in AB pairs. Ask student A to look at the questions in the green squares and student B to look at the questions in the yellow squares. They should find the answers in the units and try to memorise them. They may need longer than five minutes for this.

Step 2 Tell students to play the game in pairs. They should take turns to throw a coin and move one square for heads and two squares for tails. They should answer the question on the square they land on. Their partner should check the answer in the relevant part of the book. If they get the answer right, they move forward one square (but not answer that question until their next turn). If they get the answer wrong, their partner tells them the answer and they miss a turn – and use the coin again for their next turn. The first one to reach the last square is the winner. Students could then swap colours and play again.

Note In the next three activities, the students should work in groups of three and use the *Vocabulary Builder* to help them if they want to.

Conversation practice

Overview
In this activity, students decide for themselves which conversation they want to repeat. Two students perform the task in front of a third, who acts as 'judge'. Having an audience normally means students perform better. The judge also has to listen carefully because they have the responsibility for marking their classmates. This whole process has the added advantage of promoting learner autonomy.

Aim
To give fluency practice and to raise students' awareness of their speaking ability by asking them to observe and assess each other.

Step 1 Put students in threes. They can refer to the *Vocabulary Builder* if they wish. They should take turns to be a pair of speakers and an observer. Each pair should choose one of the topics, look back at the relevant part of the book and take a few minutes to prepare. They then conduct the conversation while the third student (the observer) listens and takes notes. At the end, the observer should give each speaker a mark out of 10 and explain the mark (10 = excellent, 1 = poor). It would be useful if the observer could also use their notes to give more detailed feedback on strengths and weaknesses / errors, but they may learn to do this better over time. Then swap. Monitor and help / prompt where necessary and give some overall feedback at the end.

Act or draw

Overview
This is an enormously popular game amongst people the world over because it is so much fun. The gap between the actor / artist's performance and the 'guesser's' ideas leads to a lot of laughter and a lot of language use as well.

Aim
To revise and practise vocabulary in a fun way.

Step 1 Put students in new groups of three or four and ask them to take turns to act or draw the words / phrases in the box, chosen at random. They should not speak while they are acting or drawing. Their partners should guess the word / phrase. Then swap.

Quiz

Overview
This game is best played in teams of two or three in order to promote speaking. It's a good idea to give students a realistic time limit. The pressure also increases energy levels and makes the game more exciting. You could also conduct this as a race between teams.

Aim
To revise and practise more vocabulary from the units.

Step 1 Put students into pairs or threes and ask them to answer as many questions as possible. You could do this as a race so that the first pair / three to finish with the correct answers are the winners.

Alternatively You could conduct this as a 'pub quiz' with you reading out the questions and groups of three or four students conferring quietly on the answers. Then in open class each group swaps their answers with another group. You read / elicit the answers and they mark each other's answers. Check with the whole group at the end. The winner is the group with the most correct answers.

Answers

1. Your **cousin** is the son / daughter of your mother's or father's brother / sister.
2. A **teenager** is 13–19.
3. You get **grades** at school, usually in exams. A good grade is A or 90–100%. A bad grade is E/F or less than 40%
4. Your parents might **force you to** study / do your homework / stay in because you have been naughty or they think it is good for you.
5. Winter clothes are **thick**. You wear them to keep warm.
6. If your trousers are too **loose** you need a smaller size. You could wear a belt.
7. **Changing rooms** are in gyms, sports facilities or clothes shops. They are for changing your clothes.
8. **Damage** is for things; **injure** is for people (n = injury).
9. Food that isn't **cooked** is raw or undercooked.
10. You need to let food **cool down** when it is too hot.
11. You can have a **steak** cooked rare, medium or well-done.
12. **Water** can be still or sparkling.
13. To **apply for** a job you need to send a CV or application form and covering letter, have an interview and accept if they offer you the job.
14. You could **install** a new computer, software or a telephone.
15. People who often have to **work shifts** are nurses, doctors, factory workers, restaurant and hotel staff.

Collocations

Overview

Collocations are words that usually go together, such as *put pressure on someone, spend time with someone*. Until relatively recently, the concept of collocation was not an area that was covered in vocabulary teaching. However, research has shown what an important force collocation is in language and how useful it is for students in helping them to understand text and express themselves fluently. This activity helps develop students' awareness of collocation in natural generation of language.

Aim

To revise some common collocations from the first four units and give students practice in using the *Vocabulary Builder*.

Step 1 Put students in pairs and ask them to take turns to test each other on collocations. One should look at Unit 1 of the *Vocabulary Builder* and read out a collocation, with a gap where there is a '~'. They should say 'blah' for the gap, and their partner should say the missing word, then the whole phrase. They could do 6–8 collocations and then swap.

Pronunciation

Overview

These activities encourage students to be reflective about sound and develop their 'inner ear'. The main aim is not to make the students sound like native speakers, but to develop their ability to understand spoken English as well as to improve their own intelligibility when speaking to other non-native and native English speakers.

Aim

To compare different pronunciations of the letter *a* and associated spelling and to encourage students to learn phonetic script.

Step 1 Elicit from students some different ways the letter *a* can be pronounced and what they notice about spelling changes. Or put some specific examples on the board (different from those in the book) and ask them how to say and spell the words.

Step 2 Ask students to look at the words and repeat them after the recording. Play the recording. Ask them to notice the phonemes and say each one separately.

R1.1

/æ/	gran	/eə/	share
/eɪ/	grade	/ɔː/	saw
/aː/	dark	/iː/	treat
/ə/	arrest		

Step 3 Put students in pairs and get them to say the words in B and decide which one sounds different in each group. Play the recording for them to check. Check with the whole group. Then read out the explanation box.

Answers

1 terrace	2 establish	3 complicated
4 active	5 research	6 persuade
7 healthy		

R1.2

1 /æ/ brand, hat, value, wrap, terrace
2 /eɪ/ behaviour, debate, creative, steak, establish
3 /aː/ argue, aunt, heart, smart, complicated
4 /ə/ annoying, pregnant, unreliable, facilities, active
5 /eː/ airline, caring, repair, wear, research
6 /ɔː/ cause, fault, install, warm, persuade
7 /iː/ colleague, disease, steal, neat, healthy

Step 4 Tell students they are going to hear eight phrases. They should listen and write them down. Play the recording. Then put students in pairs to compare what they have written. Tell them to check by looking at the audioscript on page 165.

R1.3

1 share your seat
2 wear a smart jacket
3 argue with my aunt
4 cause a lot of laughter
5 be treated for heart disease
6 accuse him of charging too much
7 have a rare steak with cream sauce
8 have a debate with my colleagues about it

Note *Listening* and the rest of the review unit could be used as the basis for a progress test. The suggested scores are given below each exercise. Alternatively, these exercises could be done in pairs or individually then checked in pairs, or you could conduct them as a quiz / competition, with students in teams. If students have problems with any of the exercises, refer them to the relevant pages in the grammar reference or the *Vocabulary Builder*.

pp. 34–35

LISTENING

Aim

To give practice in listening for gist and detail. The audio is R1.4.

Exercise A answers

a - b 4 c 1 d 2 e 3

Exercise B answers

A 3 b 1 c - d 4 e 2

GRAMMAR

Exercise A answers

1 comes, work
2 am not playing
3 have seen
4 Did you go
5 was caught
6 wasn't listening
7 didn't go
8 have they been
9 is planning
10 are you thinking

Exercise B answers

1 but this one was not as / was less
2 Shall we go
3 Neither of them are
4 is usually made with
5 Would you like
6 isn't old enough
7 Could you open
8 All of us

LANGUAGE PATTERNS

Answers

1 from 2 other 3 waiting 4 where 5 as

PREPOSITIONS

Answers

1 of
2 for
3 on
4 about
5 to
6 to
7 on
8 in
9 of

FORMING WORDS

Answers

1 choice
2 impression
3 creativity
4 unreliable
5 argue
6 anger
7 advertisement
8 confidence
9 contribution
10 training

ADJECTIVES

Answers

1 d 2 e 3 g 4 a 5 b 6 h 7 f 8 c

NOUNS

Answers

1 research
2 behaviour
3 disease
4 portion
5 repairs
6 sale
7 sauce
8 policy

VERBS

Answers

1c runs
2b employ
3a supplies
4a earn
5a stealing
6b retire
7a miss
8c persuade

VOCABULARY

Answers

1 succeeds
2 shouted
3 neat
4 sale
5 discount
6 determined

05 RELAX

UNIT OVERVIEW
The main aims of this unit are to learn how to **make plans and arrangements, make negative comments, talk about sports** and **form nouns from adjectives**. The main grammar aims are **superlatives**, ***might***, the **present continuous** and ***be going to*** **+ verb**.

Next class Make photocopies of **5A** p. 136.

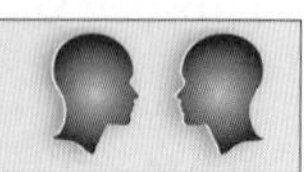

SPEAKING

Aim
To lead in to the topic and give fluency practice.

Step 1 Put students in small groups and ask them to discuss the questions in A. Conduct brief feedback.

VOCABULARY

Activities, places and equipment

Aim
To introduce and practise words and phrases associated with sports.

Step 1 Put students in pairs and ask them to look at the words / phrases in the box and complete the table. Check with the whole group, model, drill and concept check where necessary.

Note *Pool* has two possible meanings here: swimming pool, or the game pool.

Answers

Activity	Clothes	Equipment	Place
dance classes	boots	racket	golf course
basketball	trainers	bat	tennis court
fishing	shorts	golf clubs	running track
pool (game)		net	pool
cycling		cards	(swimming)
Pilates			
walking			

Step 2 Ask students to complete the sentences in B with as many different words / phrases as possible from A. Ask them to notice the collocations and grammar in the examples, e.g. *go* + verb + *-ing*. Check in pairs, then with the whole group.

Answers
1 fishing, cycling, walking
2 basketball, pool, cards
3 Pilates
4 tennis court, football pitch, pool, running track
5 bat, racket
6 golf clubs, trainers, shorts, cards

Step 3 Ask students to look at the model in C. They should answer in one of the three different ways, depending on how they feel. Model the conversation with a strong student, then in open pairs. Put students in closed pairs to continue practising. Model and correct where necessary.

LISTENING

Aim
To give practice in listening for specific information and detail.

Step 1 Tell students they are going to hear a conversation between Corinne and her friend, Maribel, who is visiting her for the weekend. Today is Thursday. Ask them to look at the list in A and tick [✓] the activities they hear mentioned. Play the recording.

Answers
relaxing and doing nothing special, buying a few things, doing some exercise, going on a trip to the country

5.1

C = Corinne, M = Maribel

C: So what are you going to do while you're here?
M: I'm just going to take it easy. I might go shopping tomorrow. You're working tomorrow, aren't you?
C: Yes – and Saturday morning, I'm afraid.
M: Oh dear.
C: I'm sorry, but some important clients are coming and I need to go and meet them at the airport and make sure everything's OK.
M: Right. What time are you going to be back?
C: Hopefully about 2.
M: That's OK, then. I don't usually get up before 11 anyway and I've brought my trainers, so I might go for a run. Is there anywhere to go near here?
C: There's actually an athletics track just down the road.
M: OK. To be honest, though, I'd prefer a park or somewhere like that.
C: Hmm. There's not much near here. I usually just run on the streets.
M: OK. Well, I'll see. Have you got any plans for us over the weekend?
C: Well, a friend is having a party for his birthday on Saturday night, if you'd like to go.
M: Yeah, great. You know I always like a dance!
C: And the forecast is really good for Sunday, so we're thinking of going for a walk in the mountains near here.
M: Oh right. That sounds nice.
C: Yeah, it's great there. There's a lovely river we can go swimming in.
M: Oh right. I haven't got my swimming gear with me.
C: That's OK. I'm sure I can lend you something.
M: Isn't the water cold?
C: A bit, but you soon warm up.
M: I must admit, I'm a bit soft. I like a heated pool.
C: Honestly, it's not so bad and the water's really clear. It's just beautiful with the mountains and everything!
M: So what time are you thinking of leaving?
C: Well, it's two or three hours by car, so if we want to make the most of the day, we need to leave about 6 o'clock.

Step 2 Put students in pairs and ask them to try to answer the questions in exercise B from memory. Then play the recording again for them to check.

Answers
1 no swimsuit, cold water, early start
2 lovely river, clear water, beautiful in the mountains

NATIVE SPEAKER ENGLISH *gear*

Ask students if they remember which phrase Maribel used for her swimsuit (*swimming gear*). Ask if they know what this means and try to elicit other examples with *gear* e.g. *running gear.* Read out the box.

SPEAKING

Aim
To personalise the topic and give fluency practice.

Step 1 Ask students to look at the questions and think about how to answer them. Then put them in small groups to discuss the questions. Conduct brief feedback.

DEVELOPING CONVERSATIONS

Introducing negative comments

Aim
To present ways of introducing negative comments.

Step 1 Ask students if they remember what reason Maribel gave for not swimming in cold water and what she said (*I must admit, I'm a bit soft. I like a heated pool.*) Read out the box and model and drill the expressions.

Step 2 Check students understand *messy* = untidy and disorganised, *unreliable* = you can't trust this person to do what they say they will do, *unfit* = not in good condition physically, *conservative* = traditional, not keen on change. Model and drill. Put them in pairs and ask them to tell each other about their own negative characteristics, using the words / phrases in A. Monitor closely and correct where necessary.

Step 3 Put students in new pairs and ask them to tell their new partner about themselves, using the sentence starters in B. Then ask them to report to the class something they found out about their partner.

GRAMMAR *might*, present continuous, *be going to* + verb

Aim
To present / revise different ways of talking about the future.

Step 1 Lead in by asking students what they are planning to do the next weekend. Try to get examples of present continuous, *going to* and *might*.

Step 2 Ask students to match each of the examples 1–6 with one of the uses (meanings) a, b or c. Check in pairs, then check with the whole group. Put the examples on the board and use them to highlight form and meaning, especially *thinking of* + verb + *-ing*. This is present continuous but not an arrangement, as it refers to something not yet fully decided.

Answers

1 a	2 b	3 b	4 c	5 a	6 c

Direct students to the grammar reference on page 144 if they still seem unsure.

Step 3 Ask students to look at the exchanges in B and put the responses a and b in the correct order. Check in pairs, then check with the whole group.

Answers
1 a Who else is going?
1 b Where are you going to have it?
2 a Who are they playing?
2 b When are you thinking of getting the tickets?
3 a How long is she going to stay?
3 b What are you thinking of doing while she is here?

Step 4 In pairs, ask students to practise the conversations in exercise B.

Step 5 Ask students to look at sentences 1–6 in D and change some words to make the sentences true for them. Tell them they can change the activity as well, e.g. *I might play tennis on Saturday*. Tell them to use *might* or *thinking of* + verb + *-ing* for plans which are not certain.

Step 6 Put students in pairs and get them to take turns to ask and tell each other about their plans. Monitor and correct where necessary. Feedback by asking each student to tell the class one thing their partner is planning, and one thing they might do.

CONVERSATION PRACTICE

Aim
To give freer practice of the target language.

Step 1 Put students in AB pairs. Student A is the host and Student B is the visitor. Ask them to imagine B is visiting A for the weekend, as in *Listening*. They should decide who and where they are and choose an activity for person A to suggest. Then ask them individually to think about what they are going to say, using the chart in File 18 on page 159.

Step 2 When they are ready, ask them to role-play the conversation. They could swap roles if there is time. Monitor and note down errors in target language for a correction slot at the end.

5A see Teacher's notes p. 122.

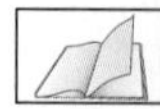
pp. 38–39

Next class Make photocopies of **5B** p. 137.
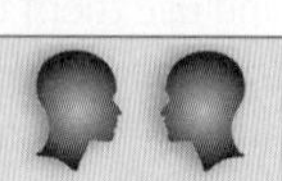

VOCABULARY Sports and games verbs

Aim
To extend the topic and lead in to the *Listening* and *Grammar* (superlatives).

Step 1 Lead in to the topic by asking about recent football – or any sporting – results. Ask students to complete sentences 1–8 with the correct word from the box. Check they know that Slavia Prague is a football team. Check in pairs then with the whole group.

Answers

1 won	4 drew	7 throw
2 scored	5 beats	8 support
3 time	6 kicked	

Step 2 Ask students to 'test' each other. Put them in AB pairs. Student A should mime or explain the verbs from A in random order. Student B should guess. You might like to demonstrate this first.

Step 3 Put students in small groups and ask them to discuss the questions in C. Conduct brief feedback.

LISTENING

Aim
To give practice in predicting and listening for specific information.

Step 1 Tell students they are going to hear a speech about why football is so popular. Put them in pairs and ask them to make a list of reasons for football's popularity and a list of why some people might not like it.

Step 2 Ask students to listen to the speech and see if the speaker mentions the same ideas. Play the recording. Check in pairs, then with the whole group.

5.2
Last night I watched the big game in England between Liverpool and Chelsea. I was one of 1 billion people watching in places as far apart as Peru, Saudi Arabia and Vietnam. It was a nil-nil draw and perhaps the most boring game I've ever seen. Football may be the most popular sport in the world, but it's difficult to know why when you see a game like that. Knowing that the players earn millions a year just makes it worse! So why do we watch when there are plenty of alternatives? The Olympics contains thirty-five sports; other countries have different national sports such as cricket; and new sports are being created all the time.

Maybe it's because football is the simplest game to play. Does anyone really understand the rules of cricket? Football doesn't need expensive equipment. In fact, it requires hardly any gear at all and you need no real skill to play – who can't kick a ball? So nearly everyone has played at least once in their life and once you've played a sport, you appreciate it more. Finally, football's different every game. Last night's game was boring, but next time Chelsea might win five-four, with a goal in the last minute! You never know.

Step 3 Ask students to look at the audioscript on page 166 and tick [✓] the ideas they agree with, put a cross [x] where they disagree and a question mark [?] where they don't understand.

Step 4 Put students in pairs / threes to discuss their responses to the speech. Conduct brief feedback.

GRAMMAR Superlatives

Aim
To introduce / revise superlatives.

Step 1 Elicit some of the things the speaker said about football in *Listening*, e.g. *the most boring game I've ever seen, Football may be the most popular sport in the world.* Try to elicit the examples in *Grammar*, or read them out. Remind students of the rules of comparatives (short adjectives = add *-er*, longer adjectives = add *more* before the adjective, adjectives ending in *-y* = change *y* to *i* and add *-er*). Ask them to discuss the question in A. Check with the whole group.

Answers
Use *the most* with three-syllable adjectives or longer, and with some two-syllable adjectives.
Use *the ... est* with one-syllable adjectives and some two-syllable ones.
Use *the ... iest* with short adjectives ending in *-y*.

Step 2 Ask students to complete sentences 1–6 with the superlative form of the adjective in brackets. Tell them not to worry about the other gaps at this point. Check in pairs then check with the whole group.

Answers
1 the tallest
2 the fittest
3 the cleverest
4 the most relaxed
5 the ugliest
6 the most exciting

Step 3 Ask students to complete the sentences in B so that they are true for them. Model what you want them to say, as in the example. Then put them in pairs to tell each other about their examples. Monitor and correct where necessary.

 **5B** see Teacher's notes p. 122.

PRONUNCIATION /ɪ/ for weak sounds

Aim
To focus on /ɪ/ for weak sounds, especially in the context of superlatives.

Step 1 Elicit the pronunciation of *the greatest* and focus on /ɪst/. Read out the explanation and model and drill.

Step 2 Ask students to look at sentences 1–4 in exercise A and underline all the /ɪ/ sounds. Check in pairs then ask them to listen and check. Play the recording. Check with the whole group. Then play the recording again and ask students to repeat after each sentence.

5.3 and answers
1 These days, people are married on average for eleven and a half years, but the longest marriage lasted eighty years!
2 English must be one of the easiest languages to learn.
3 We wanted to go there because they said it's the nicest place to eat.
4 It's the prettiest village round here, so there's often a shortage of places to stay.

READING

Aim
To read for gist and specific information and use the target language in context.

Step 1 Ask students to look at the pictures and try to identify the sports. If they can't, ask them what is happening in each picutre. Then ask them to read the texts quickly, ignoring the words in bold, and match each text with a picture. Check with the whole group.

Answers
pato = a, f Keirin = b, e Bossaball = c, d

Step 2 Ask students to read the texts again and answer the questions in B. Check in pairs, then check with the whole group.

Answers

1 Keirin	4 Pato
2 Pato / Horseball	5 Keirin
3 Bossaball	

Step 3 Ask students to look at the words in bold and try to match them with the definitions in C. Then ask them to check in the *Vocabulary Builder* on pp. 18–19 before checking as a class.

Answers

a pace	b outcome
c spectator(s)	d aim
e banned	f bet

Step 4 Put students in small groups and ask them to discuss the questions in D. Remind them to explain their choices. Conduct brief feedback.

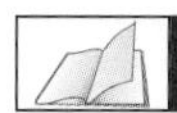 **pp. 40–41**

LISTENING

Aim

To practise predicting, listening for specific information and taking notes.

Step 1 Lead in by miming *taking a nap* in front of the students. Ask them what you are doing and why they think you are doing it. Then ask them to read the dictionary definition or read it out to them.

Step 2 Put the students in pairs / threes and ask them to discuss the questions in A. Check *productive* = efficient at producing things or ideas, *concentration* = giving your full attention to something, *opportunities* = chances. Then ask them to listen to the recording and tick the points in A that the speaker says are the actual results of napping. Play the recording. Check in pairs, then check with the whole group.

Answers

people can go out and enjoy their social lives more, people feel happier and more creative

5.4

In Spain, people typically work from nine in the morning till seven in the evening, though some start even earlier and finish even later. When people go out and relax, they often book a table in a restaurant for around ten at night or later and people frequently stay out till two, three or four in the morning. How do they do it?

In the past, the answer was the *siesta* – a short nap after lunch at around three or in the early evening. Recent research on sleep suggests the Spanish were very wise. A short nap of between 20 minutes and an hour sometime between 1 and 3 pm can increase energy levels and improve your mood and creativity.

However, nowadays more and more Spanish people are working longer and longer hours, and the *siesta* is becoming a luxury outside the summer holidays. At the moment, late nights are still common but some academics say people are going to suffer from not having enough sleep if lifestyles don't change.

Strangely, this comes at a time when other countries are finally showing more interest in the siesta. One group in Britain has launched a campaign called National Nap at Work Week. They aim to inform people of the benefits of napping – and say that workers who take naps aren't lazy. In fact, exactly the opposite is true – people who nap during work time actually work better than those who don't sleep. Tired people lose concentration and make more mistakes. Naps also bring increased happiness, and happy workers are more productive.

Elsewhere, a New York-based company called Metronaps has created a special hi-tech room for business people to nap in during the day. They are hoping to install the rooms in businesses everywhere. And in Europe a lot of offices are buying a specially designed bed, called the Ready Bed, which can be easily folded and put away.

But remember, napping isn't only about being able to work better. Research also shows health benefits. People who nap regularly are apparently less likely to have heart attacks – maybe because they're more relaxed. A nap also means you can stay awake to do the things you really enjoy instead of falling asleep in front of the TV because you're so tired after a long day's work.

Step 3 Ask students to listen again and fill in the gaps in the notes in C. Check in pairs then check with the whole group.

Answers

1 7pm
2 10pm,
3 2, 3 or 4 am
4 20 minutes
5 1–3pm
6 mood
7 creativity
8 suffering
9 the benefits of napping
10 a special hi-tech room
11 fold
12 put it away

Step 4 Put students in pairs or threes and ask them to discuss the questions in E. Conduct brief feedback at the end.

LANGUAGE PATTERNS

Aim
To draw students' attention to patterns with *more and more*.

Step 1 Ask students to look at the sentences in the box and notice the similarities (repetition of the comparative adjective for dramatic effect).

Step 2 Ask students to translate these sentences into their own language. In monolingual classes ask students to compare their translations. In multilingual classes ask students to work in pairs and tell each other if the sentences were easy to translate and whether they were able to translate them word for word.

Step 3 Ask students to cover the English translations and translate the sentences back into English using their translations. Then ask them to compare their translations in pairs against the book.

Alternatively If you prefer not to use translation, ask students to notice the patterns. Concept check any areas of difficulty and elicit a few more examples. If time, write the examples on the board and tick them if correct. If the sentences are wrong, ask the students to correct them or correct them yourself.

VOCABULARY Word families

Aim
To raise students' awareness of how to build nouns from adjectives.

Step 1 Try to elicit some nouns from the adjectives *tired = tiredness, happy = happiness* (draw their attention to the fact we remove the *-y* and add *-i + ness*), *good = goodness*. Read out the box.

Step 2 Ask students to complete the pairs of sentences with either the noun or the adjective from the words in the box. Do the first example with them. Check in pairs, then with the whole group.

Answers

1 a lazy	1 b laziness
2 a fitness	2 b fit
3 a weakness	3 b weak
4 a ill	4 b illness
5 a mad	5 b madness
6 a homeless	6 b homelessness
7 a consciousness	7 b conscious
8 a aware	8 b awareness

Step 3 Put students in pairs and ask them to think of two more nouns ending in *-ness*, for example, *sad-sadness, empty-emptiness*. Then ask them to join another pair, share their nouns and write four pairs of sentences, as in exercise A, to show how to use the adjective and noun forms. Check with the whole group.

Step 4 Put students in small groups to discuss the questions in C. Conduct brief feedback.

SPEAKING

Aim
To give fluency practice and round off the unit.

Step 1 Ask students to read the Fact File and put an exclamation mark [!] next to any facts that surprise them.

Step 2 Put students in pairs to compare their ideas. Check understanding and what facts surprised them as a class.

Step 3 Ask students to look at the questions in C and check they understand the words / phrases in bold. They could check in the *Vocabulary Builder*, or with you, if they are not sure.

Step 4 Put students in small groups of four or five to discuss the questions. Conduct brief feedback as a class.

06 HOME

UNIT OVERVIEW
In this unit, you will learn how to **explain about where you are from** and **describe your hometown and area**. You will also practise asking **useful questions when you are staying with someone** and **asking for permission**. The main grammar aims are ***have to / don't have to, can / can't*** and ***will / won't***.

SPEAKING

Aim
To lead in to the topic of home and give fluency practice.

Step 1 Ask students to think about how they would answer the questions in A. Then put them in pairs / threes to discuss them. Conduct brief feedback.

LISTENING

Aim
To give practice in predicting and listening for specific information and detail.

Step 1 Tell students they are going to hear three conversations about three different places: Treviso, Muscat and Port Isabel. Put them in pairs and ask them what – if anything – they know about these places, and where they think they are. Do not conduct feedback as they will hearing the answers to these in the next step.

Step 2 Ask students to listen to the conversations and note down where each place is. Check in pairs then as a group.

Answers
Treviso is in Italy, Muscat is in Oman, Port Isabel is in Texas (US).

6.1
Conversation 1
A: Where are you from?
B: Italy.
A: What part?
B: Treviso.
A: Where's that?
B: It's a small city in the north-east. It's about 40 kilometres from Venice. So say that's Venice, Treviso is just here to the north.
A: Oh OK. So what's it like?
B: It's great. The centre is very old with some beautiful old buildings, but the city's also quite modern. You know Benetton? The clothes?
A: Yes.
B: Well, Benetton's based in Treviso.
A: Oh wow! OK. So where do you live? In the centre?
B: Not exactly, but everything is quite near. It's small. It's easy to get round. I live near the river. You can walk along there – and there's a park. It's nice.

Conversation 2
C: Where are you from?
D: Oman.
C: Oh, OK. Oman. I'm sorry, but where is that exactly? My geography isn't very good.
D: It's in the Middle East – on the Indian Ocean. So you've got Saudi Arabia here and the UAE up here and Oman goes down here to the right.
C: Oh, OK. And where do you live?
D: The capital, Muscat, it's in the north of the country.
C: What's it like? Is it a big city?
D: Quite big – it's about a million and it spreads along the coast quite far.
C: It sounds nice.
D: It is. It's beautiful because you have the sea and the mountains behind. And it's a very exciting place because lots of people from different countries live there and, you know, there's lots to do there.

Conversation 3

E: So where are you from Chuck?
F: Texas.
E: Whereabouts?
F: I doubt you'll know it. It's a little town called Harlingen. It's right in the south – by the Mexican border.
E: Yeah, I know it. In fact, I've been there! I have a friend who lives in Port Isabel.
F: Port Isabel! Wow, that's real close. So did you like it?
E: Yeah, it was lovely. I mean, it's a bit quiet, but for a holiday it was great.
F: When were you there? What time of year?
E: February, but the climate's lovely. It's so warm. We went to the beach quite a lot.
F: Sure.
E: And we took a boat along the coast a couple of times and went fishing.
F: Did you catch anything?
E: Not much, but it was just nice to be on the sea.
F: So what's your friend called?
E: Harry Dancey
F: You're kidding me! Skip Dancey? I went to high school with him!
E: No! Really? What a small world!

Step 3 Tell students to listen again and write down anything else they find out about the three places. Check in pairs, then as a group.

Answers

Treviso: a small city in the north-east. It's about 40 kilometres from Venice. Old buildings, and a river and a park. Benetton is based there.

Muscat: in the Middle East – on the Indian Ocean, capital of the country, millions of people, beautiful – sea and mountains.

Port Isabel: lovely climate and beach, near the Mexican border.

Step 4 Put students in pairs or threes to discuss the questions in D. Conduct brief feedback.

NATIVE SPEAKER ENGLISH *Whereabouts?*

Ask students if they remember how the speaker asked Chuck exactly where he was from (*Whereabouts?*) Read out the box. Elicit more examples by getting them to ask each other where they were born / live / work, etc. followed by *Whereabouts?*

DEVELOPING CONVERSATIONS

Explaining where places are

Aim

To give practice in describing places in more detail.

Step 1 Ask students to look at the map of Germany and decide which place is being described in each of the sentences in A. Check in pairs then check with the whole group. Model and drill some of the key phrases about location, e.g. *It's a big port in the north-east; it's on the coast; it's in the west; it borders France and Germany*.

Step 2 Put students in pairs and ask them to practise having conversations about where they are from. They should cover the sentences in A and use the map and imagine they are from different places in Germany. Tell them to have conversations as in the example. Model and drill with a strong student, then in open pairs, before continuing in closed pairs. Monitor and correct mistakes in target language.

Step 3 Demonstrate to students how we often mime drawing a map when we explain where places are. Show them, using the example in the box. Then put them in small groups to practise explaining and 'drawing' using the examples in C. Model with a strong student first. Tell them to make up where the places are if they aren't sure. Ask them to check on the world map in File 6 on page 157 at the end to see how accurate they were.

VOCABULARY Cities and areas

Aim

To extend the topic and introduce more vocabulary about places.

Step 1 Ask students to look at the groups of words in A and decide which is the odd one out. Check they understand 'odd one out', e.g. student / study / desk / cinema. Which word is the odd one out? Cinema. *Why?* The other's are related to school. Do the first example with them. Check in pairs then with the whole group.

Answers

1. buildings – other words are about climate
2. a forest – others are about industry
3. dirty – others are about nature
4. churches – others are about transport
5. village – others are about city life
6. squares – others are about the countryside
7. desert – others are about the sea
8. modern – others are old
9. lovely – others are negative, about crimes
10. financial – others are about water
    (**Note** *bank* might be tricky, but here it relates to a *river bank.*)

Step 2 Put students in small groups and ask them to pick four of the descriptions in B and think of places that fit each description. Ask them to discuss what they know about the places, whether they have been there, etc. Conduct brief feedback.

Step 3 Ask students individually to write descriptions of three places in their country, using the phrases from A. In a multilingual class, they could write descriptions of places in the country where they are studying. Then put them in pairs and ask them to read the descriptions and guess their partner's places. Conduct brief feedback.

CONVERSATION PRACTICE

Aim
To give freer practice of the target language.

Step 1 Tell students they are going to practise conversations similar to the one they heard in *Listening*. Ask them to choose a country from the world map on page 157, or think about where they are really from, and to look at the questions in A and prepare to answer them.

Step 2 Put students in small groups and get them to take turns asking and answering the questions in A.

Step 3 Conduct brief feedback by asking students to tell you something they learnt about their partner(s).

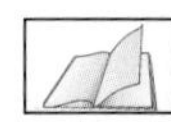 **pp. 44–45**

Next class Make photocopies of **6A** p. 138.

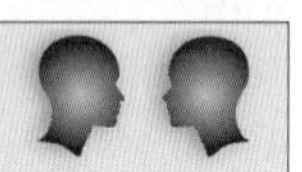

SPEAKING

Aim
To give fluency practice and lead in to *Listening*.

Step 1 Ask students to think about how they would answer the questions in A. Then put them in small groups to discuss their answers. Conduct brief feedback.

LISTENING

Aim
To give practice in listening for gist, specific information and detail.

Step 1 Tell students they are going to hear a Chinese man, Guo, talking about leaving home. Ask them to listen and decide what kind of place he's living in.

Answer
Room in student accommodation / university hall of residence, like the third picture.

6.2
I'm from Harbin, in the north-east of China, but I moved to Wales last year to do a Master's. It's the first time I've lived away from home, it hasn't been easy. The culture is different and I have to speak English all the time as well, which is tiring. The place I'm living in is nice, though. I have my own room with a basin to wash in, but I have to share the bathroom and kitchen with five other students.

The best thing for me now is the freedom. I can do whatever I want – whenever I want. I can come home late if I want to and I don't have to answer questions about where I've been. The hardest things are learning how to live on my own – I have to do everything for myself now – and living in a block with so many other students. It can be very noisy sometimes!

Step 2 Ask students to listen again and make notes on the good and bad things about where Guo lives. Check in pairs then check with the whole group.

Answers
Good: freedom, nice place, own room
Bad: has to do everything himself, e.g. housework, share bathroom and kitchen, sometimes noisy

Step 3 Ask students to complete the sentences in C from what they remember. Then tell them to look at the audioscript on page 167 to check their answers.

Answers
1 have to 2 have to 3 can 4 can 5 don't have to

LANGUAGE PATTERNS

Aim
To draw students' attention to patterns with *whenever, wherever, whoever*, etc.

Step 1 Ask students to look at the sentences in the box and notice the similarities. Ask students to translate these sentences into their own language. In monolingual classes ask students to compare their translations. In multilingual classes ask students to work in pairs and tell each other if the sentences were easy to translate.

Step 2 Ask students to cover the English translations and translate the sentences back into English using their translations. Then ask them to compare their translations in pairs against the book.

Alternatively If you prefer not to use translation, ask students to notice the patterns. Concept check any areas of difficulty and elicit a few more examples from the students.

GRAMMAR *have to, don't have to, can*

Aim
To introduce modals of obligation and permission.

Step 1 Write the examples on the board and use them to highlight form and meaning. Check especially that students understand the difference between *don't have to = it isn't necessary,* and *mustn't = you can't do it.* Read out the box or ask students to read it.

Step 2 Ask students to look at the sentences in A and complete them using the correct form of *have to, don't have to* or *can / can't.* Do the first example with them. Put them in pairs to check their answers, then check with the whole group. Direct them to the grammar reference on page 145 if they still seem unsure.

Answers
1 can
2 have to
3 don't have to
4 can
5 doesn't have to
6 don't have to
7 have to
8 can
9 have to

Step 3 Read out the pronunciation box, highlighting the weak forms. Then get students to say the sentences in A again, paying attention to the weak forms. Play the recording and ask them to repeat after each sentence.

6.3
1 We can walk there in ten minutes.
2 Do you have to pay extra for the bills?
3 I don't have to pay my parents rent.
4 Friends can stay at my house if they want to.
5 She doesn't have to do any housework at all!
6 You don't have to cook for everyone in the flat.
7 I have to help with all the cooking and cleaning.
8 I can talk to her about anything.
9 They have to find a bigger place.

Step 4 Ask students to make a list of good and bad things about where they live. They should use *have to / don't have to* and *can / can't.*

Step 5 Put students in small groups to compare their ideas. Ask them to decide who has the best life in each group and why, and to tell each other if anyone they know has a better life and to explain why using *has to / doesn't have to / can.* Conduct brief feedback.

READING

Aim
To give practice in predicting, reading for detail and responding to text.

Step 1 Tell students they are going to read an article about things you should know before you leave home. Put them in pairs / threes and ask them to imagine what advice the writer might give about the items in A.

Step 2 Ask students to look at the phrases in B and decide which item in A each one connects to. Then ask them to read the article to check their predictions and find out what the writer says about each thing. Check in pairs then as a group.

Answers
Money: a budget, a healthy bank balance – it's important to budget; **Food:** frozen meals, your weight – you should eat healthily and learn to cook; **Housework:** iron your clothes, tools – learn how to use basic tools
Flat-sharing: a pint of milk, argue – don't share with your best friends; **Loneliness:** fill your time, your own company – learn to appreciate being on your own

Step 3 Put students in pairs or threes and ask them to discuss the questions in D. Conduct brief feedback.

6A see Teacher's notes p. 122.

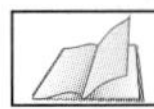
pp. 46–47

Next class Make photocopies of **6B** p. 139.
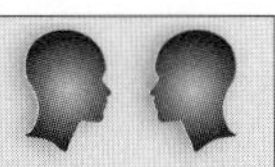

VOCABULARY Staying with people

Aim
To introduce vocabulary associated with staying at someone's house.

Step 1 Ask students to look at the sentences in A and complete each one with the correct word from the box. Check in pairs then as a group.

Answers
1 take off
2 borrow
3 sit
4 leave
5 hang
6 lend
7 lock
8 show
9 use
10 Help

Step 2 Check *guest* = person staying in someone else's home, *host / hostess* = person inviting them to their home. Ask students to read through the sentences in A again, and in pairs to discuss which of the sentences are said by the guest and which by the host. Check with the whole group.

Answers
Guest: 1, 2, 3, 6, 9 Host: 4, 5, 7, 8, 10

Step 4 Put students in pairs and ask them to think of two more things the guest might say, and two more things the host might say. Check with the whole group.

Suggested answers
Guest = Could you lend me a towel, please? Could you show me how to use the shower, please?
Host = Would you like a drink? Could you leave your shoes at the door, please?

SPEAKING

Aim
To give fluency practice.

Step 1 Ask students to think about how they would answer the questions in A. Put students in small groups to discuss their ideas. Conduct brief feedback.

LISTENING

Aim
To give practice in listening for specific information and detail, and note-taking.

Step 1 Tell students they are going to hear a student from Uzbekistan arriving at his host family's in London. Ask them to take notes on what they learn about the host family and the house rules. Play the recording. Check in pairs, then as a group.

Answers
Family: Isabel and Oliver, vegetarian; House rules: own key, no overnight guests, breakfast from 7–8 am, lock the front door at night, no smoking in room

6.4
H1 = host father, M = Maksim, H2 = host mother
H1: Hello there. Come in, come in.
M: Hello. I am Maksim.
H2: Hi. I'm Isabel and this is Oliver. How was your journey?
M: OK, but very long.
H1: I can imagine. Anyway, you're here now. Do you want me to take your coat?
M: Oh, yes. Thank you.
H1: And you can just leave your bag and things over there for now.
H2: Would you like a cup of tea or something to eat, Maksim?
M: No, thank you. I'm fine. Maybe just some water.
H2: Yes, of course. I'll just go and get some for you. There you are.
M: Thank you. Oh, I almost forgot. I brought you this. It's traditional. It's from my country.
H2: Oh thank you. That's very thoughtful of you. It's ... um ... very ... um ... interesting. I'll go and put it ... um ... somewhere.
H1: I'll show you around the house in a minute, Maksim, but first I'll just tell you a bit about the house rules.
M: OK.
H1: We'll give you your own key, so you can come and go when you want. If you come home late, though, please try to be quiet. And make sure you lock the front door.
M: From inside?
H1: Yes. here, look. Like this.
M: Ah, I see. OK.
H1: And no overnight guests are allowed in the house.
M: Guests?
H1: Yes. Um ... no-one can sleep in your room apart from you, so no friends or ...
M: Oh, OK. yes. Don't worry. No problem. No problem.
H1: And breakfast is served between seven and eight. You know we're vegetarian, don't you?
M: Veg ...?
H1: Vegetarian. We don't eat any meat.
M: No meat?
H1: No. Didn't they tell you? Oh well. Anyway, that's more or less everything, I think. I'll show you to your room. I'm sure you're very tired.
M: Yes. And I have to get up early tomorrow. Do you have a watch I can borrow?
H1: An alarm clock, you mean? Yes, I'm sure we can lend you one.
M: Thank you.
H2: And then tomorrow morning, we'll show you how to get to your school.
M: OK. One question. Do you mind if I smoke in my room?
H2: Smoke? Well, actually, I'd rather you didn't, if you don't mind. I'm sorry.

Step 2 Ask students to look at the statements in B and decide if they are true or false. Then play the recording again for them to check. Check in pairs then as a group. Ask students to correct the false sentences.

Answers
1 F = Oliver takes his coat.
2 F = He asks for some water.
3 F = His host family find the present a bit strange.
4 T
5 F = He can come home when he likes.
6 T
7 T
8 T
9 F = The host father will show him how to get to the school.
10 T

Step 3 Put students in pairs or threes to discuss the questions in C. Conduct brief feedback.

DEVELOPING CONVERSATIONS

Asking for permission

Aim

To give practice in ways of asking for permission and responding appropriately.

Step 1 Read out the box, checking understanding as you read. Elicit more examples by getting students to ask permission to do things in open pairs and respond appropriately.

Step 2 Ask students to look at sentences 1–6 in A and match them with the correct response a–f. Then ask students to listen to check their answers. Play the recording. Check with the whole group. Model and drill a few examples, especially for polite intonation.

6.5

1 Do you mind if I open the window?
a No, of course not. It is quite hot, isn't it?
2 Do you mind if I use your computer?
c No, of course not. One minute. I'll just log off.
3 Do you mind if I borrow your phone for a minute?
f Well, actually, I'd rather you didn't. I don't have much credit.
4 Is it OK if I leave class early today?
e Yes, of course. Just make sure you remember to do your homework.
5 Is it OK if I close the window?
d Yes, of course. It is quite cold, isn't it?
6 Is it OK if I stay a few more days?
b Well, actually, I'd rather you didn't. My mother is visiting tomorrow, you see.

Step 3 Put students in pairs and ask them to practise asking and answering the questions in A. Monitor and correct where necessary.

Step 4 Still in pairs, ask students to write three new questions people might ask when staying in someone's house. Tell them to use, *Do you mind if I … / Is it ok if … ?* Check as a group.

GRAMMAR *will / won't*

Aim

To introduce *will / won't* + verb to talk about spontaneous decisions, to make offers or promises and to give immediate responses.

Step 1 Read out the examples in the box, checking as you read. Elicit more examples of each use of *will / won't* from students by miming, e.g. *I'll open the door for you; I won't drop it.*

Step 2 Ask students to look at the sentences in A and to complete them using *'ll / won't* + a suitable verb. Check in pairs, then as a group. Direct students to the grammar reference on page 145 if they still seem unsure.

Answers

1 'll probably just stay
2 'll lend
3 'll call / phone
4 'll bring
5 'll just go
6 'll show
7 won't be
8 won't tell

Step 3 Put students in pairs and ask them to practise conversations, using the sentences in B as starters and giving a suitable response using *I'll … + if you want / like.*

Step 4 Ask students in the same pairs to have three-line conversations, based on their ideas in Step 3 and the sentences in B.

Step 5 Draw students' attention to the weak form of *'ll*. Model and drill a few examples from their conversations in Step 4. Ask them to listen to the recording and repeat the sentences. Play the recording.

6.6

1 I'll call you later.
2 I'll see you tomorrow.
3 I'll help you with that.
4 I'll go and get some.
5 We'll be there at 6.
6 She'll email you.
7 He'll bring it with him on Monday.
8 They'll probably forget.

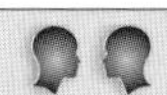 **6B** see Teacher's notes p. 122.

SPEAKING

Aim

To give fluency practice and round off the unit.

Step 1 Tell students they are going to role-play similar conversations to the one they heard in *Listening*. Put them in pairs and ask them to list five things the host mother / father should say to the student about the house rules, the area and the town / city. Ask students to choose their roles. The foreign student should ask three questions from *Developing conversations* exercise C, and both should look at the audioscript on page 168 for ideas and useful expressions.

Step 2 When ready, students role-play the conversation. When finished, they swap roles and start again. Monitor and note down errors in target language for a correction slot at the end.

Optional activity If time, ask a couple of strong pairs to role-play their conversation for the class.

07 MIND AND BODY

UNIT OVERVIEW

The main aims of this unit are to learn how to **talk about common illnesses and their symptoms**, to **give and understand medical advice** and to **give instructions**. The main grammar aims are **imperatives** and ***should, ought to*** and ***why don't you* to give advice**.

Next class Make photocopies of **7A** p. 140.

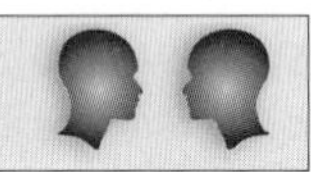

VOCABULARY

Illnesses and health problems

Aim

To introduce vocabulary for health problems.

Step 1 Ask students to look at the illnesses in the box and concept check they know what each one is. Have they or anyone they know suffered from any of these? Then ask them to look at the pictures and match each one with one of the items in the box.

Step 2 Ask students to compare / explain their ideas in pairs then check their answers as a group. Concept check, model and drill where necessary.

Answers

a asthma
b an allergy
c hay fever
d a temperature
e a headache
f a sore throat
g an upset stomach
h the flu
i a nosebleed

Step 3 Put students in pairs / threes and ask them to discuss the questions in C. Conduct brief feedback.

Step 4 Ask students to look at the sentences in D and decide whether the words in bold are adjectives, nouns or verbs. Then ask students to try and translate them into their own language. Check in pairs, then check with the whole group.

Alternatively If you prefer not to use translation, ask them to check the meaning of the words in bold in the *Vocabulary Builder*. Check in pairs, then check with the whole group.

Tip With a monolingual class ask students to compare / check their translations. With a multilingual class ask pairs to tell each other which words were easy / difficult to translate.

Answers

1 *water* = verb, *sneeze* = verb (hay fever)
2 *sick* = adjective (*be sick* = verb) (upset stomach)
3 *rash* = noun (allergy)
4 *out of breath* = adjectival phrase, *cough* = verb (asthma)
5 *last* = verb (nosebleed)
6 *aches* = verb, *appetite* = noun (flu)
7 *swallow* = verb (sore throat)
8 *sweating* = verb (temperature)
9 *concentrate* = verb (headache)

Step 4 Put students in pairs and ask them to match each of the sentences in D with the illnesses / health problems in exercise A. Check with the whole group. (Answers in brackets above.)

LISTENING

Aim

To give practice in listening for specific information and detail.

Step 1 Tell students they are going to hear two conversations about how people are feeling. Ask them to look at the questions in A and try to answer them as they listen. Check in pairs then check with the whole group.

Answers

Conversation 1
1 cold / flu
2 feels weak and tired and aching muscles
3 go home and get some rest
4 yes

Conversation 2
1 hay fever
2 sneezing, eyes watering, taking tablets
3 wear sunglasses
4 no, probably not

7.1

Conversation 1

A: Hi, how're you?
B: Not very well, actually. I think I'm getting the flu.
A: Oh no! You poor thing! Are you sure it's not just a cold?
B: It might be, I suppose, but it doesn't feel like it. I've had it for a few days now. I just feel really weak and tired all the time and my muscles ache a lot.
A: That sounds horrible. Maybe you should go home and get some rest.
B: Yes, maybe you're right.
A: No-one will thank you if you stay and spread it!
B: That's true. Could you tell Mr. Einhoff I'm sick?
A: Yes, of course.
B: Oh, and would you mind giving him my homework? Thank you.
A: That's OK. You take it easy and get well soon.
B: I'll try! Bye.
A: Bye. See you.

Conversation 2

C: Bless you!
D: Oh! I am sorry! That's the fifth time in as many minutes!
C: That's OK.
D: I always get like this at this time of year! It's awful, because I hate winter, but then as soon as the sun comes out I can't stop sneezing! And my eyes really water as well. I really want to rub them, but that just makes them worse!
C: Oh, that sounds horrible. Are you taking anything for it?
D: Yes, I went to the chemist's last year and they recommended these tablets, so I take four of these every day, and they do help, but they don't stop it completely.
C: Why don't you get some sunglasses to protect your eyes a bit?
D: That's not a bad idea, actually, but I think I'd feel a bit funny walking round in sunglasses all day!
C: Yeah, I know what you mean, but maybe you ought to try it. You never know. It might work for you.

NATIVE SPEAKER ENGLISH *Bless you!*

Mime sneezing and try to elicit what we say when someone else sneezes = *Bless you!* Ask students what they say in their own languages and whether it is similar or different to English. Ask them why they think we say these things (one ancient reason was in case someone had the plague; now it is considered good manners). Read out the box. Ask when people sneeze (when they have a cold, the flu, hay fever, allergies, etc.).

GRAMMAR Giving advice (*should, ought to, why don't you*)

Aim
To focus on and practise different ways of giving advice.

Step 1 Try to elicit some ways of giving advice by telling students you have a headache and asking them what you should do, e.g. *You should lie down; You should drink some water.* Read out the grammar box. Ask them to notice the verb form after *should, ought to, why don't you* (base form or infinitive without *to*).

Note These forms are all interchangeable but *ought to* is the most formal and *why don't you* is the least formal.

Step 2 Ask students to complete the sentences in A with only one word in each space. Do the first one with them, then check in pairs then with the whole group. Direct them to the grammar reference on page 146 if they still seem unsure.

Answers

1 should	5 don't
2 ought	6 should, ought
3 should, Why	7 to
4 should	8 A ought, B should, A you

Step 3 In pairs ask students to discuss what they think the problem is in each case in A. Check ideas as a class.

Suggested answers
1 husband has stayed out all night with his friends without calling
2 she insulted her friend
3 booking tickets for a concert
4 bad service in a restaurant
5 changing jobs
6 car needs a service
7 young man has no job and no money after university
8 she is working extra hours for no extra money.

Step 4 Ask students to look at the problems in C and think of suitable advice for each one. Check their ideas in open pairs.

Suggested answers
1 Why don't you join a gym?
2 You ought to have a hot bath before you go to bed.
3 You should see your doctor.
4 Why don't you put a bandage on it?
5 You ought to revise more.
6 Why don't you get a part-time job?

7A see Teacher's notes p. 123.

Developing conversations

Common questions about illness

Aim
To extend the topic and lead in to fluency practice.

Step 1 Ask students to look at questions 1–3 in A and match them with two possible answers a–f. Check in pairs then as a group.

Answers
1 b, f   2 c, e   3 a, d

Step 2 Put students in pairs and ask them to think of two more possible answers to the questions in A. Check their ideas as a class.

Conversation practice

Aim
To give freer practice of the target language.

Step 1 Tell students they are going to role-play conversations similar to those in *Listening*. They should each think of an illness / health problem, either from *Vocabulary*, or something else. They should think of its symptoms, how serious it is, whether they have been to the doctor's or taken anything for it, etc. Tell them to make some notes and to look at the unit for ideas.

Tip Weaker students could look at the audioscript on page 168 for useful expressions to use.

Step 2 Put students in pairs. One should start by asking, *Are you OK?* and both should use as much language from the unit as possible. When they have finished, they should swap. Monitor and note down errors in target language for a correction slot at the end.

Step 3 If time, ask a strong pair to role-play their conversation for the class.

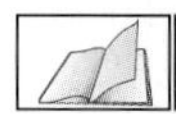
pp. 50–51

Reading

Aim
To further extend the topic into mental health. To give practice in predicting, responding to text and reading for specific information.

Note Before going into the topic of mental illnesses, remember that this may be upsetting for some students as they may have had personal experiences or be affected by this in some way.

Step 1 Ask students to look at the sentences in A and try to guess what the word / phrases in bold mean. Tell them to check in the *Vocabulary Builder* on pp. 27–28 if they are not sure. Check as a class.

Answers
1 mental illnesses = illnesses of the mind rather than physical illnesses, e.g. schizophrenia, depression
2 treatments = ways of trying to make someone better
3 cured = made better
4 recovered = returned to health
5 overcoming = dealing successfully with a problem, controlling
6 blind = unable to see
7 disability = a physical or mental condition that restricts the way someone lives their life
8 negative attitudes = being critical about something

Step 2 Put students in pairs and ask them to discuss the questions in A. Conduct brief feedback. Then ask the students to read the first paragraph of the article and discuss the questions.

Step 3 Ask students to read the second paragraph of the article and discuss in the same pairs whether it changes their attitude and why. Check their ideas.

Step 4 Ask students to read the rest of the article, ignoring the words in bold and decide whether the statements in E are true or false. Check in pairs then with the whole group.

Tip For extra practice ask them to correct the false sentences (answers included below).

Answers
1 T
2 T
3 F Many people recover fully.
4 T
5 F Men don't show emotions because of expectations from society.
6 F Science is making progress.
7 F We need to change our attitudes towards mental illnesses.

Step 5 Ask students to look at the text again and complete the sentences in F with the correct form of the correct word in bold. Check in pairs, then with the whole group. Ask concept questions, model and drill where necessary.

Answers
1 recovered
2 reaction = response
3 case = dose
4 progress = improvement
5 recognises = accepts
6 overcome
7 anxiety = feeling of worry or fear
8 attitude

Step 6 Put students in small groups to discuss the questions in G. Conduct brief feedback.

VOCABULARY Forming words

Aim
To look at some common ways of forming adjectives from verbs and nouns.

Step 1 Lead in by trying to elicit adjectives from *believe* = *believable*, *emotion* = *emotional* and *nature* = *natural*. Ask students what they notice about this (added *-able* and *-al*). Then read out the box. Try to elicit more examples of adjectives ending in *-able* and *-al*.

Step 2 Ask students to look at the words in A and decide which come from nouns, which from verbs. Check in pairs, then check with the whole group. Elicit spelling of nouns and verbs so students can see how the spelling changes. Model and drill to focus on stress changes.

Answers
All except *inevitable*, but formed in different ways. Afford (v), compare (v), advise (v), finance (n), chemical (n), centre (n), physics (n) affordable comparable advisable inevitable financial chemical central physical

Step 3 Ask students to complete the sentences in B with an adjective formed from the underlined word. Check in pairs then as a group. Model and drill and elicit the stress.

Answers

1 industrial	5 curable
2 enjoyable	6 acceptable
3 musical	7 reliable
4 cultural	8 occasional

SPEAKING

Aim
To extend the topic and give personalised fluency practice.

Step 1 Ask students to look at the joke, check students understand why it's funny (a play on *like*, the doctor likes to eat sausages, but the man likes to keep them in his living room, which is strange). Ask them to look at the questions in A and think about how they would answer them.

Step 2 Put students in groups to discuss the questions. Conduct brief feedback at the end.

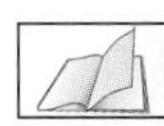

pp. 52–53

Next class Make photocopies of **7B** p. 141.

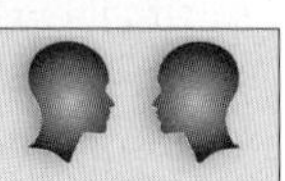

VOCABULARY Parts of the body

Aim
To revise vocabulary for parts of the body.

Step 1 Run through the vocabulary in the box and ask students to show / point to the corresponding parts of the body. Then ask students to look at the picture and label it with the words from the box.

Answers

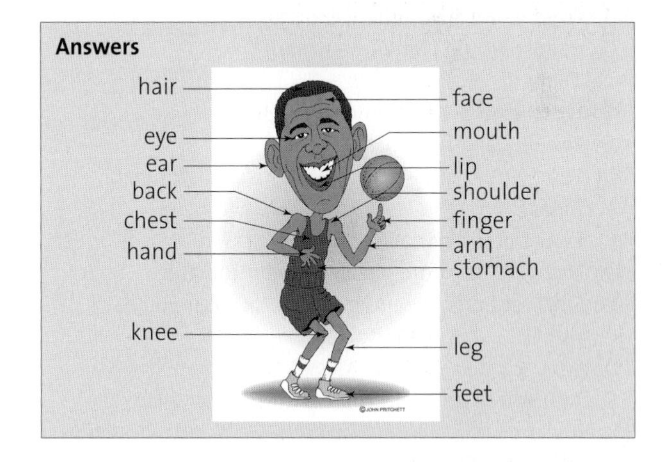

Step 2 Ask students to complete each group of collocations with the correct part of the body from A. Check in pairs, then with the whole group. Concept check where necessary, e.g. conduct as a drill, tell all students to stand up and say: *touch your nose, touch your lips*, etc.

Answers
1 back 2 feet 3 lip 4 hair 5 face 6 stomach

Step 3 Put students in AB pairs. B should close his / her book. Student A should be the 'doctor' and read out the instructions in C. Student B should do what A tells them. Monitor and check students are following the instructions correctly.

Listening

Aim
To give practice in listening for gist and detail.

Step 1 Tell students they are going to hear three conversations. They should listen and circle the correct place in A for each one. Play the recording. Check in pairs then as a group.

Answers
1 d 2 e 3 b

7.2
Conversation 1
A: Are you OK?
B: Hic! Yeah, I've just got hiccups. Oh gosh! Hic! It's really annoying.
A: Here. I know a cure. It never fails.
B: Hic.
A: Take some water in your mouth, but don't drink it.
B: Mmm.
A: Now put your fingers in your ears. Bend down and put your head between your knees and swallow the water slowly.
B: Mmmm?
A: Swallow the water!
B: Mmm.
A: OK. You can breathe now. Have you still got them?
B: Um, no. No, I don't think so.
A: You see. It works every time.
B: Maybe, but I wouldn't want to do it in public! People would think I was mad!

Conversation 2
C: Yes sir. Can I help you?
D: Yes, I would like something for a bad stomach, please.
C: Does it hurt or have you been sick?
D: Not sick. It's more gas. It's uncomfortable.
C: OK. It sounds like indigestion. It's after you eat, right?
D: Yes.
C: And you're going to the toilet normally? No diarrhoea?
D: Diarrhoea? No.
C: OK, so I think these are what you need. They're indigestion tablets. You mix them with water and drink them after your meals. They're the most effective, I think.
D: OK.
C: What flavour would you like? Orange or blackcurrant?
D: Oh, orange.
C: That'll be four twenty-five. Don't take more than four tablets a day – and if they don't deal with the problem, consult your doctor.
D: OK. Thanks. I will.

Conversation 3
E: The burn's not too bad. We'll give you some cream for it, but you'll need some stitches in that cut. It's quite deep. What happened?
F: Well, I cut my head dancing with my son.
E: I'm sorry?
F: I was dancing with my five-year-old son and I stepped on one of his toys and I fell and hit my head on the side of the table.
E: Oh dear. What about the burn, then?
F: Well, my wife came in when she heard me shout and while she was helping me stand up, she knocked a cup of coffee off the table and it went all over my leg.
E: Oh dear, I am sorry. I shouldn't laugh!
F: Don't worry. It was very stupid!
E: Nurse, could you dress the burn after I've done these stitches?
G: Of course.

Step 2 Ask students to look at the questions in B and try to answer them as they listen again. Play the recording again. Check in pairs then with the whole group.

Answers
Conversation 1
1 hiccups
2 she put some water in her mouth, her fingers in her ears and her head between her knees

Conversation 2
1 indigestion
2 take indigestion tablets mixed with water after meals

Conversation 3
1 a burn and a cut
2 he fell while dancing with his son and cut his head; his wife spilt coffee on his leg

Tip With a weaker class pause after each conversation to allow them time to answer the questions. Play the recording again if necessary.

Step 3 In pairs or small groups, ask students to act or draw what happened in each conversation. Their partner(s) should guess which conversation they're acting or drawing.

Step 4 Ask students to look at the questions in D. Check they understand *pharmacists* = people who work in chemist's, *prescription* = note from doctor with details of medicine you need to buy and take, *chemist's* = shop where you buy medicine and cosmetics. In small groups ask students to discuss the questions. Conduct brief feedback.

GRAMMAR Imperatives

Aim
To practise positive and negative imperative forms.

Step 1 Read out the box and ask checking questions as you read, e.g. *What form do we use for the imperative* (to give orders or advice)? = the base form. *What do we add to form the negative?* (*Don't.*)

Step 2 Ask students to look at sentences 1–8 in A and complete them, using an imperative form of the correct word from the box, so that they mean something similar to the instruction above them. Check *exceed* = take more than; *external* = on the body or skin; *drowsiness* = feeling sleepy. Check in pairs, then with the whole group.

Answers

1 Don't take	5 Don't drink
2 Drink	6 Wash
3 Put	7 Don't leave
4 Don't stop	8 Let

Step 3 Ask students to look at the example in B. Model the game with a strong student, using the example. Then put the students in pairs to play the game using the six sentence starters given. Remind them this is not a natural conversation. Monitor and correct where necessary. Direct students to the grammar reference on page 146 if they still seem unsure.

 **7B** see Teacher's notes p. 123.

LANGUAGE PATTERNS

Aim
To draw students' attention to patterns with verb + *-ing*.

Step 1 Ask students to look at the sentences in the box and notice the similarities (verb + *-ing*). Ask students to translate these sentences into their own language. In monolingual classes ask students to compare their translations. In multilingual classes ask students to work in pairs and tell each other if the sentences were easy to translate and whether they were able to translate them word for word.

Step 2 Ask students to cover the English translations and translate the sentences back into English using their translations. Then ask them to compare their translations in pairs against the book.

Alternatively If you prefer not to use translation, ask students to notice the patterns. Concept check any areas of difficulty and elicit a few more examples from the students. If time, write their examples on the board and tick them if correct. If the sentences are wrong, ask the students to correct them or correct them yourself.

SPEAKING

Aim
To round off the unit and give fluency practice.

Step 1 Check students understand *scar* = a mark remaining on the body after an injury or operation. Elicit different ways you can get scars. Ask them to look at the instructions in A and think about what they are going to say. They could make a few notes.

Step 2 Put students in small groups and ask them to tell their stories. Monitor and help where necessary.

Step 3 Conduct feedback by asking students which was the funniest / strangest / most interesting, etc. story they heard.

08 GETTING THERE

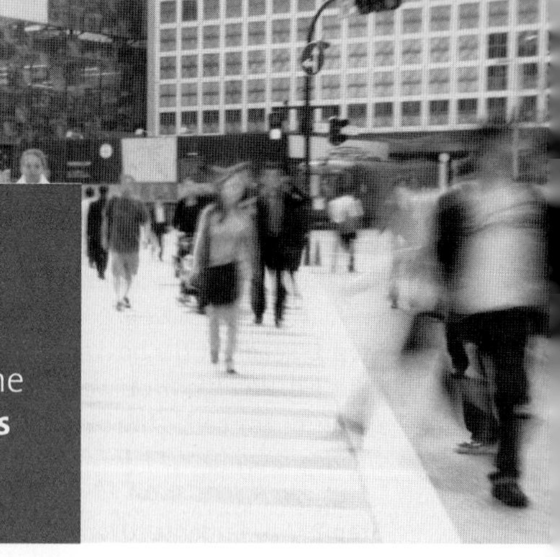

UNIT OVERVIEW
The main aims of this unit are to learn to **talk about travelling, well-known buildings and places, ask for and give directions** and **ask questions in a more polite way.** The main grammar aims are to revise the **definite and indefinite articles (*a, an* and *the*)** and the use of **quantifiers with uncountable nouns.**

VOCABULARY Places in town

Aim
To present vocabulary for places in a town and to lead in to *Listening*.

Step 1 Ask students to look at the picture and find examples of the words / phrases in the box. Check in pairs, then check with the whole group. Model and drill where necessary. Check a *subway* = way of crossing the road underground; *town hall* = headquarters of local council or local government; *playground* = place outside where children play, often attached to a school; a *roundabout* = alternative to crossroads, where two or three roads meet.

Step 2 Put students in pairs and ask them to answer the questions in B. Check with the whole group.

Answers
1 all of them
2 a bridge, a crossing (especially a level crossing, over a railway)
3 a sports ground, a playground, a monument
4 a roundabout
5 traffic lights, a subway, a crossroads
6 a church
7 a police station
8 a town hall

Step 3 Put students in pairs / threes and ask them to discuss the questions in C. Conduct brief feedback.

Tip In a multilingual class try and put students in mixed pairs. In a monolingual class tell them to talk about other cities they have been to.

NATIVE SPEAKER ENGLISH *subway*

Ask students about the word *subway*. Ask them what it is in the picture and ask if they know a different meaning (in American English = *the underground*). Ask if they know any other examples like this, e.g. *sidewalk* (British English) versus *pavement* (American English). Then read out the box.

LISTENING

Aim
To give practice in listening for specific information.

Step 1 Tell students they are going to listen to a couple asking a number of different people for directions. Ask them to look at the questions in A and try to answer them as they listen. Play the recording. Check in pairs, then with the whole group.

Answers
1 the museum
2 it's a long way, they didn't listen, they got off at the wrong stop
3 to the bus stop, to another bus stop (67), to the museum

8.1

Conversation 1

A: Listen, we're obviously lost – ask this guy.
B: OK, OK. ... Sorry. Do you speak English?
C: Sure.
B: Oh, great. Do you know the way to the museum from here?
C: Yes, but it is far. It's better to get a bus.
B: OK. So how do we get to the stop?
C: Down this road. Take the second on the right then cross, turn left and then left and it's directly opposite the town hall.
B: OK great.
C: No problem.
B: So did he say second right or second left?
A: I don't know I wasn't really listening, I thought you were! What bus did he say we should catch?
B: No idea! Listen, it's down here somewhere anyway.

Conversation 2

B: It's your turn. Ask that old lady.
A: Excuse me. Is this the right bus stop for the museum?
D: Eh?
A: The bus? Brmm To the museum?
D: Eh?
A: To the museum?
D: Eh?
E: You want the number 67 bus.
D: Oh thanks.
E: You have to go over the road. This stop, it goes the wrong way. Go over the crossing. It's after the traffic lights.
A: I see it. Thanks.
E: They come often.
A: Thanks.

Conversation 3

A: Excuse me, sorry. Do you speak English?
F: Sure I do. How can I help?
A: Do you know where the museum is? Is it near here?
F: Yes, quite near, but you got off at the wrong stop, really. Go down this road until you come to a church. Then turn left. It's quite a big road. You'll go past a monument and a football ground. Just keep going. It's maybe half a mile. It's on the right. You can't miss it.
B: I told you that was it! Why do you never listen to me?

Step 2 Ask students to look at the sentences in B and try to choose the correct word from memory. Play the recording again for them to check.

Answers

1 way	6 where the museum is
2 It's	7 near
3 Take	8 got off
4 did he say	9 going
5 right	10 miss

Step 3 Put the students in small groups and ask them to discuss the questions in C. Conduct brief feedback.

Language patterns

Ask students to look at the questions in the box and notice what they have in common (*Do you know...?*). Ask them to write the questions in their own language.

Step 2 Ask students to cover the English translations and translate the sentences back into English using their translations. Then ask them to compare their translations in pairs against the book.

Alternatively If you prefer not to use translation, ask students to ask each other questions using *Do you know...?*

Developing conversations

Giving directions

Aim

To practise asking for and giving directions focusing on prepositions.

Step 1 Ask students if they remember any phrases used in *Listening* to give directions. *You have to go over the road; Go down this road until you come to a church*, etc. Read out the box, modelling and drilling the prepositional phrases.

Step 2 Ask students to complete the directions in A, using the correct preposition from the box. Check in pairs, then check with the whole group.

Answers

1 over	5 to
2 through	6 at
3 along	7 on
4 past	8 opposite

Step 3 Ask students to draw a map to illustrate the directions given in A. Put them in pairs to compare their maps.

Tip Bring a map of the area you're teaching in to class and use it to give students directions to the school.

Step 4 Ask students to choose one of the places in C and write a short email giving directions from their home to this place. Monitor and help as they write. Then put students in pairs and ask them to swap emails, check they are clear and correct any mistakes.

Tip You could ask them to write these emails as homework and then compare them in the next class.

Conversation practice

Aim
To give freer, more communicative practice of the target language.

Step 1 Tell students they are going to role-play several conversations between a local person and someone new to the area.

Step 2 Put students in AB pairs. Student A should look at the map in File 4 on page 156 and Student B should look at the map in File 20 on page 160. They should take turns asking for and giving directions to various places, using the structures given in A. Monitor and note down errors in target language for a correction slot at the end.

pp. 56–57

Next class Make photocopies of **8A** p. 142.

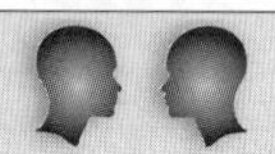

Speaking

Aim
To lead in to the reading and the topic of travel.

Step 1 Put students in pairs / threes and ask them to look at the quotes about travel in A and discuss what they mean and whether they agree or disagree. Monitor and make sure they understand all the language. Conduct brief feedback.

Reading

Aim
To give practice in predicting, reading for gist and detail.

Step 1 Tell students they are going to read a folktale about travelling and that the last paragraph is missing. They should read it and guess how the story ends. Put them in pairs to compare their ideas. Then ask them to read the ending in File 3 on page 156.

Step 2 Ask students in the same pairs to decide which of the six quotes in *Speaking* A best illustrates the story. Check with the whole group.

Suggested answer
'Travel makes wise people better and stupid people worse.'

Step 3 Ask students to look at the adjectives in D and decide which aspects of the story they describe. Check in pairs, then with the whole group.

Answer
brief: story is brief, conversation with farmer is brief
keen: traveller to rest his feet
glad: second person farmer meets
disappointed: first stranger when farmer tells him the people in the next town are the same
selfish: first stranger
dusty: road
happy: farmer / second stranger
hard-working: farmer

Step 4 Ask students to complete the sentences in E with the correct adjective from D. Check in pairs, then with the whole group.

Answers
1 happy
2 glad
3 keen, disappointed
4 hard-working
5 brief
6 selfish
7 dusty

Note Students may find question 3 hard as *very happy to meet me* almost works. Try and encourage them to use *keen* instead.

Grammar articles (*a*, *an*, and *the*)

Aim
To revise the rules for using the definite and indefinite articles.

Step 1 Read out the box, asking checking questions and eliciting other examples as you read. For example hold up pen and ask *What's this?* (A pen.) *Where's the pen?* (It's in your hand.) Why did you use *a* first and then *the*? (*A* introduced something new; *the* because it's already been mentioned and the listener knows which pen it is.)

Step 2 Ask students to complete the sentences in A with the correct article. Check in pairs then check with the whole group.

Answers
1 a, the
2 the, the, a
3 a
4 an, a, a, the
5 a, the, a, the, a
6 A the, the
B the, the, a, the, the

Step 3 Ask students to look at pairs of sentences 1–5 in B and cross out *the* where it isn't necessary. Do the first example with them and concept check the difference between 1A and 1B (general versus specific). Check in pairs, then check with the whole group. Direct students to the grammar reference on page 147 if they still seem unsure.

Answer
Cross out *the* in 1a 2a, 3b, 4a, 5a

Step 4 In pairs ask students to discuss which of the sentences in exercise B they agree with. Conduct brief feedback.

8A see Teacher's notes p. 123.

PRONUNCIATION *the*

Aim
To focus on the two different pronunciations of *the*.

Step 1 Read out the box and elicit / model a few examples, e.g. *the Spanish language, the English language; the orange, the lemon, the computer, the Internet.*

Step 2 Put students in pairs and ask them to look at the phrases in A and decide how *the* is pronounced.

Step 3 Play the recording and ask students to listen, check their ideas and repeat after each one.

8.2
the black forest /ðə/
the Great Wall /ðə/
the Mediterranean /ðə/
the Indian Ocean /ði/
the great Barrier Reef /ðə/
the Canary Islands /ðə/
the Alps /ði/
the Amazon /ði/
the Nile /ðə/
the Eiffel Tower /ði/
the equator /ði/
the Sahara /ðə/
the Andes /ði/
the Thames /ðə/
the Pyramids /ðə/
the Caribbean /ðə/
the Arctic /ði/
the Himalayas /ðə/

Step 4 Put students in small groups and ask them to discuss the questions in C. Conduct brief feedback.

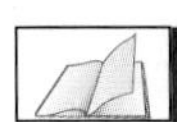

pp. 58–59

Next class Make photocopies of **8B** p. 143.

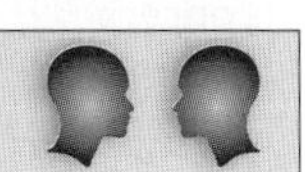

VOCABULARY Transport

Aim
To extend the topic and introduce forms of transport and associated words.

Step 1 Lead in to the topic by asking students how they got to class. The ask them to match 1–10 in A with the forms of transport in the box. Check in pairs, then with the whole group. Check *coach* = a long-distance bus.

Answers

1 foot	6 train
2 taxi	7 car
3 coach	8 bus
4 plane	9 boat
5 bike	10 motorbike

Step 2 Put students in pairs / small groups and ask them to take turns acting or drawing one of the forms of transport from exercise A. Their partner should guess. Then they swap and repeat.

Step 3 Tell students to think of places they have been using six of the forms of transport. Model the conversation in C with a strong student, then continue in open pairs. Then in closed pairs, ask students to practise conversations, using different modes of transport. Monitor and correct where necessary.

8B see Teacher's notes p. 123.

LISTENING

Aim
To give practice in predicting, listening for gist and detail.

Step 1 Tell students they are going to hear the travel news on the radio, followed by an interview with Ellen MacArthur, the famous round-the-world British sailor. Put them in small groups and ask them to look at the travel problems in A and think of as many possible reasons for them as they can. Check these as a class.

Note Ellen MacArthur broke the world record in 2005 for the fastest sailing around the globe.

Step 2 Ask students to listen to the news and decide how many items there are and which ones are good / bad travel news. Play the recording. Check in pairs, then with the whole group.

Answer
seven; only one good piece of news – London-Birmingham rail services reopening

8.3
M = Mark; L = Lisa

M: In a moment we'll be with Ellen McArthur, interviewing her about her latest adventure – sailing round the globe on her own – so if you have any questions for her, ring 9873-7373 or email us at may@bbd.net. But first, the travel news from Lisa Verity.

L: Thanks Mark. Not much good news, I'm afraid. Getting anywhere today is going to feel a bit like sailing round the world for many people. Terrible problems in a lot of places at the moment.

Starting with the airports. The air traffic controllers' strike in France is continuing to cause complete chaos. Many flights are being delayed and quite a few cancelled because only a few planes can fly over France and others have to be diverted to avoid French air space. Passengers who are flying at any time in the next few days are asked to ring their airline or consult their airline's website.

A lorry has crashed on the A516 entering Milton Keynes and lost its load of watermelons. Lanes in both directions are shut at the moment while police try to clear up the mess – a big mess I would imagine too! Avoid the area, if you can.

The M6 motorway between junctions 5 and 6 is completely closed for repairs. A diversion is in operation, but expect delays all day there. Traffic moving very slowly, so best to take other routes.

Large sections of the Northern Line in London are closed today because of continuing repair work to renew the underground. A replacement bus service is in operation. And East Ham station is closed because of a flood. A burst water pipe there.

Better news elsewhere. The rail service between London and Birmingham is now running normally after a fallen tree was removed from the line. And there aren't any more problems on the A6 now that the traffic lights are working again at the crossroads with the B761. The traffic's moving freely there.

Finally, two events tonight to tell you about. Just to remind those travelling to Wembley for the big concert there – there's no parking in or around the stadium. Police will be operating in the area to remove cars, so go on foot or take public transport. And lastly, in central London, a demonstration by cyclists is likely to cause some traffic problems from 5 o'clock, so avoid driving or leave work early. That's all from me – back to Brian.

M: That's pretty awful for those going on holiday. Any idea when the air traffic controllers might end their strike?

L: Well, negotiations are continuing, but there's little hope of a deal yet. We'll give you more news when we have it.

M: OK, thanks. Well, strikes were probably one thing she didn't have to deal with, but she had plenty of bad weather, storms, ten-metre high waves and more. Ellen McArthur, it doesn't sound like much fun! Why do you do it?

Step 3 Ask students to look at the table in C and complete it as they listen again. Play the recording. Play it again if necessary. Check in pairs, then with the whole group.

Answers

Place	Problem	Cause	Solution / advice
Airport	flights delayed / cancelled	strike in France	check with airline
A516	closed lanes	lorry crashed	avoid area
M6 junctions 5–6	diversion	repairs	take other routes
Northern Line	sections closed	repairs	take replacement bus
East Ham station	closed	flood, burst water pipe	[none]
Wembley concert	no parking	too crowded	take public transport
Central London	traffic problems	bike demonstration	avoid driving or leave work early

Step 4 Ask students to match a verb in column A with a noun phrase in column B to form phrases from *Listening*. Play the recording again and ask them to look at the audioscript on pp. 169–170 to check their answers. Check as a class.

Tip Tell students the phrases come in the same order as the questions.

Answers

1 e	2 d	3 f	4 a	5 h	6 c	7 b	8 g

Optional extra For extra practice, ask students to tell you what each of the phrases in D are referring to in *Listening*.

Answers
1 boat
2 strike in France
3 strike in France
4 lorry (watermelons)
5 spilt watermelons
6 the A516 entering Milton Keynes
7 railway tracks
8 air traffic controllers' strike

Step 5 Put students in small groups and ask them to tell each other about any similar situations that have happened to them. Conduct brief feedback at the end.

Alternatively If they haven't experienced any of these, they can use an example of someone they know, or make something up.

Grammar

Quantifiers with uncountable nouns

Aim
To focus on quantifiers with countable / uncountable nouns.

Step 1 Read out the examples in the box, checking and eliciting other examples as you read, e.g. ask for more uncountable nouns (traffic, transport) and more countable ones (trains, cars). What else can you have *many* of (problems, delays) and *not much of* (time, money).

Step 2 Ask students to complete sentences 1–10 in A by choosing the correct alternative. Do the first one with them. Check in pairs, then with the whole group.

Answers

1 any	6 little
2 much	7 many
3 any	8 much
4 a few	9 some, many
5 few	10 any

Direct students to the grammar reference on page 147 if they still seem unsure.

Step 3 Ask students to look at the sentence beginnings in B and think of as many possible endings as they can. These should be true for themselves as far as possible, otherwise they can invent them. Then put students in pairs to try to 'beat' each other. They should read out their sentences and the one with the most true ones wins. If they think their partner is lying, they should challenge them by asking questions. Monitor and help / correct where necessary.

Step 4 Conduct brief feedback and do a correction slot at the end.

Speaking

Aim
To round off the unit and give fluency practice.

Step 1 Ask students to look at the questions in A and think about how they would answer them. Check they understand words like *reliable* = you can believe such a person will do what they say they are going to do, *banned* = not allowed, *policy* = set of plans or ideas on which a decision is based. Ask them to make a few notes, using language from the unit where possible.

Step 2 Put students in small groups to discuss the questions. Monitor and note down errors in target language for a correction slot at the end.

Alternatively If you don't have time to discuss all nine questions, ask students to choose in their pairs the four / five questions they think are most interesting to discuss.

02 REVIEW

LEARNER TRAINING

Aim

To make students more aware of different ways of learning and practising grammar.

Step 1 Lead in by asking students how they feel about learning grammar, what different strategies they use to help them, etc. Read out the ideas and ask students if they have any preferences.

Step 2 Ask students to look at the statements and look back at the units to find examples of each thing mentioned. Ask them to think about why the book works like this and about which of these sections they like / dislike and why.

Step 3 Put students in small groups to discuss their ideas. Conduct brief feedback at the end.

GAME, CONVERSATION PRACTICE & ACT OR DRAW

For aims and suggested procedures see Review 01, pp. 32–33.

QUIZ

Answers

1 Three activities with **a net** are tennis, table tennis and badminton.
2 A **draw** is 0–0 or 1–1, etc.
3 If someone **cheats** they break the rules – they are punished if caught.
4 People might want to **raise awareness** of problems or issues or learning styles / strategies, as in learner training. They would do it by asking questions or giving exercises / tasks.
5 In a **rural** area you could find farms, lakes, rivers, mountains, fields, villages.
6 A budget is to help people control their spending. You **keep to** one by saving and not spending too much.
7 You would tell someone to **go ahead** if you want them to go in front of you or answer a question.
8 The **host** invites someone; the **guest** is invited.
9 **A sneeze** is through your nose; **a cough** is through your mouth.
10 Yes, it is a good thing to **overcome** a problem.
11 If people **panic**, they get very anxious and lose control.
12 A doctor gives you a **prescription**, and you take it to the chemist to get your medicine.
13 You would **report** a crime at a police station.
14 Two kinds of **lane** are a bus lane and a motorway lane – or a country lane.
15 There might be a **traffic jam** because of repairs or an accident, or just too many cars.

COLLOCATIONS

For aims and suggested procedure see Review 01, pp. 32–33.

PRONUNCIATION Words containing *o* or *u*

For aims and suggested procedure see Review 01, pp. 32–33.

R2.1

/ɒ/	golf
/uː/	pool
/ʌ/	lovely
/ə/	spectator
/ɔː/	shorts
/ɜː/	work
/ʊ/	put
/əʊ/	throw
/aʊ/	out
/ɔɪ/	boy

Answers

1 couple
2 wood
3 move
4 swallow
5 factory
6 cause
7 flu
8 mouth
9 launch
10 coincidence

R2.2

1 /ɒ/ concentrate, forest, cough, foreign, couple
2 /uː/ loser, remove, statue, mood, wood
3 /ʌ/ countryside, budget, brush, month, move
4 /ə/ season, recognise, contain, freedom, swallow
5 /ɔː/ forecast, score, court, shortage, factory
6 /ɜː/ burst, murder, worst, survey, cause
7 /ʊ/ put, pull, full, wool, flu
8 /əʊ/ mouth, boat, ocean, shoulder, progress
9 /aʊ/ doubt, allow, town hall, ground, launch
10 /ɔɪ/ noisy, annoy, voice, avoid, coincidence

R2.3

1 score a goal
2 hurt your shoulder
3 bounce up and down
4 drop the ball on the ground
5 reduce pollution from factories
6 the forecast is for snow
7 brush the dust from the floor
8 a good cure for an upset stomach

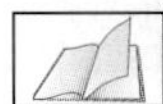 **pp. 62–63**

Listening

For aims and suggested procedure see for the rest of the review see Review 01, pp. 32–35. The audio is R2.4.

Exercise A answers
a 1 b 4 c - d 2 e 3

Exercise B answers
a 4 b 3 c - d 2 e 1

Grammar

Exercise A answers
1 I might
2 We are going to have
3 can't
4 the easiest
5 correct
6 I'll bring
7 correct
8 correct
9 I'll see
10 will be
11 are coming
12 correct

Exercise B answers
1 much
2 any
3 many
4 few
5 lots
6 some
7 a
8 the

Exercise C answers
1 Why don't you
2 the most intelligent person
3 don't make a noise
4 ought to do
5 are no

Prepositions

Answers
1 through
2 along
3 at
4 On
5 on
6 from
7 on
8 on

Language patterns

Answers
1 more
2 whatever
3 wherever
4 playing
5 if / whether
6 is

Forming words

Answers
1 illness
2 central
3 financial
4 consciousness
5 advisable
6 depression
7 treatment
8 comparable

Adjectives

Answers
1 tiny
2 right
3 sore
4 brief
5 spare
6 foreign
7 weak
8 dry

Nouns

Answers
1 pollution
2 progress
3 budget
4 back
5 case
6 motorway
7 appointment
8 line

Verbs

Answers
1 b catching
2 b drop
3 c banned
4 c cheated
5 a raced
6 b beat
7 b delayed
8 c crossing
9 a support

09 SCIENCE AND NATURE

UNIT OVERVIEW

The main aims of this unit are to learn to **talk about the weather, animals and pets, science and research** and to **discuss and respond to news stories**. The main grammar aims are to introduce **the past perfect simple** and **reported speech**.

VOCABULARY Science and nature

Aim

To introduce vocabulary associated with different aspects of science and nature.

Step 1 Lead in by writing the word *nature* on the board and brainstorming words and phrases students associate with it. To help, you might like to write different categories like *animals, weather, science* on the board.

Step 2 Ask students to put the words from the box in A in the correct column. Check in pairs, then check with the whole group. Model, drill and concept check where necessary.

Answers

Science	**The weather**	**Animals**
a discovery	freezing	a horse
experiments	snow	mosquitoes
investigate	boiling	a bee
a rocket	a storm	protect
space	windy	extinct
nuclear	sunny	a whale
	rain	pets

Step 3 Ask students to look at the weather words and the questions in B and think about a time when they experienced each kind of weather. You might like to model this by telling them about some bad weather you've experienced. Put them in small groups to talk about their experiences. Conduct brief feedback at the end. *What is the worst weather anyone in the class experienced?*

Step 4 Ask students to complete the sentences in C with one of the words from A. Check in pairs, then with the whole group.

Answers
1 horse
2 a rocket
3 extinct
4 experiments
5 nuclear
6 investigate
7 discovery
8 mosquitoes
9 pets

Step 5 Put students in small groups and ask them to discuss / vote on whether they agree with each of the sentences in C. Conduct brief feedback by asking how many in each group agreed / disagreed with each statement.

LISTENING

Aim

To give practice in listening for gist and specific information.

Step 1 Tell students they are going to hear four short conversations about science and nature in the news. Ask them to look at the topics in A and number them in the order they are mentioned. Play the recording. Then check in pairs, then with the whole group.

Answers
1 3 2 4 3 2 4 1

9.1

Conversation 1

A: Did you read this article about bees?
B: No.
A: They're all dying for some unknown reason.
B: Really? That's terrible!
A: I know. It's really bad news because we really depend on bees. If bees become extinct, we won't have any fruit or vegetables.
B: I hadn't thought about that. They should do something – fund research or something.
A: Absolutely.

Conversation 2

C: Did you see the forecast for tomorrow?
D: No.
C: It's going to be nice – really hot and sunny.
D: Really? That's great!
C: I know. It's good. It's been so wet and windy recently.
D: We should go out, then – go to the beach or somewhere.
C: Yeah, that's a good idea.

Conversation 3

E: Did you hear what they want to do in Morovia?
F: No. What?
E: It said on the news that they're going to pull down a lot of the horrible houses they've built along the coast and create a national park instead.
F: Really? That's great.
E: I know. It's good news.
F: They should do more to protect the countryside here too.
E: Definitely. We need more green spaces.

Conversation 4

G: Did you see they've discovered a new way to kill the mosquitoes that spread malaria?
H: No.
G: Yeah, it said it could save millions of lives.
H: Really? That's great.
G: I know. It's really good.
H: It makes a change to hear some good news.
G: Absolutely.

Note Monrovia is the capital city of the West African nation of Liberia.

Step 2 Put students in pairs and ask them to make notes on what they remember about the details of each conversation. What were they talking about and how did the speakers feel about it? Play the recording again for them to check their ideas. Check as a group.

Answers

1 bees are becoming extinct, speakers think they should do research to stop this
2 hot and sunny forecast for tomorrow, speakers might go to the beach
3 they're going to pull down a lot of the horrible houses they've built along the coast in Monrovia to create a national park instead, speakers think this is good and they should do more to look after their own countryside
4 they've discovered a new way to kill the mosquitoes that spread malaria, speakers are very pleased, this could save millions of lives

LANGUAGE PATTERNS

Aim

To draw students' attention to patterns with *something, someone, somewhere*, etc.

Step 1 Ask students to look at the sentences in the box and notice the similarities (all use *some*-). Ask students to translate these sentences into their own language. In monolingual classes ask students to compare their translations. In multilingual classes ask students to work in pairs and tell each other if the sentences were easy to translate and whether they were able to translate them word for word.

Step 2 Ask students to cover the English translations and translate the sentences back into English using their translations. Then ask them to compare their translations in pairs against the book.

Alternatively If you prefer not to use translation, ask students to notice the patterns. Concept check any areas of difficulty and elicit a few more examples. If time, write their examples on the board and tick them if correct. If the sentences are wrong, ask the students to correct them or correct them yourself.

DEVELOPING CONVERSATIONS

Responding to news and comments

Aim

To present and practise natural responses to news and comments.

Step 1 Lead in by making an announcement like *My sister got married yesterday* and try to elicit suitable responses, e.g. *Really? That's good / great news*. Then read out the box, modelling and drilling the phrases as you read.

Step 2 Ask students to look at the audioscript on pp. 170–171 and underline examples of each kind of response. (The answers are underlined in audioscript 9.1.) Put them in pairs to check and then read out the four conversations together. Monitor and correct their pronunciation where necessary.

Step 3 Ask students to look at the sentences in B and write a suitable response to each one. Then put them in pairs to practise saying the sentences with their responses. Monitor and correct where necessary. Check their ideas as a class.

Suggested answers
1 Really? That's great news.
2 I know, it's terrible.
3 Absolutely. Good idea.
4 I know! It's really good news.
5 I know.
6 Really? That's interesting.
7 Really? That's bad news!
8 Good idea.

CONVERSATION PRACTICE

Aim
To give further practice in telling someone about the news and responding naturally.

Step 1 Tell students they are going to have similar conversations to the ones in *Listening*. Ask them to look at the outline to help them. Then put students in AB pairs. Student A should look at the news in File 11 on page 158 and Student B should look at the news in File 13 on page 158. They should take turns telling each other their stories and responding, using the outline. Monitor and help where necessary.

pp. 66–67

Next class Make photocopies of **9A** p. 144.
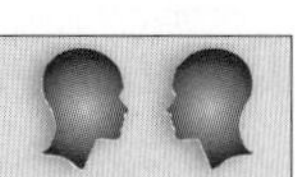

VOCABULARY Animals

Aim
To extend vocabulary about animals and lead in to *Reading*.

Step 1 Ask students to look at the pictures and say which of the animals in the box they can see. Check in pairs then with the whole group. Model, drill and concept check where necessary.

Answers
shark, parrot, lion, sheep, fly, rat

Step 2 Put students in pairs and ask them to categorise the animals in A into pets, insects, wild animals and farm animals. Point out that many can belong to more than one category. Check with the whole group.

Answers
pets: dog, rabbit, parrot, rat
insects: fly
wild animals: rat, shark, pigeon, lion, rabbit, parrot
farm animals: dog, cow, sheep

Step 3 In the same pairs, ask students to add two more words to each category. Check with the whole group. Model, drill and concept check where necessary.

Tip Tell weaker students to look back at their list of animals from *Vocabulary* A (page 64) for ideas.

Suggested answers
pets: cat, horse, goldfish
insects: mosquito, spider, bee
wild animals: tiger, whale
farm animals: pig, goat

Step 4 Ask students to look at the questions in D and think about how they would answer them. Then put them in small groups to discuss the questions. Conduct brief feedback.

READING

Aim
To give practice in predicting, reading for gist and responding to text.

Step 1 Tell students they are going to read some short newspaper stories about animals helping humans. Ask them to read the stories quickly, ignoring the words in bold for the moment and match each story with one of the headlines. One of these is not needed. Check in pairs then with the whole group.

Answers
1 Wedding goes with a 'woof'
2 Dinner not well done
3 Tips for birds
4 From zero to hero
5 Milk of human kindness
6 Barking witness

Step 2 Put students in pairs to discuss the questions in B. Check with the whole group. Help with meaning where necessary. (Text about parrots is invented – although a Japanese restaurant did train monkeys to do a similar job.)

Step 3 Ask students in the same pairs to try to guess what the words in bold mean. They should then check in the *Vocabulary Builder* on page 35. Check as a class.

Answers
insisted on = you say very strongly that something must happen
cage = container with bars, for keeping animals / birds in
sense of smell = your ability to notice things with your nose
detect = if you detect something, you find it when it is not easy to see or hear
boost = improve
suspected of = if you suspect someone of something bad, you think that they did it

Step 5 Ask students to look at the questions in D and think about how they would answer them. Then put them in small groups to discuss the questions. Conduct brief feedback.

NATIVE SPEAKER ENGLISH *the big day*

Read out the box and ask students whether they would say something similar in their own language. If not, how would they say it? Elicit more examples of when you would use *the big day* (birthdays, anniversaries, exam days, results days, etc.).

GRAMMAR The past perfect simple

Aim
To introduce the past perfect and give practice.

Step 1 Ask students if they know what the past perfect is and how to form it (*had / hadn't* + past participle). Then read out the box. Ask them to find other examples of the past perfect in the news stories.

Suggested answers
Story 1: (the dogs) *had brought the couple together*
Story 3: *the parrots had previously lived in a cage*

Step 2 Ask students to match sentences 1–8 with the correct sentence a–h. Check in pairs and ask students to discuss which tense is used and why in a–h. (Past perfect, because they all contain a past action / event previous to the past action / event in sentences 1–8.) Check with the whole group.

Answers
1 b 2 g 3 e 4 d 5 a 6 c 7 h 8 f

Direct them to the grammar reference on page 148 if they still seem unsure.

Step 3 Ask students to look at the sentences in C and write possible endings using the past perfect. Put them in pairs to compare / check their ideas. Check quickly as a class.

Step 4 Put students in small groups and ask them to discuss what they think had happened before each of the situations in D. Then tell them to read the endings in File 7 on page 157 to find out what really happened.

9A see Teacher's notes p. 124.

SPEAKING

Aim
To give fluency practice and extend the topic.

Step 1 Ask students to look at A and B and choose one to talk about. Then put them in pairs to tell each other their stories. Conduct feedback at the end, by asking who told / found the best story.

Tip If students choose to research their story on the Internet, ask students to do this for homework and come to class with their stories already prepared.

Alternatively Ask students to talk about A in class (they can make something up if they don't have a story) and then ask them all to do B for homework and bring it to the next lesson.

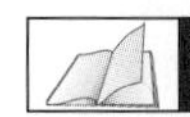
pp. 68–69

Next class Make photocopies of **9B** p. 145.
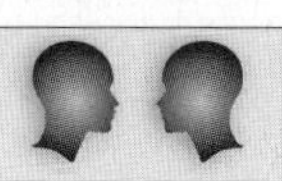

READING

Aim
To give practice in reading for specific information and detail and responding to text.

Step 1 Ask students to read the text quickly first, ignoring the gaps. Check they understand *psychologist* = someone who makes a scientific study of the mind. Ask them to find out what the experiment was really about (how tolerant people were to giving other people electric shocks).

Step 2 Ask students to complete the text by putting the correct word from the box in each gap. Check in pairs then with the whole group.

Answers
1 experiment 4 button
2 purpose 5 participants
3 list 6 results

Step 3 Ask students to label the picture in B. Put them in pairs to check and discuss the role of each person in the experiment. Check with the whole group.

Step 4 Put students in pairs or threes and ask them to discuss the questions in C. Conduct brief feedback at the end.

LISTENING

Aim
To give practice in predicting, listening for gist and specific information and detail.

Step 1 Tell students they are going to hear two radio extracts giving more information about the Miligram experiments. Ask them to listen and check whether their ideas about what happened in the experiments were correct or not. Play the recording.

9.2
The people who were the teachers believed that the learners were receiving real electric shocks, but, in fact, there were none. When the 'teacher' pressed the electric shock button, it simply turned on a light in front of the 'learner'. After a while, the actor who was playing the 'learner' started to bang on the wall between him and the 'teacher' and to shout in pain. At one point, the 'learner' – who was an actor, remember – then complained about having a heart problem. Then, as the false shocks got stronger and stronger, the 'learner' went silent.

Some of the 'teachers' began to laugh nervously or show other signs of stress when they heard the screams coming from the 'learner'. Many people asked to stop the experiment and wanted to check that the learner was OK. However, the 'scientist' told them to "please continue". When the 'teachers' asked the 'scientist' if he was sure, the 'scientist' said that the experiment required them to continue. He then said it was absolutely essential that they continued. Finally, the scientist told any people who still complained, "You have no other choice. You must go on."

At the end of the experiment, 65% of participants had given the final 450-volt shock, although many were very uncomfortable doing so; at some point, every teacher stopped and questioned what the purpose of the experiment was, but only one person out of the forty absolutely refused to give shocks before reaching the 300-volt level – a level which could still kill you.

Step 2 Ask students to look at the statements in B and decide whether they are true or false. Check in pairs, then play the recording again for them to check. Check with the whole group.

Tip For further practice ask students to correct the false statements (answers included below).

Answers
1 T
2 F they were all actors
3 F no, they sometimes laughed nervously
4 T
5 T
6 F no, 65% gave the maximum shock

Step 3 Ask students to look at the words / phrases in C and decide how each one fits into the next extract they are going to hear about the experiments. Check their ideas briefly and then play the recording for them to check if they were correct.

9.3
So what *was* the real purpose of the experiment? During the Second World War soldiers had participated in some terrible crimes that caused the deaths of millions of innocents. People couldn't understand it. How could they all be so cruel? Why didn't anyone stop the killing? Milgram wanted to investigate these issues.

The experiment showed that people found it very difficult to say no to people in authority – people more important than them and who wore a uniform. All the ordinary people who took part in Milgram's experiment agreed to cause pain to another person just because a 'scientist' in a white coat told them to. Most continued long enough to kill someone.

Step 4 Put students in small groups and ask them to discuss how the words in C were really connected to the story.

Answers
the Second World War: soldiers had participated in terrible crimes
cruel: soldiers
cause pain = ordinary people will cause pain to others if a 'scientist' tells them to
people in authority = people find it hard to say no to them
kill someone = most continued long enough to kill someone

Step 5 Ask students in their groups to discuss the questions in F. Conduct brief feedback.

Tip While students are discussing these questions, write the examples from the next exercise, *Grammar*, on the board.

GRAMMAR Reporting speech 1

Aim
To introduce basic rules of reported speech.

Step 1 Ask students what verbs we usually use to report what people say: *say, tell, ask.* Read out the box, checking as you read, or put the examples on the board and use them to highlight form and meaning.

Step 2 Ask students to complete the sentences in A with the correct form of *say, tell* or *ask*. Do the first one with them. Check in pairs then with the whole group.

Answers
1 told
2 asked, told
3 A did / say; B told
4 told
5 asked, tell, said
6 said
7 asked, said
8 asked

Direct students to the grammar reference on page 148 if they still seem unsure.

Step 3 Ask students to complete the sentences in B in interesting or funny ways, so that they are true for them. You might like to model the first one for them, e.g. *My parents always told me to eat carrots so I could see in the dark*. Monitor and help as they write.

Step 4 Put students in small groups to compare their ideas. Conduct feedback by asking whose idea was the funniest / most interesting, etc. in each group.

 **9B** see Teacher's notes p. 124.

SPEAKING

Aim
To give fluency practise and round off the unit.

Step 1 Put students in new small groups and ask them to discuss the questions in C. Elicit what they know about the famous people in the box. Conduct brief feedback at the end.

Tip Try and put students in multilingual groups if possible.

Note Archimedes (c. 287–212 BC) = a Greek mathematician, philosopher and inventor;
Issac Newton (1642–1727) = English mathematician and physicist, discovered the laws of Gravity;
Louis Pasteur (1822–95) = French chemist who proved the theory of germ disease;
Charles Darwin (1809–82) = British scientist who first proposed the theory of evolution, wrote the famous *The Origin of Species*;
Guglielmo Marconi (1874–1937) = Italian physicist, he also discovered radio waves and the wireless;
Galileo Galilei (1564–1642) = Italian astronomer, made many discoveries in astronomy;
Ivan Pavlov (1849–1936) = Russian psychologist, discovered 'conditional training' of dogs;
Marie Curie (1867–1934) = Polish-born scientist, her experiments led to the invention of x-ray machines (two Nobel prizes);
Alexander Fleming (1881–1955) = Scottish scientist who discovered penicillin;
Albert Einstein (1879–1955) = German-born scientist who developed the theory of relativity.

10 EDUCATION

UNIT OVERVIEW
In this unit, students learn how to **talk about academic experiences** and **future plans, the school system in their country, explain what they use computers for** and to **respond with surprise to negative sentences**. The main grammar aims are **first conditionals** and ***had to / could*** to talk about past ability / obligation.

Next class Make photocopies of **10A** p. 146.

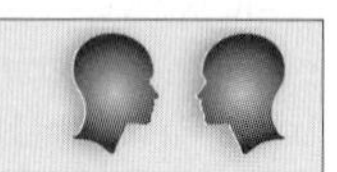

VOCABULARY School and university

Aim
To introduce phrases about education.

Step 1 Lead in by asking students what kind of schools they went to, whether they enjoyed them, etc. Check *Master's* = a qualification you do after your undergraduate (first) degree. *PhD* = the highest form of university qualification. Ask them to look at the sentences in A and put them in the correct order. Check in pairs, then as a group. Model, drill and concept check where necessary.

Answers
3, 8, 9, 1, 5, 7, 4, 2, 6

Step 2 Put students in pairs and ask them to discuss how old they think each person is in A. Check their ideas.

Suggested answers
1 17 / 18
2 any age, probably over 22
3 5 / 6
4 any age, probably 21 / 22
5 18 / 19
6 any age, probably over 25
7 early 20s
8 11
9 14

Step 3 Put students in small groups and ask them to discuss the questions in C. In a multilingual class, mix up the nationalities as much as possible. Conduct brief feedback.

NATIVE SPEAKER ENGLISH *graduate*

Ask students when they think people usually *graduate*. Then read out the box.

LISTENING

Aim
To give practice in listening for specific information and using language in context.

Step 1 Tell students they are going to hear three people taking about university. Ask them to look at the questions and try to answer them as they listen. Play the recording.

Answers
1 1 yes; 2 yes; 3 no
2 1 OK– some bits are good, 2 likes it, 3 quite liked it but thinks they've learnt more working
3 1 Spanish, Art, favourite subjects, History is also ok, Business – dad wants him to study; 2 Pure Maths – the subject he is studying, Astrophysics – might do a Master's in it; 3 International Law – the subject he studied at university
4 1 Yes – to study Business at university; 2 Yes – to do a Master's in Astrophysics; 3 No

10.1
Conversation 1
A: So how's school, Ollie? Your father told me you're doing well.
B: It's OK, I suppose. Some bits are good.
A: Yeah? What're your favourite subjects?
B: Spanish and Art. And History's OK as well.
A: And what year are you in now?
B: Year Nine.
A: So how long have you got left?

B: Two more years.
A: What are you going to do when you finish? Have you got any plans?
B: Well, if I can save enough money between now and then, I'll try and take a year off. Dad doesn't want me to, though.
A: No?
B: No, he just wants me to stay in the system and go straight to university and study Business or something and graduate and become just like him.
A: Yeah, well. He's probably just worried about you.
B: Yeah, right. Whatever!

Conversation 2
C: So what course are you doing, Pep?
D: Pure Mathematics.
C: Wow! OK. That sounds hard.
D: Yeah, it can be, but I'm really enjoying it. To be honest, the most difficult thing for me is doing the whole degree in English, but my tutors are great. Everybody has been very supportive.
C: What year are you in?
D: My third, unfortunately. I've got my finals next April!
C: Oh, OK. Well, good luck!
D: Thanks!
C: What're you going to do after you graduate? Any plans?
D: Well, if I get the grades I want, I'll probably do a Master's somewhere.
C: Oh, OK. What in? The same subject?
D: Maybe. I'm not sure. I'm thinking of maybe doing Astrophysics, actually.
C: Oh, right. Have you applied anywhere yet?
D: No, I haven't, actually – not yet. But I probably should!

Conversation 3
E: So did *you* go to university, Dhanya?
D: Yes, I did. The Paul Cézanne University in Marseille. It's one of the oldest universities in France.
D: Oh, OK. What did you study?
F: International Law.
D: And did you enjoy it?
F: Yes, up to a point, I suppose, but to be honest, it was quite theoretical. It wasn't very practical and I think I've learned much more since I started working.
D: I know what you mean! I mean, I left school at 16 and started working straight away. To begin with, I did lots of horrible jobs, but I learnt a lot as well and it made me hungry for success. I was running my own business by the time I was 22. I'm not sure many university graduates can say the same!
F: You can't beat the university of life, eh!

Step 2 Put students in pairs and ask them to try and complete the conversations in B from memory. Then play the recording for them to check. Check with the whole group.

Answers
1 're your
2 have you got
3 when you finish
4 are you doing
5 are you in
6 applied anywhere
7 to university
8 did you
9 you enjoy

Step 3 Put students in pairs and ask them to try to remember the answers to the questions in B. Then ask them to look at the audioscript on page 171 to check.

Step 4 Ask students to look at the questions in D and think about how they would answer them. Then put them in groups to discuss the questions. Conduct brief feedback.

LANGUAGE PATTERNS

Aim
To draw students' attention to patterns with *left* meaning *remaining*.

Step 1 Ask students to look at the sentences in the box and notice the similarities. Ask students to translate these sentences into their own language. In monolingual classes ask students to compare their translations. In multilingual classes ask students to work in pairs and tell each other if the sentences were easy to translate and whether they were able to translate them word for word.

Step 2 Ask students to cover the English translations and translate the sentences back into English using their translations. Then ask them to compare their translations in pairs against the book.

Alternatively If you prefer not to use translation, ask students to notice the patterns. Concept check any areas of difficulty and elicit a few more examples. If time, write their examples on the board and tick them if correct. If the sentences are wrong, ask the students to correct them or correct them yourself.

PRONUNCIATION School subjects

Aim
To focus on the pronunciation and stress on the names of school subjects.

Step 1 Ask students to listen to the recording and mark the stress on the school subjects. Play the recording. Check in pairs then check with the whole group. Check they know what the initials stand for: PE = Physical Education (sports), RE = Religious Education, IT = Information Technology. Also check *sociology* = the study of society or the way people live.

Answers
Geography, Economics, History, Biology, Mathematics, Chemistry, Physics, Latin, Sociology, PE, RE, IT

10.2
Geography
Mathematics
Sociology
Economics
Chemistry
PE
History
Physics
RE
Biology
Latin
IT

Step 2 Ask students to listen again and repeat each one. Play the recording again.

Step 3 Put students in pairs and ask them to discuss the questions in C. Conduct brief feedback.

DEVELOPING CONVERSATIONS *No?*

Aim
To present a simple and natural way of responding to negative comments.

Step 1 Read out the box and focus on the rising intonation. What does it mean when we say *no* like this? (*No, why?*) Give a few prompts to get students to respond with *No?* and the correct intonation.

Step 2 Put students in pairs and get them to take turns reading out a sentence in A and responding with *No?* Ask them to offer explanations. Monitor and correct, especially the use of intonation.

GRAMMAR First conditionals

Aim
To present / revise first conditionals.

Step 1 Read out the box, checking as you read. Or put the examples on the board and use them to highlight form and meaning. *If I get the grades I want, I'll probably do a Master's; You won't pass if you don't start working harder! What will you do if you don't get into university?* Are we talking about the present or the future? (Future.) How many clauses are there? (Two – *if* clause and main clause.) What tense do we use in the *if* clause? (Present simple.) Which tense do we use in the main clause? (*Will* + base form.)

Step 2 Ask students to complete the sentences in A using the correct form of the verbs in brackets. Check in pairs then check with the whole group. Direct students to the grammar reference on page 149 if they still seem unsure.

Answers
1 need, will work
2 pass, will buy
3 don't get, will retake
4 don't get, won't get into
5 won't consider, miss
6 A will do
B happens, will probably just start

Step 3 Put students in AB pairs. Student A is an *optimist* = someone who sees thing positively and B is a *pessimist* = someone who sees things negatively. Ask them to take turns completing the sentences in B with *will / won't* + verb according to their character. Conduct feedback at the end by eliciting some of their ideas.

CONVERSATION PRACTICE

Aim
To give freer, personalised practice of the target language.

Step 1 Ask students to look back at the conversations in *Listening* exercise B and choose the questions they would like to ask other students. They should also think about how they would answer the questions that apply to them.

Tip Tell weaker students to look at the audioscript on page 171 and underline any useful expressions they could use.

Step 2 Put students in small groups and get them to take turns asking and answering the questions they have chosen. Monitor and note down errors in target language for a correction slot at the end.

10A see Teacher's notes. 124.

pp. 72–73

VOCABULARY
Computers and the Internet

Aim
To introduce and practise using vocabulary about computers.

Step 1 Ask students to match the verbs in A with the most suitable endings. Check these quickly and then get students to do the same for B. Check in pairs then as a group. Model, drill and concept check where necessary.

Answers

1 b	3 a	5 c	7 j	9 g
2 d	4 e	6 h	8 i	10 f

Note They might choose *visit a blog*, which could be correct but *write chat rooms* is incorrect so *write a blog* is the best answer.

Step 2 Put students in pairs and ask them to talk about which of the activities in A they do, or how they feel about them. Tell them to try to develop conversations by asking / telling each other as much as they can. Conduct brief feedback.

Speaking

Aim
To develop fluency, personalise the topic and lead in to *Reading*.

Step 1 Ask students to look at the questions in A and think about how they would answer them. Then put them in small groups to discuss the questions. Conduct brief feedback.

Reading

Aim
To give practice in reading for gist and specific information and responding to text.

Step 1 Ask students to read the text quickly, ignoring the words in bold, and list good and bad things about the Internet it mentions. Check in pairs then check with the whole group.

Answers
Bad: lack of parental control, wasting time on computer games, teachers worry it makes cheating easier, plagiarism, sale of homework
Good: parents can use controls to stop children accessing harmful sites, software detects plagiarism, can teach children life and social skills

Alternatively Before going on to Step 1 ask students what they think the title means and what the article might be able. Elicit, point out the pun on *web* = *web* as in *spider web*, *web* as another name for the Internet.

Step 2 Put students in pairs to discuss the questions in B. Check with the whole group.

Answers
1 Copying someone's work and pretending it's your own; Internet makes it easier.
2 Parents can use the software to stop children accessing harmful sites.
3 Students use perfect English, above their level; sometimes leave 'clues' from original.
4 As an example of how the Internet can be used positively in education.
5 He's doing a project about trees; making a website, talking on messenger and doing a PowerPoint presentation.

Step 3 Put students in new pairs / threes to discuss the questions in C. Conduct brief feedback.

Note If students are unsure how to quote properly, tell them they must put the other's person's writing in quote marks and make sure they clearly say who said the words.

Step 4 Read out the box. Elicit more examples of words which can be both verbs and nouns, especially words connected with computers, e.g. *chat, search, google*. Ask students to look back at the text and decide if the words in bold are being used as verbs or nouns. Put them in pairs to compare and explain their answers. Check with the whole group.

Answers

1 worry – n	5 mix – v
2 increase – n	6 quote – v
3 copy – v	7 photograph – v
4 harm – n	8 cheat – v

Step 5 Ask students to complete the sentences in E with the correct form of one of the words from D. Check in pairs, then check with the whole group.

Answers

1 copy	5 mix
2 quote	6 increased
3 worry	7 harm
4 photographs	8 cheat

Step 6 Put students in pairs and ask them to think of five more words that can be both verbs and nouns. If they need help, ask them to look at the words on this page to give them ideas (e.g. *form, test, interview, tax, show, cook*). Conduct this as a race – the first pair to finish should put their hands up / shout *finished!* Check with the whole group.

Speaking

Aim
To extend the topic with freer, more personalised practice.

Step 1 Ask students to look at the questions and situations in A and think about how they would answer them. Then put students in small groups to discuss the questions. Conduct brief feedback.

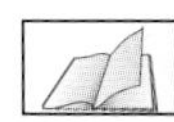

pp. 74–75

Next class Make photocopies of **10B** p. 147.

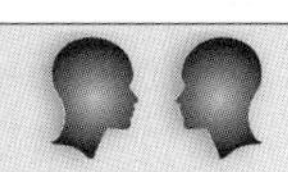

LISTENING

Aim
To give practice in listening for specific information and detail and responding to text.

Step 1 Tell students they are going to listen to an interview with Rebecca, who has been educated in both England and Spain. Ask students to decide which of the items in A they feel are positive in relation to school in their country. Put them in pairs / threes to discuss their ideas.

Tip With weaker students, put monolingual pairs together to discuss their ideas first, then try and put them in a multilingual group to compare their schooling systems.

Step 2 Ask students to listen to the interview and tick the things in A which Rebecca mentions. Play the recording.

Answers
Relationships, homework, approach to teaching, school hours, holidays

10.3
I = Interviewer, R = Rebecca

I: So how did you find school when you came here?
R: A bit mixed. I made friends quickly. I knew a bit of Spanish and people were friendly, but I remember that to begin with, my brother just stood in the corner of the playground watching everyone play. It was sad!
I: But he made friends in the end?
R: Yeah.
I: So you could speak Spanish?
R: A bit, but in class I hardly understood anything. It was horrible, but I sat with a girl that had an Australian dad and she sometimes translated for me.
I: That's lucky. Were classes very different?
R: Primary was. For some reason, I did the last year of primary here, although I'd already done it in England. Maybe it was because they have five years of secondary school in England, but there are only four here. Sorry, what was the question?
I: Were classes different?
R: Oh yeah. Basically, in primary in England we had the same teacher all day, but here we changed teachers. I liked some, but some – like Don Miguel – were really boring! He just read from the book. We didn't use textbooks much in England – we did more group work and arty things.
I: Right.
R: And we had lots of homework! I hardly had any in primary in England – maybe some reading or sums and once a term we did a project. Here, I had loads – maybe an hour or more each night. I remember really crying about it. My friends in England complain when they have to do 45 minutes in secondary school and I often have two hours – and we study for tests all the time.
I: So which do you prefer?
R: It's difficult to say. Now I'm at instituto ...
I: Instituto?
R: Sorry, secondary school. We finish at two o'clock every day and then we get almost three months off in the summer whereas in England my friends finish at four and they only get six weeks' summer holiday. I chat to my friends in England on Messenger and they say school is boring too and they get stressed when they have assignments, but then they have this thing here, where if your teacher fails you some subjects, you have to repeat the whole year! I don't like that stress.

Step 3 Put students in pairs and ask them to look at the statements in C and decide from memory if they are true or false. Play the recording again for them to check.

Tip Ask students to correct the false statements (answers included below).

Answers
1 F – Rebecca did, her brother didn't
2 T
3 T
4 T
5 T
6 T
7 T
8 F – all think school is boring
9 F – only true of Spanish schools

Step 4 Tell students they are going to hear Rebecca's father talking about education. Ask them to look back at the list in A and note the ones he mentions and whether he is positive or negative about each one. Play the recording and ask students to read the audioscript on page 172 as they listen. Check as a group.

Answers
resources: mostly positive (but there are fewer resources in Spain)
approach to teaching: positive
class sizes: good
holidays: bad
relationship between students: positive
textbooks: negative, has to buy them all in Spain

> 10.4
> You hear politicians and parents here saying education is bad, but you get the same complaints in Britain where there are generally more resources. Parents send their kids to private schools or move house to be near good state schools.
>
> From what Rebecca says, Spanish teachers are generally more traditional in their approach, but that's OK. Students probably learn to listen and concentrate better and get more knowledge. It all depends on the teacher – and the students, of course. There's good and bad everywhere. Luckily, Rebecca's very responsible and she has some great teachers. She's happy and the school has a good atmosphere, small classes and there's no violence or bullying – that's the most important thing.
>
> The only policies I don't like here are books and holidays. I spend 400 euros on books every year. In Britain, they're free. Schools buy the books and the students borrow them. Then in summer here, it's difficult looking after the kids for three months when both parents work.

Step 5 Put students in small groups and to discuss the questions in F. Conduct brief feedback.

Tip If you are teaching Spanish students, ask them if they agree with what Rebecca and her father said about Spanish schools.

VOCABULARY Students and teachers

Aim
To introduce and practise some common collocations related to education.

Step 1 Ask students to look at the groups of words in A and match each one with the correct verb from the box. Check in pairs, then as a group. Concept check where necessary.

Answers

1 subject	5 course
2 assignment	6 class
3 textbook	7 school
4 test	8 approach

Step 2 In pairs ask students to decide which collocations apply to students and which to teachers. Check with the whole group.

Answers
Teachers = 2 (set an assignment, mark some assignments), 4 (set a test) 5 (design a course, teach on the course), 6 (give a class, control the class) 7 (the head of a school) 8 (take a traditional approach)

Students = 1, 2, 3, 4, 5, 6, 7, 8

GRAMMAR *had to / could*

Aim
To introduce *had to* and *could* to talk about past obligation and past ability / possibility.

Step 1 Lead in by asking students what they *had to / could* do at primary school. Then read out the box and ask checking questions as you read. Or put the examples from the box on the board and use them to highlight form and meaning.

Step 2 Ask students to complete the sentences in A using *had to, didn't have to, could* or *couldn't*. Check in pairs then with the whole group.

Answers
1 couldn't, had to
2 couldn't, Did you have to
3 had to
4 didn't have to
5 had to, could
6 had to, couldn't

Step 3 Tell students to look at B and choose two pairs. Ask them to write as many sentences as they can, comparing the two items in each pair. Point out that they will need to use the present simple to talk about current experience. Monitor and help as they write. Direct them to the grammar reference on page 149 if they still seem unsure.

Step 4 Put students in pairs or threes to tell each other their sentences. They should try to develop conversations by asking follow-up questions. Conduct brief feedback.

10B see Teacher's notes p. 124.

SPEAKING

Aim
To round off the unit and give fluency practice.

Step 1 Ask students to read the questionnaire and circle the best answer for themselves. Check vocabulary, *swot* = a student who works hard and gets high marks, and who is usually not very popular; *skip class* = miss class because you don't want to attend; *neatly* = in a tidy way; *plays* = dramas, e.g. *Hamlet*.

Step 2 Put students in small groups to compare their answers and explain them to each other. Ask them to tell the rest of the class who is the best student in their group and why.

Step 3 In new pairs, ask students to think of someone they know who would answer the questions differently to them and why. Conduct brief feedback.

11 PLACES TO STAY

UNIT OVERVIEW
The main aims of this unit are to learn how to **talk about places you stay,** explain and deal with **problems in hotels, talk about past habits** and to **give bad news politely**. The main grammar aims are using **second conditionals** to talk about hypothetical situations and give advice and ***used to*** **to talk about past habits** and states.

SPEAKING

Aim
To lead into the topic and give fluency practice.

Step 1 Ask students to think about what kinds of places they like staying in when they go on holiday and what they think is important when choosing a holiday. Then ask them to look at the items in A and give them a mark according to how important they consider them to be when choosing where to stay: 0 = not important at all, 5 = very important. Check *convenient location* = somewhere close and easy to what they want to do / see.

Step 2 Put students in pairs / threes to compare their answers to A. Then ask them to discuss the questions in B. Conduct brief feedback in open class.

LISTENING

Aim
To give practice in predicting, listening for specific information and note-taking.

Step 1 Tell students they are going to hear a conversation between a hotel receptionist and an English man, David. Ask them to read the introduction and then list the questions David might ask about rooms, cars, facilities or services. Put them in pairs to compare their lists.

Step 2 Ask students to listen and take notes on David's questions and answers. Play the recording. Put students in pairs and ask them to check their answers and discuss what they think David's colleague will decide to do and why. Check with the whole group.

Answers
No triple rooms, only doubles – can get a double with an extra bed, 110 euros per night, breakfast is extra, Wi-Fi costs £12, parking costs £15, they can't hire a car though the hotel, and none of the weekends they want are free and they have to pay 10% now, which they'll lose if they cancel.

Colleague might choose to stay somewhere else – not very cheap / convenient.

11.1
R = receptionist, D = David
R: Hillborough Hotel.
D: Oh, hello. I'm ringing on behalf of a colleague. He wants some information.
R: Sure. What would you like to know?
D: Um, well, do you have any triple rooms available in August?
R: I'm afraid not. We only have doubles.
D: Oh right. Is it possible to get a double with an extra bed? They have a small kid.
R: That should be possible.
D: And how much would that be per night?
R: 110 euros per night, with a supplement for the cot.
D: Sorry. Does that includes the cost of the extra bed or not?
R: It does include it, yes.
D: And breakfast?
D: I'm afraid breakfast is extra. What dates are they thinking of coming?
D: Um, Tuesday the 12th to the 17th.
R: OK. Let me just check our availability. Hmm, I'm afraid we're fully booked that weekend.
D: So does that include Friday night?
R: That's right, yes. Sorry.
D: And what if they came earlier? Would that be better?
R: Again, the previous Saturday we're full, but we have rooms available from the Sunday night.
D: So that's the 10th, right?
R: That's correct.
D: OK. I'll need to check with them about that. And just a couple of other things.
R: Sure.
D: Do you have Wi-Fi or Internet access?
R: There is Wi-Fi in rooms for a fee.
D: So you have to pay, right?

R: I'm afraid so. It's 12 euros a day, or four euros for half an hour.
D: And do you have parking facilities?
R: Not at the hotel itself, but we have an arrangement with a local car park. They offer a reduced rate of 15 euros per day.
D: And what if they wanted to rent a car once they're in Dublin? Could they do that through the hotel?
R: I'm afraid not, but there are several car hire places nearby, or they could try through the Internet.
D: OK – and what about getting from the airport?
R: There's a shuttle bus, which serves a number of hotels including ours. It costs three euros – or they could take a cab.
D: OK. Let me just talk to my friends. Could you tell me your name if I call back?
R: Yes, it's Jackie, but any of my colleagues can deal with the booking.
D: Oh wait, sorry – one last thing. Will they need to make a payment when they make the booking?
R: Yes, we'll need to take a 10% deposit on a credit card.
D: So if for whatever reason they didn't come, they'd lose that money?
R: If the cancellation was made within two weeks of the arrival date, then yes, that's right.

Step 3 Ask students to look at the audioscript on page 172 and find five words or expressions they would like to remember. Put them in pairs to compare their choices and help each other with meaning. Tell them to check in the *Vocabulary Builder* on pp. 42–43 or with you if they are not sure.

Language patterns

Aim
To draw students' attention to patterns with *Let me / us* + verb.

Step 1 Ask students to look at the sentences in the box and notice the similarities. Ask students to translate these sentences into their own language. In monolingual classes ask students to compare their translations. In multilingual classes ask students to work in pairs and tell each other if the sentences were easy to translate and whether they were able to translate them word for word.

Step 2 Ask students to cover the English translations and translate the sentences back into English using their translations. Then ask them to compare their translations in pairs against the book.

Alternatively If you prefer not to use translation, ask students to notice the patterns. Concept check any areas of difficulty and elicit a few more examples. If time, write their examples on the board and tick them if correct. If the sentences are wrong, ask students to correct them or correct them yourself.

Developing conversations

Giving bad news

Aim
To introduce and give practice of softening bad news.

Step 1 Read out the box, checking as you read. Elicit a few more examples of *I'm afraid so / I'm afraid not* by asking questions like *Will it be sunny tomorrow? Do you have an exam next week?* etc. Then get students to ask and answer similar questions in open pairs.

Step 2 Put students in closed pairs to practise, using the question prompts in A. Monitor and correct where necessary.

Step 3 Put students in small groups and ask them to think of as many things as they can that a hotel employee might say, beginning *I'm afraid* ... Stop them after three minutes. The group with the most correct ones is the winner. Conduct feedback by asking students which one they think is the funniest / most surprising, etc.

Pronunciation Spelling and numbers

Aim
To practice the pronunciation of letters and numbers.

Step 1 Lead in by asking students to spell a few items in the classroom. Then ask them to listen and repeat the vowel sounds. Play the recording.

11.2
/iː/
/eɪ/
/e/
/aɪ/
/əʊ/
/uː/
/ɑː/

Step 2 Put students in pairs and ask them to say the letters of the alphabet to each other and write them next to the correct phoneme. Check with the whole group.

Answers
/iː/ b, c, d, e, g, p, t, v
/eɪ/ a, h, j, k
/e/ f, l, m, n, s, x, z
/aɪ/ i, y
/əʊ/ o
/uː/ q, u, w
/ɑː/ r

Step 3 Tell students they are going to hear the receptionist taking David's credit card details. Ask them to complete the form as they listen. Play the recording.

Answers
Name on the card: Mr D E Gwaizda
Card number: 1003 6566 9424 8307
Security number: 718
Expiry date: 06/17
Contact number: 0044 796 883 412

11.3
R = receptionist, D = David
R: OK, so can I take your credit card details for the deposit?
D: Sure.
R: What kind of card is it?
D: Visa.
R: And the name on your card?
D: Mr D E Gwaizda. That's G - W - A - I - Z - D - A.
R: OK. That's an unusual name.
D: Yeah, it's Polish originally.
R: OK. And the card number on the card?
D: 1003 6566 9242 8307.
R: And the security number on the back of the card – the last three digits there?
D: 718.
R: And the expiry date?
D: O – 6 Seventeen
R: And can I just take a contact number in case there are any problems?
D: Sure. 0044 796 883 412.

Step 4 Ask students to say the phone number again. Then read out the explanation box. Practise by asking students their phone numbers. If they don't want to give their real number, tell them to use an old number or make one up.

Step 5 Ask students to write (secretly) the details of an invented card. Then put them in pairs and ask them to take turns asking and noting down the details. At the end, ask them to compare what they have written.

CONVERSATION PRACTICE

Aim
To extend the topic and give freer practice.

Step 1 Tell students they are going to have similar conversations to the one they heard in *Listening*. Put them in AB pairs. Student A should read the role card in File 8 on page 157 and Student B should read the role card in File 5 on page 156. Both should individually write down the questions they want to ask.

Step 2 When they are ready, ask students to take turns being the receptionist and role-play the conversations. The receptionist should give at least two pieces of bad news, beginning *I'm afraid*. Monitor and note down errors in target language for a correction slot at the end.

pp. 78–79

Next class Make photocopies of **11A** p. 148.
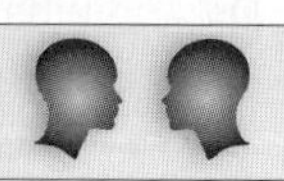

VOCABULARY Hotel problems

Aim
To introduce vocabulary associated with hotel problems.

Step 1 Lead in by asking students to look at the pictures in A and describe the problems the people in each picture are having.

Step 2 Ask students to look at the sentences in B and complete each using the correct pair of words. Do the first one with them to demonstrate. Check in pairs then check with the whole group. Model, drill and concept check where necessary.

Answers
1 main road + noisy
2 wake-up call + missed
3 boiling + air conditioning
4 bill + overcharged
5 filthy + insects
6 toiletries + reception
7 available + booking
8 fixed + low

Step 3 Put students in pairs or threes and ask them to discuss the questions in C. Conduct brief feedback.

GRAMMAR Second conditionals

Aim
To introduce second conditionals to talk about hypothetical present or future situations.

Step 1 Read out the box, checking form and meaning as you read. Or put the examples on the board and use them to highlight form and meaning.

Note We generally use *were* for the second conditional of *to be*, though some people use *was* for first and third persons singular. *Were* is still considered to be more standard.

Step 2 Ask students to complete the sentences in A by choosing the correct alternative. Check in pairs then check with the whole group. Check students understand question 1 as this is a metaphorical use, meaning 'under any circumstances'. Direct students to the grammar reference on page 150 if they still seem unsure.

Answers
1 would not stay, paid
2 A would stay, could; B would do, weren't
3 A would move, had; A were, would tell
4 B Would it be, had; A would be, would drop, stayed

Step 3 Put students in pairs and ask them to take turns asking each other about the problems in *Vocabulary* exercise B. They should try to develop conversations by asking follow-up questions. Model with a strong student, then in open pairs, then put them in closed pairs to continue. Monitor and correct where necessary.

Step 4 Ask students individually to write three questions beginning *What would you do if ...?* Then put them in small groups to ask and answer the questions. Conduct brief feedback by asking *What was the best question in each group? And the best answer?*

Step 5 Ask students if they know a way of giving advice using second conditionals. Then read out the box. Model and drill the examples, paying attention to the weak form of *were* /wə/.

Step 6 Put students in pairs and ask them to take turns giving each other advice in response to the prompts in D. Model with a strong student, then in open pairs, then put them in closed pairs to continue. Monitor and correct mistakes in target language.

 **11A** see Teacher's notes p. 124.

Listening

Aim

To give practice in predicting, listening for gist and specific information.

Step 1 Tell students they are going to hear a conversation between a guest and a hotel receptionist. In pairs ask them to look at the pictures in A and discuss how they might be connected to the conversation.

Step 2 Ask them to listen and check their predictions. Check with the whole group.

Answers
bunch of roses – Lady Zaza wants 100 bunches delivered to her room; *chocolates* – she also wants chocolates, with the peanut ones removed;
a *light bulb* – she wants them changed; *kittens* – she wants a white one delivered; *the gym* – she wants to use it at 4 a.m.

11.4

R = receptionist, M = manager, L = Lady Zaza

R: Hello. Reception.
M: Hi. I'm calling on behalf of Lady Zaza, in the presidential suite.
R: Oh yes. It's a real pleasure to have her in the hotel.
M: Yeah, well, there was no way we could stay in that last place. The service there was a joke!
R: Well, I hope everything's OK with our rooms. We really didn't have much time to prepare them.
M: Yeah, everything's fine, basically, but there are just a couple of things she's asked for.
R: OK.
M: Well, first, can you ask room service to send some fresh flowers to the room? Lady Zaza enjoys arranging them. It relaxes her, you know? She'd like a hundred bunches of red flowers, eighty bunches of white and fifty bunches of yellow.
R: Certainly. I'll send someone up with them in a minute.
M: And tell them to bring more of her favourite chocolates too, please. With the peanut ones removed. There were two left in the ones that were in the room, and she almost ate them! She has a really bad nut allergy!
R: I'm so sorry to hear that. I'll sort that out at once.
M: Oh, and no green ones either, please. She can't stand the colour green!
R: Of course.
M: She'd also like the light bulbs in her room changed. She said it's too dark. And can you bring her a kitten?
R: Er, a kitten?!
M: Yeah, a white one.
R: I ... um ... well, I'll see what I can do.
M: Oh, and one last thing. Can she get a wake-up call at four a.m., please? She'd like to use the gym.
R: Well, the gym doesn't usually open until 6, but I'm sure we can organise something for her.
M: Great. That's it for now. Oh, wait. Just one second. She's saying something.
L: They did it again! You've got to do something!
M: Yeah, OK. OK. Hello?
R: Yes, hello,
M: Lady Zaza can hear the people downstairs. They're talking or watching TV or something and wants them to be moved.
R: Moved? I'm afraid that's just not possible.
M: Sure it's possible. You've got hundreds of rooms in this place.
R: I know, but I'm afraid we're fully booked. We don't have any other rooms available.
M: So you're telling me you can't move them?
R: I would if I could, but I'm afraid I can't. I'm terribly sorry.
M: Well, that's just not good enough. I'd like to talk to the manager.
R: He's not here at the moment, I'm afraid, but I'm sure that if he was, he'd tell you exactly the same thing.
M: Is that right?
R: I'm afraid so, yes.
M: OK. Well, I'll tell her ... but she's not going to like it.

Step 3 Ask students to look at the sentences in C and try to number them in the order in which they heard them. Play the recording again for them to check.

Answers

1 d	5 c
2 g	6 a
3 b	7 h
4 f	8 e

Step 4 Put students in pairs and ask them to discuss which of the adjectives in D they think describes Lady Zaza and why. Check they understand *selfish* = thinking only of oneself, inconsiderate; *tidy* = organised, neat; *ambitious* = keen to do well in life, especially academically or professionally; *demanding* = wanting everything to be provided. Conduct brief feedback.

Step 5 Put students in small groups and ask them to discuss the questions in E. Conduct brief feedback.

Native speaker English

One second / a minute

Read out the box, checking as you read. What does *one second / a minute* mean here? = a very short period of time. Elicit a few more examples from students.

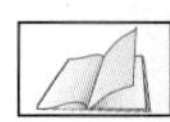

pp. 80–81

Next class Make photocopies of **11B** p. 149.

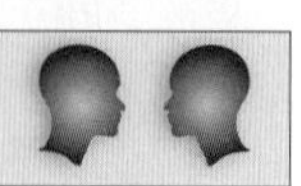

Reading

Aim

To give practice in predicting, reading for specific information and exchanging information.

Step 1 Tell students they are going to read about people's experiences of camping. Lead in by asking who has been camping, whether they liked it, etc. If they haven't been, ask if they think they would like it and why / why not?

Step 2 Put students in small groups and ask them to make a list of good and bad points about camping.

Suggested answers

Good: fun, nice to be close to nature, something different, an adventure

Bad: might be cold / uncomfortable in the tent, might get animals around the tent in the night, no proper bathrooms

Step 3 Divide the class into two groups, A and B. Ask the A students to read about Andro and Falah and the B students to read about Sherise and Marcia in File 14 on page 158. All should match each text with a picture and check whether their people mention any of the good and bad points they listed earlier. Check in same-letter pairs, then with the whole group.

Step 4 Put students in same-letter pairs and ask them to answer the questions in C as if they were the people they read about. Do not check the answers.

Step 5 Put students in AB pairs and ask them to take turns interviewing each other as if they were the people they read about. They should use the questions in C but try not to look at the texts as they answer. Conduct brief feedback as a class on which sounds like the best place.

Step 6 Ask students to look at the items in E and try to match two items with each of the people in the texts. Then put them in AB pairs again to compare and explain their choices.

Answers

Falah: a city boy, peace
Andro: hide and seek, a cold atmosphere
Sheries: cool down, comfort
Marcia: a fire, an achievement

Step 7 Put students in small groups and ask them to discuss the questions in F. Check they understand Girl Guides / Boy Scouts. Boy Scouts = organisation founded by Baden Powell, to help young boys to learn a variety of new skills and be more active and helpful in their community. Girl Guides = equivalent organisation for girls. Conduct brief feedback at the end.

GRAMMAR *used to*

Aim

To introduce *used to* for talking about past habits and states.

Step 1 Ask students to look at the sentences from the texts in A and match each one with one of the uses. Then read out the box, checking as you read. Emphasise that *used to* is only used to talk about the past and does not have a present form in English and that for the present form we use *usually / never*. Alternatively, put the examples on the board and use them to highlight form and meaning.

Answers
1 habit in past
2 habit in past (ran)
3 habit in present
4 habit in past
5 single action / event in past

Step 2 Ask students to complete the sentences in B using *used to*, *never used to* or *usually*. Check in pairs, then with the whole group.

Answers
1 used to
2 used to
3 never used to
4 never used to, used to
5 usually

Step 3 Ask students to look at the sentences in C and rewrite all the ones they can, using *(never) used to*. Check in pairs then check with the whole group.

Answers
1 I never used to like
2 I used to go rock climbing
3 no change
4 he used to smoke
5 I used to have
6 It never used to be very crowded.
7 no change
8 I never used to go away

Direct them to the grammar reference on page 150 if they still seem unsure.

Step 4 Put students in pairs and ask them to discuss what they think happened to cause the changes in 1–8. Conduct brief feedback.

Suggested answers
1 Had a good time camping once which has changed his / her mind – or has children now.
2 Stopped because she got married and husband thought too dangerous.
3 The weather forecast was worse than usual.
4 He gave up smoking when he had children.
5 He had his hair cut because he needed to look smart and serious.
6 Someone wrote an article recommending the place.
7 It rained all the time.
8 She has now left home so she went on holiday with her friends.

Step 5 Ask students to look at the items in E and think about what they are going to say. Give them some time to do this.

Step 6 When they are ready, put students in small groups of three or four to share their ideas. Monitor and note down mistakes in target language for a correction slot at the end. Conduct brief feedback on some of the things they talked about.

 **11B** see Teacher's notes p. 125.

12 PHONE

UNIT OVERVIEW
The main aims of this unit are to learn how to **give and take phone messages**, to **explain where people are**, to **use sentence stress for key words** and to **form negative adjectives**. The main grammar aims are to focus on the tense shift in **reported speech** and ***just, already*** and ***yet*** with the present perfect simple and ***still*** with the present continuous and present simple.

Next class Make photocopies of **12A** p. 150.

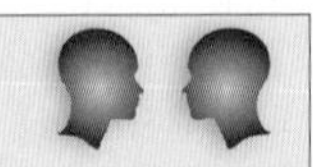

VOCABULARY Using phones

Aim
To introduce students to the topic of the lesson and words and phrases connected with using phones.

Step 1 Ask students to look at the sentences in A and guess the meaning of the words in bold from the context. Ask them to translate them into their own language, then check in the *Vocabulary Builder* on page 46. Ask them to check the meaning in pairs and then check answers as a class.

Alternatively If you prefer not to use translation, asks students to discuss in pairs what they think the words mean, then check in the *Vocabulary Builder* page 46.

Answers
text = send a written message on a mobile phone
on hold = waiting to speak to someone on the phone
line (is) *busy* = a telephone connection that is being used when you try to call
get cut off = phone suddenly stops working
call (you) back = phone (you) later
coverage = the area where there is a strong signal
signal = electrical waves that carry sound or pictures
put through = connect to the person you want to talk to
hang up = end a phone conversation suddenly

Step 2 Put students in small groups and ask them to discuss the questions in B. Conduct brief feedback.

LISTENING

Aim
To give practice in listening for detail and note taking.

Step 1 Tell students they are going to hear two short telephone conversations. Ask them to look at the messages left after each conversation and complete them as they listen. Play the recording. Check in pairs, then with the group.

Answers
1 Brendan
2 seven
3 eight
4 Lincoln
5 The price
6 the details
7 07729-651-118
8 away on holiday from

12.1
Conversation 1
A: Hello.
B: Hi, it's Brendan. Is Neil there?
A: No, he's not up yet. Is it urgent?
B: No, it's OK. Just tell him we're meeting earlier – at seven, not eight. And tell him he's very lazy! 12 o'clock and still in bed!
A: Well, he was out late last night. Has he got your number, Brendan?
B: Yeah, he has. So what time will he be up?
A: I imagine in about an hour. He didn't get back home till four.
B: Oh right. Well, I'll see him later. Thanks.
A: That's OK. I'll give him your message. Meet at seven, not eight.
B: Yeah.
A: Bye now.

Conversation 2

C: Good morning, D B B. How can I help you?
D: Yeah hi. Could I speak to Jane Simpson, please?
C: Of course. I'll just put you through to her.
D: Thanks.
E: Hello.
D: Hi, Jane?
E: No, it's actually Poppy. I'm afraid Jane's out visiting a client. Would you like to leave a message?
D: Yeah, could you tell her Diane called. I've already spoken to my boss and he's fine with the price, so we can go ahead with the work. Can you ask her to phone me when she gets back so we can sort out the details?
E: Of course. Has she got your number?
D: I don't think she has my mobile. It's 07729-651-118.
E: OK. 07729-651-118. And what was your name again? Sorry.
D: Diane Lincoln. L-I-N-C-O-L-N. So when will she be back?
E: Probably later this afternoon. I think she said she was going for lunch.
D: Oh right. Well, hopefully I can speak to her today. I'm actually away on holiday from tomorrow.
E: Oh right. Well, I'll let her know anyway.
D: OK. Thanks. Bye.
E: Bye.

PRONUNCIATION Sentence stress

Aim

To focus on the way key words are often stressed in sentences.

Step 1 Write the first two lines of the dialogue on the board. Read out this sentence and ask students which words are stressed, *Hi, it's Brendan. Is Neil there?* Why are they stressed? (They are the key words.) Then read out the box. Model and drill the examples with exaggerated stress.

Step 2 Ask students to look at the audioscript on page 173 and notice how the key words are stressed.

Step 3 Put students in pairs to practise reading the conversations, paying particular attention to sentence stress. Monitor and correct their stress / pronunciation where appropriate.

DEVELOPING CONVERSATIONS
Asking for people and explaining where they are

Aim

To practise asking for people on the phone and explaining where they are if they're not there.

Step 1 Lead in by eliciting how you ask for someone on the phone *Is ... there? Hello, is that ... ?* and some things you might say if they are unable to answer. Try and elicit we explain where people are if they are not able to answer. Then read out the box and model and drill the examples.

Step 2 Ask students to complete the sentences in A with the correct preposition or adverb from the box. Check in pairs then check with the whole group.

Answers

1 out	5 off
2 away	6 up
3 in	7 from
4 of	

Step 3 Put students in pairs and ask them to practise the conversations in A. They should try to reply to the questions and continue each conversation for as long as they can. Model with a strong student, then in open pairs, then continue in closed pairs. Monitor and correct where necessary.

Tip Write the examples from the next exercise in *Grammar* on the board while students are discussing this.

GRAMMAR *Just, yet, already* and *still*

Aim

To introduce adverbs and their associated tenses, commonly used on the phone.

Step 1 Read out the box, checking as you read. Model and drill the examples. Alternatively, write the examples on the board and use them to highlight form and meaning.

Step 2 Ask students to complete the sentences in A by choosing the correct alternative. Check in pairs then check with the whole group.

Answers

1 already
2 still
3 yet
4 just
5 still
6 yet
7 already, still
8 just, just, yet

Direct students to the grammar reference on page 151 if they still seem unsure.

 **12A** see Teacher's notes p. 125.

CONVERSATION PRACTICE

Aim
To practise leaving and taking messages.

Step 1 Tell students they are going to role-play similar conversations to the one they heard in *Listening*. Ask them to begin individually by writing two messages they want to leave for different people, one for a friend and one in a business situation.

Tip Tell weaker students to look at the audioscript on page 173 for ideas and useful expressions to use when holding their conversations.

Step 2 Put students in pairs and ask them to role-play their conversations, using the plan in File 19 on page 159 and their messages. They should take turns to start. Monitor and note down errors in target language for a correction slot at the end.

Optional extra Ask strong students to role-play their conversations for the class.

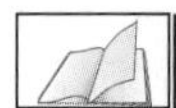 **pp. 84–85**

READING

Aim
To give practice in recognising topic sentences, predicting and reading for specific information.

Step 1 Tell students they are going to read three short news stories about phones and emergencies. Begin by reading out the explanation box. Then ask students to read the first sentence of each of the stories and guess the answers to the questions in A. Put them in pairs to compare ideas, but don't conduct feedback.

Step 2 Ask students to read the complete stories, ignoring the words in bold, to check their predictions. Ask each pair how many they guessed correctly.

Answers
1 a 999
  b to make unimportant complaints and requests
  c leaflets and fines
2 a fell off bike and hit head
  b to make hole in head – didn't have proper medical one
  c to consult a colleague
3 a in a pub in south-west England
  b he was bitten by a spider
  c huge and poisonous
  d scientists recognised the species and gave him a cure

Note You might like to point out that 999 is the emergency number for the UK and that the number varies in each country. For example, students might know the American number 911 from TV programmes.

Step 3 Put students in pairs and ask them to discuss the meaning of the words in bold. Then ask them to complete sentences 1–8 in C with the correct word. Check with the whole group.

Answers
1 fines
2 collapsed
3 reported
4 despite
5 species
6 transferred
7 rushed
8 swelling

Step 4 Put students in pairs and ask them to choose a different character from the list in D. Tell them they are going to role-play a conversation with a friend about their day. Give them a few minutes to re-read the relevant story and think about what to say. When they are ready they should take turns to begin, as in the example. Monitor, but don't intervene / correct unless absolutely necessary.

LANGUAGE PATTERNS

Aim
To draw students' attention to patterns with compound adjectives formed with numbers (no *s* because they are adjectives).

Step 1 Ask students to look at the sentences in the box and notice the similarities. Note that the compounds are singular in form because adjectives in English do not take a plural form.

A 50-metre pool. [✓]
A 50-metres pool. [×]

Ask students to translate these sentences into their own language. In monolingual classes ask students to compare their translations. In multilingual classes ask students to work in pairs and tell each other if the sentences were easy to translate and whether they were able to translate them word for word.

Step 2 Ask students to cover the English translations and translate the sentences back into English using their translations. Ask them to compare their translations in pairs against the book.

Alternatively If you prefer not to use translation, ask students to notice the patterns. Concept check any areas of difficulty and elicit a few more examples. If time, write their examples on the board and tick them if correct. If the sentences are wrong, ask the students to correct them or correct them yourself.

VOCABULARY Forming negatives

Aim
To show students how we often form negative adjectives by adding a prefix.

Step 1 Lead in by eliciting the opposite of *necessary* = *unnecessary*, *polite* = *impolite*, *legal* = *illegal*, etc. Highlight the use of prefixes here, then read out the box.

Step 2 Ask students to write the opposites of the adjectives in A by adding or removing a prefix. Check in pairs then check with the whole group. Model and drill, paying attention to word stress. Concept check by asking for examples.

Answers
1 unwise
2 legal
3 unfortunate
4 impolite
5 unhappy
6 unexpected
7 impractical
8 unfair
9 uncomfortable
10 common
11 impatient
12 convenient
13 impossible
14 unnatural
15 rational
16 pleasant

Step 3 Ask students to work individually and write five sentences using the words with prefixes. Check in pairs, then check briefly as a group.

Tip If time, ask students if they know any other adjectives or adverbs that use *un–*, *im–*, *in* or *–ir* to mean *not*.

SPEAKING

Aim
To give fluency practice and personalise the topic.

Step 1 Ask students to look at the questions in A and think about how they would answer them.

Step 2 Put students in small groups to share their ideas. Conduct brief feedback. Ask one student from each group something interesting that they talked about.

pp. 86–87

Next class Make photocopies of **12B** p. 151.

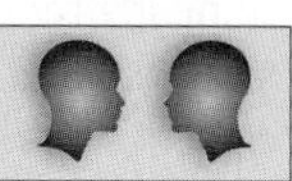

SPEAKING

Aim
To give fluency practice and lead in to *Listening*.

Step 1 Ask students to look at the places / people in the box and briefly discuss their experiences of phoning any of these as a class. Check *embassy* = building where government officials from another country work; *landlord* = a man that has a flat, room or house that people can rent.

Step 2 Put students in small groups and ask them to discuss the questions in A. Conduct brief feedback.

LISTENING

Aim
To give practice in listening for specific information and lead in to *Grammar* (reporting speech).

Step 1 Tell students they are going to listen to a woman calling World Mail, an international postal service. Read out the introduction then ask them to listen and decide which button Jaslyn should press. Play the recording. Then put them in pairs to check and explain.

Answer
3

12.2
Hello – and welcome to the World Mail enquiry service.

If you require general information about any of our products, including international mail, or need a redelivery service if you are moving house, please press 1. If you'd like to obtain a postal code or to check the status of a recorded or special delivery item, please press 2. If you need to talk to us about problems you're having with your mail or with one of our services, please press 3. To listen to information about what is available on our website, please press 4. To hear these options again, press 5.

Step 2 Ask students to look at the questions in B and answer them as they listen to Jaslyn's conversation with an employee. Play the recording. Check in pairs then with the whole group.

Answers
1 nearly two months ago
2 Flat 13, 30 Bedford Way, Walford E25 4QW
3 in main sorting office in Manchester
4 They will go out this week.

12.3
H = help desk; J = Jaslyn
If you'd like to obtain a postal code, please press 1. If you'd like to check the status of a recorded or special ...
H: Hello. World Mail. How can I help you?
J: Oh hi. I'm trying to find out what's happened to two packages that my parents sent me from Singapore.
H: OK. How long ago were they sent, because obviously international mail can take a lot longer sometimes?
J: It's nearly two months now, and they were sent by registered airmail post, so they should be here by now, really.
H: Hmm. Yes, that does sound strange. Can I take your address, please?
J: Sure. It's Jaslyn – that's J-a-s-l-y-n – Wang and my address is Flat 13, 30 Bedford Way, Walford – that's W-a-l-f-o-r-d, London E25 4QW.
H: Right. Let me just check that on my computer. Yes. OK. I've got them. It seems they entered England on June the 16th, which is five weeks ago now and they're now being held in our main sorting office in Manchester.
J: OK. Do you know why?
H: I have no information on that, I'm afraid, but they're going out this week. They'll be with you by the end of the week, the 25th. Oh, and you'll have to pay eight pounds seventy for one of them as well, because of insufficient postage.
J: Oh, OK. That's strange. Thanks anyway, though.

Step 4 Read out the next part of the story in C. Then put students in pairs and ask them to try to complete the extract. Play the last part of the recording for them to check their answers.

Alternatively With a weaker class, put the following phrases on the board and ask students to complete the text with them: *were going out, had arrived, 'd be with me, were being held*... .

Answers
1 had arrived
2 were being held
3 were going out
4 'd be with me

12.4
H = help desk; J = Jaslyn
H: If you can just wait one more minute. I'm just checking everything now. The system's a bit slow today, I'm afraid. OK. So one of your packages has been returned to Singapore and the other one is in our main sorting office in Manchester ...
J: No, that's not possible! Look, the last time I called, the man I spoke to said my packages had entered England on June the 16th, I think, and were being held in Manchester. He said they were going out that week and promised me – promised me – that they'd be with me by the end of that week.
H: Ah, well ... I don't know what's happened, but obviously something has gone wrong. What I can do is I can ...

Step 5 Put students in pairs / threes to discuss the questions in E. Conduct brief feedback.

GRAMMAR Reporting speech 2

Aim
To focus on the tense shift in reported speech.

Step 1 Ask students to look back at the extract in *Listening* exercise C and elicit what the speakers actually said in the first conversation. Ask what they notice about changes in verb forms and why this happens (the tense 'goes back', e.g. present simple = past simple when the conversation is being reported). Then read out the box. Alternatively, put the direct and indirect speech examples on the board and use them to elicit the tense changes.

Step 2 Ask students to re-write the second sentences in A in reported speech, so that they mean the same as the first. Check in pairs then check with the whole group.

Answers
1 were installing
2 had tried
3 had (already) arrived
4 would be
5 could offer

Direct students to the grammar reference on page 151 if they still seem unsure.

Step 3 Ask students to look at the email in B and decide what the exact words in the five questions were. Ask them to underline how they found this information. Check in pairs then check with the whole group.

Answers
1 How well do you know the area?
2 Can you work nights?
3 What kind of exercise do you usually do?
4 Why should we give this job to someone who will probably leave in a few months?
5 Do you have any questions?

Step 4 Put students in small groups to discuss the questions in C. Conduct brief feedback.

 **12B** see Teacher's notes p. 125.

SPEAKING

Aim
To create opportunities for students to use Reporting speech and to give fluency practice.

Step 1 Tell students they are going to role-play a phone conversation between Jim, a Canadian student in London, and World Mail. Ask them to read the advertisement he saw and tell you why they think he chose World Mail as his Internet provider.

Answers
Cheap, fast installation, free extras, no tie-in for new customers

Step 2 Ask students to listen to the message Jim left on a friend's answering machine and note down the problems he has had with World Mail. Play the recording.

Answers
took three weeks to deliver; the wireless box didn't work properly; no reply or automated response when he phones; bill for £80

12.5
T = Trish, J = Jim
T: Hi there. Sorry I can't get to the phone at the moment, but if you'd like to leave a message, please do so after the tone.
J: Hi Tricia. It's me, Jim. Sorry I haven't been in touch. I wanted to email you, but I'm having all kinds of problems with my Internet connection. I signed a contract with World Mail the other week, but they've been awful. They took about three weeks to deliver everything, and then the wireless box didn't work properly. I've tried calling them, but I always just get this automated system, which drives me mad! Then this morning I got a bill for £80. Thirty for installation and fifty for the first month! I couldn't believe it! It's so annoying. Anyway, sorry. I didn't mean to complain. Listen, I'll ... Oh. Um.

Step 3 Put students in AB pairs. Tell them that Student A works for World Mail and needs to explain the problems to Jim when he calls. Ask them to make notes on what they will say and how they will explain the problem. Tell them their aim is to make Jim happy. Student B is Jim. Tell them that they are very unhappy about the service provided and to think of what they are going to complain about. Tell both of them to read the information in B and to individually to think about what they are going to say. Tell them to look at the audioscript on page 174 and back at the unit for more ideas.

Step 4 When students are ready, ask them to role-play the conversation. They should try to use reported speech, e.g. *But your advertisement said... To begin with I was told..., but now you're telling me.* When they finish, they could swap roles and start again. Monitor and note down mistakes, especially in the use of language from the unit, for a correction slot at the end.

Optional activity Ask a strong pair to role-play the conversation for the class.

NATIVE SPEAKER ENGLISH

drives me mad

Step 1 Ask student to look at the sentences and notice what they have in common (something or someone *drives me mad* = makes me very angry or annoyed).

Step 2 Elicit a few examples from students beginning *It drives me mad when...* .

03 REVIEW

LEARNER TRAINING

Aim
To help students think about problems they might have when listening and possible reasons for them and to improve their listening strategies.

Step 1 Lead in by asking students what they listen to in English inside and outside class, what problems they have and what strategies they use. Read out the points.

Step 2 Ask students to look at the strategies and tick the ones they already do or think are a good idea and put a question mark by the ones they aren't sure about.

Step 3 Put students in small groups and ask them to discuss the strategies and reasons why they think the ones they have ticked are a good idea. Ask each group to come up with one more listening strategy. Get groups to report back to the rest of the class at the end.

GAME, CONVERSATION PRACTICE & ACT OR DRAW

For aims and suggested procedures see Review 01, pp. 32–33.

QUIZ

Answers
1 The opposite of **boiling** is freezing.
2 Species, animals, birds, dinosaurs can all be **extinct**.
3 You can be **suspected of** a crime, a murder, stealing, cheating.
4 **Cruel** people hurt other people or animals.
5 You might **make a speech** at a wedding or a party, or when leaving a job.
6 **RE** = Religious Education (religion and culture), **IT** = Information Technology, **PE** = Physical Education (gymnastics and sports).
7 It is good to be **supportive** because it means helpful and understanding.
8 The opposite of an **optional** assignment is a compulsory assignment.
9 If someone **overcharges** you, they ask you to pay too much.
10 **Toiletries** are soap, shampoo, shower gel.
11 An **expiry date** is on packets of food.
12 You can get **bitten** by an insect, mosquito, snake, dog, cat.
13 You might need to **apologise** if you have done something wrong.
14 An **irrational fear** is a phobia, e.g. fear of spiders or flying.
15 You might have to **sign a contract** when you buy / rent a house or flat, get a job, buy a mobile phone, etc.

COLLOCATIONS

For aims and suggested procedure see Review 01, pp. 32–33.

PRONUNCIATION Words containing *e* or *i*

For aims and suggested procedure see Review 01, pp. 32–33.

R3.1

/e/	pet
/iː/	retake, mosquito
/ə/	fisherman, authority
/ɪ/	rocket, windy
/ɜː/	term, first
/aɪə/	environment
/eɪ/	jail

R3.2
1 cancer / discovery
2 convenient / investigate
3 system / rocket
4 flowers / bunches
5 heated / trained
6 bee / reason
7 extracts / effects
8 finals / primary
9 redelivery / item
10 sight / witness
11 biology / meanwhile
12 introduce / identified
13 recovery / improper
14 assignment / responsible

Exercise B answers
1 same
2 different
3 different
4 different
5 different
6 same
7 different
8 same
9 different
10 different
11 same
12 different
13 same
14 same

R3.3

1 increase available resources
2 receive an urgent message
3 a poisonous species of snake
4 unbelievable success in business
5 a fixed minimum term
6 experiments by nuclear scientists
7 soldiers during the First World War
8 she went to jail on thirteen occasions

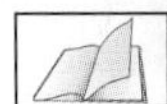 pp. 90–91

Listening

For aims and suggested procedure see Review 01, pp. 32–35. The audio is R3.4.

Exercise A answers

a 4 b 2 c 1 d - e 3

Exercise B answers

a 3 b - c 2 d 4 e 1

Grammar

Exercise A answers

1 forgot / had forgotten
2 'll call
3 've seen
4 haven't decided
5 would email
6 wouldn't worry
7 Is, raining
8 's, gone

Exercise B answers

1 had
2 asked
3 still
4 've
5 could
6 yet
7 just
8 'll

Exercise C answers

1 If I had
2 we could start
3 we didn't have to wear
4 correct
5 correct
6 tell

Language patterns

Answers

1 someone
2 Let
3 hour
4 something
5 left
6 minute

Prepositions

Answers

1 off
2 for
3 from
4 at
5 in
6 on
7 in
8 in
9 from

Forming words

Exercise A answers

1 achievement
2 coverage
3 theoretical
4 confirmation
5 scientific
6 payment
7 participants
8 cancellation
9 finances
10 findings

Adjectives

Answers

1 demanding
2 first-choice
3 long-term
4 remote
5 suitable
6 desperate
7 urgent
8 ordinary

Nouns

Answers

1 homework
2 environment
3 location
4 resources
5 uniform
6 challenge
7 delivery
8 fine

Note Direct students to units 9–12 in the *Vocabulary Builder* if they need more help with this.

Verbs

Answers

1c investigating
2a rejected
3b protect
4b questioned
5a launched
6b persuade
7c fund
8c reduce
9a boost

13 CULTURE

UNIT OVERVIEW

The main aims of this unit are to learn how to **talk about different kinds of films, favourite things and feelings** and to **explain what you have heard about things**. The main grammar aims are to understand and practise ***-ed* and *-ing* adjectives** and the **present perfect continuous** to talk about actions or situations that started in the past and are still ongoing.

Next class Make photocopies of **13A** p. 152.

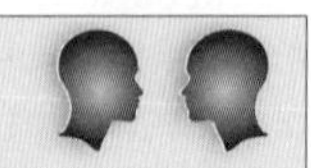

SPEAKING

Aim
To lead into the topic and give fluency practice.

Step 1 Lead in by asking students what kinds of films they like. Then put them in small groups and ask them to discuss the questions in A. Conduct brief feedback.

VOCABULARY Films

Aim
To introduce types of films and associated vocabulary.

Step 1 Put students in pairs and ask them to think of an example of each type of film in A, and any other types of films not listed. Check their answers and model, drill and concept check.

Possible answers
genres not listed: detective or crime film, cartoon / animated film, a blockbuster, etc.

Step 2 Put students in new pairs or threes to discuss the questions in B. Conduct brief feedback.

Suggested answers
amazing special effects: horror, action, science fiction, action or war movie
happy ending: romantic comedy, musical, comedy
complicated plot: all except musicals
car chases and explosions: thriller, action and science fiction movies
amazing costumes: historical drama
set in space: science fiction movie
scary: horror, thriller;
violent: war, action, martial arts
predictable: romantic comedy, martial arts movie
boring: all (depends on student's tastes)

LISTENING

Aim
To give practice in listening for specific information and note-taking.

Step 1 Tell students they are going to hear a conversation about films. Check they understand *movie* = another name for *film*. Ask them to listen and answer question 1 (what they hear about each film) as they listen. Play the recording. Check in pairs then check with the whole group.

Answers
1 *Dust and Heat*, directed by Umberto Collocini, set in the Sahara, great costumes, slow, predictable ending, stars Scottish actor Bryan McFletcher.

The Redeadening, a horror movie, really scary.

It's a Love-Hate thing, comedy; set in Paris and New York, stars Beatrice Binoche and Brad Schmidt.

13.1

A: What a boring lecture!
B: I know. It wasn't very good. I was starting to fall asleep near the end!
A: So what're you doing this afternoon? Have you got any plans?
B: Yeah, I'm thinking of going to see a movie and ... um ... listen, would you like to come with me?
A: Maybe. What's on?
B: Well, there's this film called *Dust and Heat* – directed by Umberto Collocini. It's supposed to be really good.
A: Yeah, I've seen it already, actually. I saw it the other day.
B: Oh yes? What was it like?
A: Not bad, but not as good as everyone is saying. The costumes were great and it's set in the Sahara, so it looks amazing.
B: Yeah, that's what I'd heard. So what was wrong with it?
A: Oh, I don't know. I just found it a bit too slow. I got a bit bored with it after a while – and the ending was very predictable.
B: Oh, right.
A: And that Scottish actor's in it as well. You know. What's his name?
B: Bryan McFletcher?
A: Yeah, that's him. I just find him really, really annoying. He can't act! Anyway, what else is on?
B: Um ... let me see. Oh, there's *The Redeadening*.
A: Yeah? What's that?
B: It's a new horror movie. It's supposed to be really scary.
A: OK. To be honest, I don't really like horror movies. I'd rather see something a bit lighter, if possible.
B: OK. Right. Well, how about this? *It's A Love-Hate Thing*. It's a romantic comedy set in Paris and New York and it stars Béatrice Binoche and Brad Schmidt.
A: That sounds more like it! Where's it on?
B: The Galaxy in Cambridge Road.
A: OK. And what time does it start?
B: There's one showing at 2.30 and then another one at quarter to five.
A: So shall we try the half past two one? We could go and have a coffee or something first.
B: OK. Great.

Step 2 Ask them to listen again and answer questions 2, 3 and 4. Play the recording. Check in pairs, then check as a class.

Answers
2 *It's A Love-Hate Thing*
3 The Galaxy in Cambridge Road.
4 2.30

NATIVE SPEAKER ENGLISH *on*

Ask students how A asked where the film was showing = *Where's it on?* Then read out the box. Get students to practise by asking each other where, what time, which channel films and TV programmes are *on*.

DEVELOPING CONVERSATIONS

supposed to

Aim
To introduce a way of saying what we have heard about something or someone that we don't have first hand experience of, especially in the context of entertainment.

Step 1 Read out the box, checking as you read. Elicit a few more examples of *It's supposed to* + verb by asking questions like *Have you seen...?* about new films, TV programmes, etc. Then get students to ask and answer similar questions in open pairs.

Tip Bring some newly released film posters / articles, or CDs into class and ask students to discuss what they know about them.

Step 2 Ask students to match the sentence beginnings in 1–6 with the correct endings in a–f. Check in pairs then check with the whole group.

Answers
1 d 2 b 3 f 4 c 5 a 6 e

Step 3 Ask students individually to think of one example of each thing in B and what each one is supposed to be like. They could make a few notes.

Step 4 Put students in pairs to share their ideas. Conduct brief feedback.

GRAMMAR *-ed* and *-ing* adjectives

Aim
To introduce the difference between adjectives ending in *-ed* and those ending in *-ing*.

Step 1 Write up the examples on the board and use them to check the difference. Ask students to underline the other examples of *-ing* and *-ed* adjectives in the audioscript on page 175 (answers underlined in audioscript 13.1). Check their answers and concept check by asking whether this is about the feeling (end in *-ed*) or the thing or situation that causes it (end in *-ing*). Then read out the box.

Step 2 Ask students to complete the sentences with the correct one of the pair given. Check in pairs then with the whole group.

Answers

1a tired	1b tiring
2a surprising	2b surprised
3a excited	3b exciting
4a boring	4b bored
5a interested	5b interesting

Direct them to the grammar reference on page 152 if they still seem unsure.

Step 3 Ask students to look at the items in B and think about what they are going to say. Then put them in pairs / threes to share their ideas. Conduct brief feedback.

13A see Teacher's notes p. 126.

CONVERSATION PRACTICE

Aim

To give personalised practice of the target language.

Step 1 Tell students they are going to role-play conversations similar to the one they heard in *Listening*. Ask them individually to think of three films they would like to see and make notes on what they know about them, using the prompts in A.

Step 2 Put students in pairs to role-play the conversation. They should decide whose films they are going to talk about first. In their conversation, they should choose a film to see, invent where it's on and decide what time to see it. One student should begin, *So what are you doing this afternoon? Have you got any plans?* When they have finished, students should swap roles. Monitor and note down mistakes in target language for a correction slot at the end.

Tip Tell weaker students to look at the audioscript on page 175 for a model conversation.

pp. 94–95

Next class Make photocopies of **13B** p. 153.

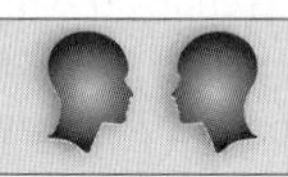

VOCABULARY Music, art and books

Aim

To introduce and practise vocabulary associated with entertainment.

Step 1 Lead in by asking students to tell you what kind of music / books / art they like. Then ask them to look at the words in A and write them in the correct column. Direct weaker students to the *Vocabulary Builder* on pp. 50–51 if they need help. Check in pairs, then check with the whole group.

Music	Art	Books
composer	sculpture	crime
album	painting	biography
voice	photographer	comedy
instrument	auction	author
concert	exhibition	novel
landscape	portrait	publish
singer		
rehearse		

Step 2 Ask students to look at the expressions in B. Check they understand all the meanings, e.g. *I'm a big fan of* = I really like..., *my all-time favourite* = the one I like best of all. Then ask them individually to look at the questions and think about how they would answer them. You could model by telling them your favourite something, using the expressions in B.

Step 3 Put students in small groups to talk about their favourites, using some of the expressions. Monitor but don't intervene unless absolutely necessary. Conduct brief feedback at the end.

LISTENING

Aim

To give practice in listening for gist, specific information and detail, and lead in to *Grammar* (present perfect continuous).

Step 1 Tell students they are going to hear four people talking about their favourites. Ask them to listen and match each speaker with one of the pictures. Check in pairs then with the whole group.

Answers

Peter: favourite singer is Sertab Erener, all-time favourite song is *Life doesn't wait – Hayat Beklemez* (picture: top right)
Gustavo: favourite composers are Shostakovich and Stravinsky (pictures: bottom right / top middle)
Zelda: favourite author is the Swedish crime writer Henning Mankell, especially his stories with the detective *Wallander* (picture: bottom left)
Mary: favourite artist (at the moment) is Swiss sculptor Alberto Giacometti, especially a sculpture called 'Cat'. (pictures: top left / bottom middle)

13.2

Peter

I'm a big fan of a Turkish singer called Sertab Erener. I first heard her in 2003 when she won the Eurovision Song Contest and I've liked her ever since then. I think she's got amazing voice. She actually trained as an opera singer. I've got five or six of her albums and last year I went to Istanbul to see her sing live. In fact, I've been learning Turkish for the last two years because I've discovered Turkey through her music and want to spend time there – and I can understand her songs better. My all-time favourite song is *Life doesn't wait – Hayat Beklemez*. Excuse my bad pronunciation.

Gustavo

I've been playing the trumpet for ten years now with *El Sistema*, which is a programme that helps young people from poor backgrounds learn classical music. I really really love playing and without *El Sistema* I would probably be in a bad situation! When I joined, I was only eight, but I was already in trouble with the police. My favourite composers are Russian – Shostakovich and Stravinsky. We've been rehearsing *The Rite of Spring* recently for a concert. It's fantastic – the best.

Zelda

My favourite author is the Swedish crime writer Henning Mankell, especially his stories with the detective *Wallander*. The stories are good thrillers. They're unpredictable, but they're also about social issues, which makes them extra interesting. For the last few weeks, they've been showing a series on TV based on the books. It's OK, but the main character is different to the character in my imagination and, of course, there's less suspense because I've already read the books! I don't know if I'll keep watching.

Mary

I'm at art school, where I'm studying Fine Art. I've known I wanted to be an artist since I was three. I've always been more of a painter, especially people – portraits, but recently I've become much more interested in sculpture. I think my favourite artist at the moment is a Swiss sculptor called Alberto Giacometti. He does these beautiful, strange, thin sculptures. I saw an exhibition of his work last year. I don't know why I liked it so much, I just did – especially a sculpture called Cat.

Step 2 Put students in pairs and ask them to try to answer the questions in B together. Check with the whole group.

Answers

1 Zelda – the TV series isn't as good as the books
2 Gustavo – by playing the trumpet with El Sistema
3 Peter – because he likes Turkish music and Turkey generally
4 Mary – used to be a painter, but now prefers sculpture

Step 3 Ask students to look at the sentences in C and try to complete them. Check in pairs then play the recording again for them to check.

Answers

1a have liked her	1b for two
2a for ten years	2b rehearsing, recently
3a have been showing	3b 've read
4a since I was three	4b 've always been

GRAMMAR The present perfect continuous

Aim

To introduce the present perfect continuous to talk about actions or situations which started in the past and are still ongoing.

Step 1 Ask students to look again at the sentences in *Listening* C. Elicit which tenses these are and what they are used for here. You could ask about other things they notice such as the use of *for* and *since*. Then read out the box, checking form and meaning as you read. Or put the examples on the board and use them to highlight form and meaning.

Step 2 Ask students to write *how long* questions for 1–8 by using the verb in brackets in the present perfect simple or continuous. Check in pairs then check with the whole group.

Suggested answers

2 How long have they been doing them?
3 How long has she been learning English?
4 How long have you been playing the drums ?/ How long have you played the drums for?
5 How long have you been training for?
6 How long have you known him?
7 How long have they been going out?
8 How long have you been married for?

Step 3 Put students in pairs and ask them to take turns asking each other the questions. A should answer using *for* and B should answer using *since*. Monitor and correct mistakes in target language. Check in open pairs at the end.

Step 4 Put students in new pairs and get them to ask each other the questions in C. If their partner answers *yes*, they should ask a *how long* question, as in the example. Model with a strong student then in open pairs, before continuing in closed pairs.

Step 5 Put the two sentences from the explanation box on the board and elicit the differences. Then ask students to look at D and choose the correct form. Check in pairs then with the whole group.

Answers
1 for
2 has produced
3 has been conducting
4 has had
5 has been writing
6 started
7 has won
8 since
9 loved
10 since
11 has been shown

Direct students to the grammar reference on page 152 if they still seem unsure.

13B see Teacher's notes p. 126.

SPEAKING

Aim
To personalise the topic and give fluency practice.

Step 1 Put students in pairs / threes and ask them to choose either question 1 or question 2 and discuss it. Conduct brief feedback at the end.

Tip Put students in multilingual pairs if possible to compare their countries.

pp. 96–97

SPEAKING

Aim
To lead in to *Listening*.

Step 1 Ask students to look at the questions and think about how they would answer them. Then put them in small groups to discuss their answers. Feedback briefly as a class.

READING

Aim
To give practice in predicting, reading for gist and specific information.

Step 1 Put students in pairs and ask them to discuss what they know about Nigeria and its film industry. Then ask them to read the article by Femi Abulu quickly and check their predictions and also what else they find out about Nigeria.

Step 2 Ask students to look back at the questions in *Speaking* and discuss how the writer, Femi Abulu, might answer them. Check ideas as a class.

Suggested answers
1 yes, third biggest in the world
2 straight to DVD
3 voodoo horror movies
4 they're fantasies where bad people are punished and the good people are rewarded
5 possibly *Living in Bondage*
6 Chico Eijiro
7 over eighty movies
8 probably
9 certain subjects are avoided and occasionally films are banned because they might cause tension in the country

Step 3 Ask students to match a verb in the first column with the correct noun / noun phrase in the second column to form phrases used in the article. Check in pairs and ask them if they remember who or what does / did each of the things in C. They should look back at the text to help them.

Answers
1e (Nigerian film industry)
2d (English)
3g (Hollywood)
4h (the man in *Living in Bondage*)
5b (Some Nollywood films/dramas)
6a (certain subjects)
7f (Nigeria)
8c (an evil love rival)

Step 4 Ask students to look at the questions in E and think about how they would answer them. Put them in pairs or threes to share their ideas. Conduct brief feedback.

Language patterns

Aim
To draw students' attention to patterns with *such as* meaning *for example*.

Step 1 Ask students to look at the sentences in the box and notice the similarities.

Step 2 Ask students to translate these sentences into their own language. In monolingual classes ask students to compare their translations. In multilingual classes ask students to work in pairs and tell each other if the sentences were easy to translate and whether they were able to translate them word for word.

Step 3 Ask students to cover the English translations and translate the sentences back into English using their translations. Then ask them to compare their translations in pairs against the book.

Alternatively If you prefer not to use translation, ask students to notice the patterns. Concept check any areas of difficulty and elicit a few more examples. If time, write the examples on the board and tick them if correct. If the sentences are wrong, ask students to correct them or correct them yourself.

Vocabulary Compound nouns

Aim
To show how compound nouns are formed.

Step 1 Read out the box. Elicit a few more examples from the article. Make sure students understand the difference between a compound noun and a strong collocation (*compound noun* = one meaning / item composed of two parts; *strong collocation* = two items often found together but still separate).

Step 2 Ask students to look back at the article and find eight examples of compound nouns. Put them in pairs to compare their answers. Check with the whole group.

Answers
Hollywood movie; video cameras; video cassettes; street stalls; action movies; black magic; religious cult; sound quality; horror movies; gangster movies; women's rights; success story; civil war; special effects.

Step 3 Ask students to look at the compound nouns in B and say where they think the stress is. Then play the recording for them to check.

13.3
business opportunity
security system
social life
heart disease
marketing manager
sunglasses
cash machine
swimming pool
tennis court
traffic lights
city centre
fast food

Step 4 Ask students to listen again and repeat after each one. Play the recording again.

Step 5 Give the students two minutes to try to memorise the words in B. Then put them in AB pairs. As should close their book while Bs test them. B should give an example or definition and A should try to remember the word. Then swap.

Step 6 Put students in small groups and ask them to generate more compound nouns by using either the first part or the second part of the words in B and a different beginning / ending, as in the example in E. The first group with 12 should shout *finished* and if they are all correct they are the winners.

Suggested answers (many possibilities)
- *business*: businessman, business woman; *opportunity*: golden opportunity
- *social*: social worker; *life*: working life, university life
- *heart*: heartbreak; *disease*: liver disease, fatal disease
- *marketing*: marketing strategy; *manager*: sales manager
- *sun*: sun cream, sun lotion, sun shade; *glasses*: wine glasses
- *cash*: cash prize; *machine*: washing machine
- *swimming*: swimming costume; *pool*: seawater pool, heated pool
- *tennis*: tennis racquet, tennis player; *court*: basketball court, law court
- *traffic*: traffic problems; *lights*: street lights, Christmas lights

Speaking

Aim
To round off the unit and give fluency practice.

Step 1 Ask students to look at the questions in A and think about how they would answer them. They could make a few notes.

Step 2 Put students in small groups to discuss their ideas. Conduct brief feedback.

14 THINGS

UNIT OVERVIEW
The main aims of this unit are to learn how to **explain where things are, to talk about common household objects** and **the environment and environmental issues**, and to **describe people, places** and **things that you don't know the name of**. The main grammar aims are to use ***must / mustn't*** to talk about obligation, and to present defining **relative clauses**.

Next class Make photocopies of **14A** p. 154.

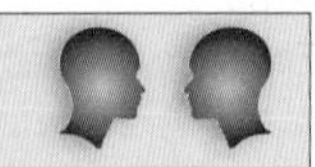

GRAMMAR Relative clauses

Aim
To introduce students to the topic, and to present and practise defining relative clauses.

Step 1 Lead in by asking students the names of a few tricky objects in the classroom, or in pictures if you have them, e.g. *What do you call ...?* Then put students in pairs and ask them to try to answer the questions in A.

Step 2 Ask students to match the definitions in A with the words in B. Check in pairs then check with the whole group. Model and drill and elicit the stress.

Answers
1 forecast
2 shelf
3 drawer
4 mortgage
5 refugee
6 neighbour
7 witness
8 pitch
9 library
10 court

Step 3 Ask students what they notice about the sentences in A. Try to elicit relative pronouns / clauses. Elicit what the relative pronouns are and what they refer to (*which / that* for things, *who / that* for people). Write a few examples on the board and use circles and arrows to show what the pronouns refer back to. Then read out the box.

Step 4 Ask students to complete the sentences in C using *which, who* or *where*. Ask students to check their answers in pairs, then check them with the whole group.

Answers
1 which
2 who
3 where
4 which
5 who
6 where
7 which
8 where
9 who

Step 5 Ask students to look at the items in D and try to write a definition for each word which includes a relative pronoun. Tell them to use the structure of the sentences in C as a guide and remind them to look at the *Vocabulary Builder* on pp. 54–55. if they need help understanding the words. Put them in pairs to compare their sentences. Check a few sentences with the whole group.

Step 6 Ask students to look at exercise E and tell them to discuss a thing that is important to them, a person who has influenced them and a place where they were very happy. Give them time to think about what they are going to say. Tell them to make some notes and remind them that they have to explain their ideas. Then put them in groups to share their ideas. Monitor as they talk for their use of relative pronouns. Conduct brief feedback.

LISTENING

Aim
To give practice in listening for specific information and note-taking.

Step 1 Tell students they are going to hear a conversation between three new flatmates planning a shopping trip. Ask them to listen and decide which of the objects in the pictures they want to buy and why. Play the recording. You may like to play the recording again before checking their answers. Check in pairs then check with the whole group.

Answers
dustpan and brush: to sweep the floor
iron and ironing board: to iron clothes
shower curtain and rail: to prevent the water splashing on to the floor
kettle: to make tea and coffee.

14.1

A: It's nice.
B: Yes, it is, but it's also very dirty!
C: I know. We'll have to give everything a good clean and sort the place out. Maybe we should go into town and buy some stuff.
A: Yeah, it's a good idea. One minute. I'll get a pen and we can write a list. OK. So ... .
B: Well, we need those things for cleaning. A brush and a ... I don't know the name. The thing that you put rubbish in. What's the name?
C: Do you mean a rubbish bin?
B: No, not that. You use it to get rubbish from the floor with the brush.
C: Oh, you mean a dustpan. A dustpan and brush.
B: A dustpan and brush. Yes, that's very useful.
C: And maybe we should get some cleaning stuff as well. Have we got any bleach?
A: What is bleach?
C: Oh, it's a kind of liquid that's really good for cleaning things, you know, like for cleaning the floor and the toilet. It's a kind of chemical. Quite strong.
A: Oh, we have some. It's in the kitchen. In the cupboard under the sink.
C: Oh, OK. I didn't notice that, but that's good.
B: We need to buy that machine that you use for the clothes. After you wash them. I can't remember the name. Oh, and I know this word as well.
A: You mean an iron?
B: Yes, an iron! And also the thing that you put the clothes on when you use the iron.
C: Yeah, an ironing board. OK. What else?
A: Oh, for the bathroom we need a thing for the shower. You know, the plastic thing that stops the water from leaving the shower – and the metal thing that holds it.
C: A shower curtain and a shower rail. Yeah, I noticed there wasn't anything like that in the bathroom. It's crazy, isn't it? Why doesn't the landlord provide things like that? It's so basic.
B: I know!
A: We should charge the landlord for these things.
B: Oh, one more thing. Before I forget. We need the machine that makes hot water – to make tea and coffee.
C: Oh, yes, of course. A kettle! I can't live without a kettle! I need my tea in the morning!

Step 2 Ask students what the other things in the pictures are called. Model and drill where necessary. Put them in pairs and ask them to take turns describing the items in the picture. Their partner should guess what they are talking about.

Answers
a kettle, a mop and bucket, a saucepan, an iron, a bin, a shower rail, a dustpan and brush, an ironing board, a needle and thread, a bottle of bleach

VOCABULARY Things in the house

Aim
To introduce and give practice in vocabulary used to talk about household objects.

Step 1 Ask students to look at the rooms and places in the home in exercise A and check understanding. Put students in pairs and ask them to discuss which of these places they have in their houses. Check briefly as a class.

Step 2 Ask students in the same pairs to look at the items in exercise B and say which ones they can see in the pictures and where in A they would expect to find each one. Check their answers and model, drill and concept check the vocabulary as necessary.

Answers
a mop and bucket: kitchen, bathroom
an iron: kitchen
a bin: office or bathroom
a needle and thread: bedroom, living room

Step 3 In pairs ask students to discuss where in their houses they would put the rest of the items in B. Check answers briefly as a class.

Suggested answers
a vacuum cleaner: kitchen / living room
a desk: a bedroom / an office
a towel: bathroom / bedroom
a hairdryer: bathroom / bedroom
a cloth: kitchen
a plaster: kitchen / bathroom
a torch: garage
a pan: kitchen
a duvet: bedroom / spare room
a stapler: an office
a rubber: an office

Step 4 Ask students to complete the questions in D with the correct word or phrase from exercise B. Ask students to check their answers in pairs then check them with the whole group.

Answers
1 a towel
2 a cloth
3 a plaster
4 a pan
5 a torch
6 a needle and thread
7 a mop and bucket
8 a vacuum cleaner

14A see Teacher's notes p. 126.

DEVELOPING CONVERSATIONS

Explaining where things are

Aim

To show how we explain where things are in two different ways.

Step 1 Read out the explanation box, checking as you read. Then ask students to choose the correct preposition to complete the sentences in A. Check in pairs then check with the whole group.

Answers

1 in, on	5 in
2 under	6 in, under
3 on	7 in, above
4 on	8 by

Step 2 Put students in pairs and ask them to take turns asking the questions in *Vocabulary* exercise D. They should give answers which are true for them, choosing from the prepositional phrases in A. Model with a strong student, then in open pairs, before continuing in closed pairs. Monitor and correct mistakes in target language.

CONVERSATION PRACTICE

Aim

To give students an opportunity to have freer practice of the target vocabulary.

Step 1 Tell students they are going to have a similar conversation to the one in *Listening*. Put students in AB pairs and ask them to look at the pictures of the things they want to take on a picnic. Student A should look at File 15 on page 159 and Student B in File 1 on page 156. Give them time to think about what they want to say. They might like to make a few notes.

Step 2 When ready, tell students to discuss in their pairs what they want to take, explain what the objects are and make sure their partner understands. They should then decide where to go and how to get there. Tell them to look back at their notes for Unit 13, *Listening* and *Conversation practice* (pp. 92–93) for language to decide where to go and how to get there. Monitor and note down errors in target language for a correction slot at the end.

Step 3 Conduct brief feedback and if time ask a strong pair to role-play their conversation for the class.

pp. 100–101

Next class Make photocopies of **14B** p. 157.

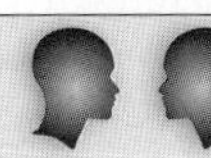

VOCABULARY Containers

Aim

To introduce common containers for food.

Step 1 Ask students to look at the pictures of three families' shopping and label them with the items in the box. Check in pairs then check with the whole group. Model and drill, paying attention to the stress on both nouns and the weak form of *of*/əv/.

Step 2 Put students in pairs and ask them to discuss what each of the containers is usually made of (some can be either). Conduct brief feedback.

Answers
metal: can, tin
glass: jar, pot
plastic: pot, carton, packet, tray
cardboard: box, packet, carton
cloth: sack

Note Ask students which one is not a container = *bar of chocolate*, which usually comes in a foil wrapper.

Tip This would be a good opportunity to introduce *it's / they're made of*, a very useful phrase.

Step 3 Put students in pairs or threes and ask them to discuss the questions in C. Conduct brief feedback at the end. There are no correct answers to these questions, but encourage students to provide the reasoning behind their ideas.

READING

Aim
To give practice in predicting, reading for gist and specific information.

Step 1 Tell students they are going to read an article about the effect of people's shopping on the environment. Put students in small groups and ask them to discuss where their family shops. Do they shop at a supermarket? If so, which one and why? Then tell them to make a list of issues they think the article might mention.

Step 2 Ask students to read the article quickly to check their predictions. Tell them to find four things they shouldn't buy and explain why. Check in pairs then check their answers as a class.

Answers
shouldn't buy food that has travelled a long way and is packaged in plastic; aluminium cans are bad, and so are small bottles and packets; shouldn't buy meat as it's bad for the environment.

Step 3 Put students in pairs and ask them to look at the statements in C and decide whether they are true or false, according to the article. Check with the whole group, asking to say which part of the text gave them the answer.

Optional activity For further practise ask students to correct the false sentences.

Answers
1 T – everything we consume leads to waste
2 F – the kiwi fruits come from New Zealand, which is thousands of miles away
3 F – recycles bottles and cans
4 T
5 T
6 T
7 T
8 T
9 F – the newspaper was 30 years old

Step 4 Ask students to look at the questions in D about the families in the pictures. Then put them in small groups to discuss the questions.

Step 5 Put students in new pairs or threes and ask them to look at the Fact File together in E. Ask them to discuss the questions. Conduct brief feedback at the end.

NATIVE SPEAKER ENGLISH *loads*

Ask students to look at the sentences and elicit another way of saying *loads* = lots. Check that students understand this is informal. Elicit a few more examples.

GRAMMAR *Must / mustn't*

Aim
To revise *must / mustn't* to talk about obligation or necessity and give practice.

Step 1 Read out the box, checking as you read. Or put the examples on the board and use them to highlight form and meaning. Concept check: Can you use *don't have to* instead of *mustn't*? (No.) Why not? *Don't have to* means *it isn't necessary*, *mustn't* means *you cannot.*

Step 2 Ask students to look at the sentences in A and choose the correct form. Check in pairs then check with the whole group.

Answers

1 must	5 must
2 mustn't	6 mustn't
3 mustn't	7 don't have to
4 must	8 must

Step 3 Ask students to write four laws about improving the environment or reducing waste beginning *People must / People mustn't...* Monitor and correct as they write. Then put them in small groups to compare their ideas and choose the best four laws between them. Check briefly as a class. Direct students to the grammar reference on page 153 if they still seem unsure.

Optional activity You could ask students in groups to write their laws to reduce waste on posters and display them around the class. You could then ask them to walk around looking at each poster and to vote on the best law.

14B see Teacher's notes p. 126.

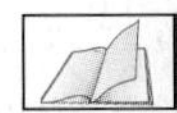
pp. 102–103

SPEAKING

Aim

To lead in to *Listening* and give fluency practice in talking about giving and receiving presents.

Step 1 Lead in by asking students when they usually give / receive presents and whether they think it is better to give or to receive. Put them in small groups to discuss the questions in A. Conduct brief feedback as a class.

LISTENING

Aim

To give practice in listening for specific information and detail.

Step 1 Tell students they are going to hear four people talking about presents. Ask them to look at the questions in A and note down the answers for each speaker as they listen. Play the recording. Check in pairs then with the whole group. Listen again if necessary before checking the answers.

Answers

1 a website
b mountain bike
c iron / dress
d rock
2 a birthday
b Christmas
c birthday
d first date
3 a yes – exciting / something they could do together
b yes – helps him save money and keep fit
c no – presents were more to please boyfriend than her
d no – embarrassing (at first), maybe yes now

14.2

1 For my birthday this year my big sister bought me my own website. She's really good with computers and I'm not, but the website has become something fun we work on together. I also loved the way she told me. She sent me an email where she gave me clues about the present for me to guess what it was, but I didn't know. Then she sent me another email with a link to a website. When I clicked on the link I understood everything and I realised that the site was the present. I was really excited! It's my favourite ever gift because, as I said, it's something we do together.

2 I got a mountain bike for Christmas a few years ago and it's been one of the most useful presents ever. Over the last year, I've lived close enough to work to be able to cycle and so I've saved loads of money on petrol. A birthday present that also saves me money! Excellent. I'm also fitter and have lost weight.

3 One of my ex-boyfriends was the king of bad presents. One year, he gave me an iron for my birthday! An iron! I mean, what kind of message does that send about our relationship and the way that he saw me? The following year, he bought me a dress that HE really liked and told me that he wanted me to start wearing more clothes like that from then on – because they would make me more attractive. I couldn't believe it! A couple of weeks after that, we broke up!

4 A few years ago, I went out with a girl and as we were getting out of the taxi to go to dinner, she suddenly said, "I got you a present". I was quite embarrassed because it was our first date and I hadn't thought of getting her anything. Then she handed me a rock from a beach. I was confused. Why had she given me this thing? She said, "I wanted to give you something you'd never forget and you could tell your children about." I said thanks to be polite, but I actually thought it was a bit stupid and it was a bad start to the evening! Now, though, I use that rock to stop papers on my desk blowing away and that girl is my wife!

Step 2 Put students in pairs and ask them to look at the words in B and try to remember how they were used in *Listening*. Then play the recording again and let the students read the audioscript on page 176 at the same time to check their ideas. Check in pairs, then check as a class.

Answers

1 *clues* – her sister sent her an email with clues about the present; *link / click* – she clicked on the link and found the website.
2 *close* – he lives close enough to work to cycle; *petrol* – he saves on petrol; *weight* – he's lost some weight from cycling.
3 the iron sent her a *message* that she was a housewife; *attractive* – her boyfriend wanted her to wear clothes that would make her more attractive; *broke up* – they broke up because she realised what he was really like.
4 *taxi* – he gave her the present as they were getting out of the taxi; *polite* – he said thanks to be polite; *papers* – he uses the rock to hold his papers down now.

Step 3 Ask students to look at the questions in D and to think about how they would answer them. Then put them in new pairs or threes to discuss their answers. Check briefly as a class.

Language patterns

Aim

To draw students' attention to patterns with adjective + *at / with* to talk about abilities.

Step 1 Ask students to look at the sentences in the box and notice the similarities. Check they understand the difference between adjective + *at* (with a subject or skill) and adjective + *with* (with people or things).

Step 2 Ask students to translate these sentences into their own language. In monolingual classes ask students to compare their translations. In multilingual classes ask students to work in pairs and tell each other if the sentences were easy to translate and whether they were able to translate them word for word.

Step 3 Ask students to cover the English translations and translate the sentences back into English using their translations. Then ask them to compare their translations in pairs against the book.

Alternatively If you prefer not to use translation, ask students to notice the patterns. Concept check any areas of difficulty and elicit a few more examples. If time, write the examples on the board and tick them if correct. If the sentences are wrong ask the students to correct them or correct them yourself.

Vocabulary Verbs with two objects

Aim

To introduce verbs which take both a direct and an indirect object.

Step 1 Write the two sentences with *bought on the board:*

My big sister bought me my own website.
My big sister bought a website for me.

Ask students what they notice about the objects (one is direct – *my own website*, the other is indirect – *me* = to me / for me). Then read out the explanation box, checking as you read.

Step 2 Ask students to look at the sentences in A and complete each one with the correct pair of sentences from the box. Do the first one with them. (Do you mind if I *ask* you a *personal question*?) Monitor and help with any problems. Check in pairs then with the whole group.

Answers

1 ask + personal question
2 read + bedtime story
3 buy + car
4 cook + dinner
5 lend + some money
6 pour + a drink
7 make + a cup of tea
8 give + something special
9 tell + a secret
10 send + a card

Step 3 Ask students to look at the questions in B and think about how they would answer them. Then put them in pairs / threes to discuss their answers. Monitor and note down mistakes in target language for a correction slot at the end.

Speaking

Aim

To give fluency practice, personalise the topic and round off the unit.

Step 1 Ask students to look at the scenarios in A and choose a suitable present, with reasons. They could make a few notes.

Step 2 Put students in small groups to discuss their ideas. Tell them they have to choose one present for each scenario between them.

Step 3 Get them to report back to the other groups on what they chose for each scenario, and why. Then, as a class, get them to choose the best presents for each of the situations in exercise A overall.

15 MONEY

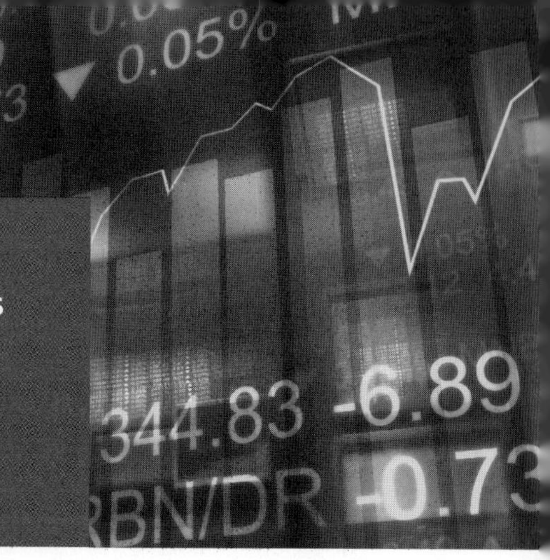

UNIT OVERVIEW
The main aims of this unit are to learn how to **talk about money issues and problems, describe the economy, compare prices** and **pronounce different kinds of numbers**. The main grammar aims are **present tenses in future time clauses** and **common time phrases with their associated tenses**.

Next class Make photocopies of **15A** p. 156.

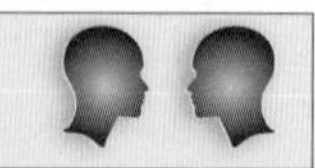

VOCABULARY

The economy and quality of life

Aim
To introduce words and phrases about the economy and lead in to *Listening*.

Step 1 Lead in by asking students about the state of the economy where they come from. Then ask them to look at the words in A and translate them into their own language. In a monolingual class ask students to compare their translations in pairs.

Alternatively If you prefer not to use translation, ask students to try to think of a definition or example for each one. They can do this in pairs and use the *Vocabulary Builder* for help.

Step 2 Put students in pairs and ask them to discuss whether each item in A means the economy is doing well or badly and to help each other with any words they are not sure of. Check with the whole group or ask them to check in the *Vocabulary Builder* on page 58.

Answers
Well: low inflation; strong currency; high average salaries.
Badly: a lot of unemployment; high cost of living; unemployment has gone up; weak currency.

Step 3 Check students understand the words / phrases in exercise C, e.g. *job security* = feeling of confidence that you will not lose your job; *pace of life* = speed at which we conduct our lives, for example: *The pace of life is usually slower in the country than in a city*. Model and drill where necessary. Put them in small groups to discuss the questions. Conduct brief feedback.

LISTENING

Aim
To give practice in listening for specific information and detail.

Step 1 Tell students they are going to hear a conversation between two people–Aidan who works in a school in a country called Freedonia, and Laima who is on holiday there. Ask them to look at the questions in A and answer them as they listen. Play the recording. Check in pairs then check with the whole group.

Answers
1 good, but not as good as it used to be
2 not very well
3 because he has better opportunities at home in Canada and he misses his friends and family

15.1
L = Laima; A = Aidan
L: So how long have you been living here?
A: Almost two years.
L: Wow! You must like it.
A: Yeah, it's nice. I have a good quality of life here – warm climate, near the beach, not too much work.
L: It sounds fantastic.
A: Yeah, it's great, but I'm actually going back to Canada in a few months.
L: Forever?
A: Yeah, I think so.
L: Why? It sounds perfect here.
A: Well, the economy's doing quite badly at the moment. I mean, unemployment has gone up quite a lot over the last few months, so I'm not sure I'm going to have a job in a year's time.
L: Really?

A: Yeah, and also salaries aren't so high here, you know. I could get paid a lot more back home.
L: Sure, but I bet the cost of living's a lot higher in Canada as well. Everything's so cheap here. I mean, eating out is twice the price in my country. You can get a three-course meal for about six dollars here.
A: Yeah, that's true, but it used to be cheaper in the past. Inflation's gone up over the last two years and if it stays high, well, you know, it won't be so cheap.
L: I know, but it's still a big difference, no?
A: Yeah, maybe, but anyway, in the end, I miss my family and friends and maybe money isn't so important, but I'll still have more opportunities back home, I think, so work might be more interesting there.
L: I guess so. It seems a shame, though. It's so nice here. Won't you miss the heat?
A: Yeah, probably, but I don't mind the cold weather so much. You get used to it after a while.
B: Mmm.
A: So what about your country? How are things there? Is it a good place to live?

Step 2 Ask students to look at the sentences in B and choose the correct answer. Then play the recording again for them to check. Check in pairs then check with the whole group.

Answers

1 at the	5 twice
2 in	6 in
3 last few months	7 in
4 back home	8 while

Step 3 Put students in pairs / threes to discuss the questions in C. Conduct brief feedback.

GRAMMAR

Time phrases and tense

Aim

To revise common time phrases and associated tenses.

Step 1 Ask students to look at the audioscript on page 176 and underline some of the time phrases. (Answers underlined in audioscript 15.1 above.) Ask them to notice the tense which goes with them e.g. *in a few months* + present continuous. Ask students to read the examples in the box and elicit a few examples from them of things they are doing now, things that are ongoing, things they will do in the future and things in the past.

Step 2 Ask students to complete the sentences in A by using the verbs in brackets in the correct tense. Check in pairs then check with the whole group.

Answers

1 is doing
2 has fallen
3 has gone up
4 used to be
5 is going to be
6 is currently losing
7 is going to fall
8 used to be
9 is getting
10 used to have

Step 3 Put students in small groups to discuss which of the ten sentences in A are true for their country. Monitor and conduct brief feedback at the end.

Tip In a multilingual class, mix up the nationalities as much as possible.

DEVELOPING CONVERSATIONS

Comparing prices

Aim

To show how we compare prices in different places and times.

Step 1 Read out the box, checking as you read. Then ask students to choose the correct word and invent a price to complete the sentences in A. Do the first example with them to demonstrate ... *You can get a designer suit for 50 euros*. Check in pairs then check with the whole group.

Answers

1 suit	5 litre
2 packet	6 pair
3 can	7 digital camera
4 laptop	8 kilo

Step 2 Put students in pairs and ask them to take turns starting conversations as in the example, using ideas from A. Model with a strong student, then in open pairs, before continuing in closed pairs. Monitor and correct mistakes in target language.

Step 3 Put students in groups to discuss the questions in C. Remind them to give examples, then compare ideas as a class.

CONVERSATION PRACTICE

Aim
To give freer practice.

Step 1 Tell students they are going to have a similar conversation to the one they heard in *Listening*. Put students in AB pairs and ask them to prepare to talk about the economy and quality of life in their own country. Student A should talk about their country and Student B should look at the role card in File 17 on page 159. When they are ready, they should have the conversation. Monitor and note down errors in target language.

Step 2 Student A should look at the role card in File 10 on page 158, while Bs prepare to talk about their own country. When they are ready they should start again. Monitor and note down errors in target language, then hold a correction slot on all the errors noted while monitoring.

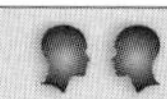 **15A** see Teacher's notes p. 127.

 **pp. 106–107**

READING

Aim
To give practice in predicting, reading for gist and specific information.

Step 1 Tell students they are going to read a story about a woman reading her father's will. Check they understand *will* = instructions left by someone about what they want to happen to their money and property after they die. Ask a few questions about why people make wills, what happens if people don't leave a will, etc. Put students in small groups to discuss the questions in A.

Step 2 Ask students to read the story quickly and find out why the author was surprised. Conduct brief feedback.

Answer
Because her father left nearly three million pounds but they had lived like poor people.

Step 3 Put students in pairs and ask them to look at the questions in C and answer them together. Check with the whole group.

Answers
1 *money's silver but a needle's thread and gold* = money isn't as important as being able to fix / mend things.

Early to bed, early to rise, makes a man healthy wealthy and wise = getting a good night's sleep and getting up early is good for you.

Never buy what you can borrow, never throw away what you can repair = borrow, re-use and recycle things.

2–4 students' own answers.

LISTENING

Aim
To continue the story and give practice in listening for specific information.

Step 1 Tell students they are going to listen to the rest of the story. Ask them to look at the statements in A and decide whether they are true or false as they listen. Check they understand *shares* = parts of company that people can buy / invest in so they get a share of the profits. Then play the recording. Ask them to correct the false statements. Check in pairs then check with the whole group.

Answers
1 F – he earned the money
2 F – they went from 0.8p to £4.12
3 T
4 F – she's had a happy childhood and the money can help other children
5 T
6 F – she doesn't know what to spend it on

15.2
The lawyer continued reading. It seemed Dad had actually been a good salesman. He earned quite a good salary, but he just preferred to save it. And he had been good at investing money too. The most expensive technology he had was a radio, but he bought shares in some camera and electronic shops. In 1965, the shares cost eight pence each and he sold them 35 years later for four pounds twelve each.

Of the 2.7 million pounds he was leaving, he had decided to give two million to a charity that looked after teenagers with problems. The rest was divided between me and my sisters.

For a moment, I felt angry. Why hadn't he said anything? Why had we lived like poor people? Why was he giving the money to other children? But then I thought, it's stupid to think like that. Really, I had a happy childhood and I'm very happy now. I remembered my parents reading us books they'd borrowed from the library and the hours we played cards together. It was fantastic what my parents had done. The love we had was more important than money, but now maybe the money they saved can bring some love to others.

The only problem I have now is what to do with a quarter of a million pounds – when I honestly don't really need anything!

Step 2 Put students in pairs / threes to discuss the questions in B. Conduct brief feedback at the end.

VOCABULARY Money verbs

Aim
To practise verbs commonly used to talk about money.

Step 1 Ask students to look back at the story and the audioscript on page 177 and underline any verbs connected with money (e.g. *leave, give, divide, save*). Put them in pairs to compare and explain any words they are not sure about.

Step 2 Ask students to look at the conversations in B and complete them using the correct form of the verbs in the box. Check in pairs then check with the whole group, perhaps in open pairs.

Answers
1 A borrow; B owe
2 B save
3 A won; B invest; A buy
4 A give; B earn
5 A worth; B left

Step 3 Put students in pairs or threes and ask them to discuss the questions in C. Conduct brief feedback at the end.

Alternatively You could conduct exercise C as a race, i.e. the first pair / three with correct answers for each question is the winner.

PRONUNCIATION Numbers

Aim
To help students with the pronunciation of different types of numbers.

Step 1 Ask students to look at the numbers from the story in A and pronounce them. Then play the recording for them to check.

15.3
1 Two million pounds
2 Seven hundred and eighty-one thousand
3 Six hundred and fifty-three
4 Nineteen Sixty-Five
5 Four pounds twelve
6 Two point seven
7 A quarter

Step 2 Ask them to listen to the next recording and write down the numbers they hear. Play the recording. Then ask to students to check by saying the numbers to each other. Check and drill with the whole group. (Answers underlined in audioscript 15.4.)

15.4
1 The minimum wage at that time was five pounds seventy-three an hour.
2 Inflation fell to three point four per cent last month.
3 The government is going to invest seven hundred million in schools.
4 Three-quarters of the population support owning a car.
5 The new factory will create eight hundred and twenty-five jobs.
6 The house cost three hundred and sixty thousand euros.
7 We borrowed a hundred and ninety-four thousand from the bank.
8 We'll finally pay back the mortgage in twenty fifty-one.

SPEAKING

Aim
To lead in to *Listening* and give fluency practice.

Step 1 Lead in by asking students about common money problems (debt, not earning enough to cover basic expenses, losing your credit cards etc). Then put them in small groups of three / four to discuss the questions in A. Conduct brief feedback.

Tip If there is not enough time to discuss all the questions, ask students in their groups to choose four questions to discuss.

pp. 108–109

Next class Make photocopies of **15B** p. 157.

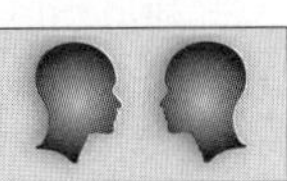

LISTENING

Aim
To give practice in predicting, listening for gist, specific information and detail.

Step 1 Tell students they are going to hear four conversations about money problems. Put them in groups to discuss the questions in A. Check their ideas as a class.

Step 2 Ask students to look at the pictures and match each one with one of the conversations as they listen. Play the recording. Check in pairs then check with the whole group.

Answers

Conversation 1: picture 2	Conversation 2: picture 3
Conversation 3: picture 1	Conversation 4: no picture

15.5

Conversation 1

A: Yes, sir?
B: Can we get the bill, please?
A: Certainly. One moment.
B: Thanks.
C: How much is it?
B: Don't worry. I'll get this. It's my treat.
C: Are you sure? I don't mind paying half.
B: No, really. It's fine. After all, I asked you out.
C: Thanks. It's really kind of you.
B: Oh no!
C: What's up?
B: I've just realised I left my wallet in my other jacket. It's got all my credit cards and cash in it! I'll have to go and get it.
C: Don't be silly. It's too far to go. I'll pay today.
B: Are you sure? I'll pay you back as soon as I can, I promise.
C: No, it's fine. Honestly. Oh! Wow! Right. That's a lot! I hope they accept my credit card!

Conversation 2

D: That looks great on you.
E: Really?
D: Yeah. Really suits you.
E: Maybe. How much is it?
D: Well, it's vintage sixties.
E: Sorry?
D: It's very old. From the nineteen sixties. It's hard to find things like that in this condition.
E: Oh. Yes. So how much?
D: Let's call it two hundred.
E: Pounds?
D: Yes, of course pounds.
E: Two hundred pounds! But it's not in perfect condition. Look – there's a mark here.
D: OK. So let's say one eighty.
E: No, sorry. It's too much. Thank you.
D: OK, OK. The best price I can manage is a hundred and fifty. Any lower than that and I'll lose money.

Conversation 3

F: But if I don't buy it, someone else will.
G: So you've said, but a thousand pounds is a thousand pounds.
F: I know, but if I don't have a car, then I'll have to keep getting the bus into town. And that's not cheap either. Fares have just gone up.
G: OK, OK. Look, you did well in your exams and we'd be happy to help, but it is a lot of money. You're working now, so why don't you pay half?
F: I would if I could, mum, honestly, but I haven't managed to save much yet!
G: Well, maybe we can borrow some money from the bank.
F: Really? Oh, that'd be brilliant!
G: And you pay us half back when you have the money, OK?

Conversation 4

H: Your card was cancelled because of some irregular activity that we noticed.
I: Irregular activity? What do you mean?
H: Well, for instance, did you have lunch in Singapore last week?
I: No. I've never been there in my life.
H: Exactly. We suspect that your card was copied sometime last month and that someone then used it overseas.
I: Oh no! How did they manage to do that? And will I get a refund?
H: Everything is covered by your insurance and we're sending out a new card today. You'll receive your new PIN number after you get the card. They're sent separately for security reasons.

Step 3 Put students in pairs and ask them to try to complete the sentences in C together. Play the recording again for them to check. Check with the whole group.

Answers

1 treat
2 up
3 left
4 condition
5 mark
6 manage
7 fares
8 managed
9 borrow
10 irregular
11 suspect
12 insurance

Step 4 Ask students to look at the questions in D and think about how they would answer them. Then put them in new pairs or threes to discuss their answers. Conduct brief feedback.

NATIVE SPEAKER ENGLISH *What's up?*

Ask students for another way to say *What's up?* (*What's the matter? What's wrong?*). Read out the box. Elicit a few more examples from students. Point out that *something's up* = something's wrong.

LANGUAGE PATTERNS

Aim

To draw students' attention to patterns with *manage* + *to*-infinitive to talk about things which are difficult to do.

Step 1 Ask students to look at the sentences in the box and notice the similarities. Ask students to translate these sentences into their own language. In monolingual classes ask students to compare their translations. In multilingual classes ask students to work in pairs and tell each other if the sentences were easy to translate and whether they were able to translate them word for word.

Step 2 Ask students to cover the English translations and translate the sentences back into English using their translations. Then ask them to compare their translations in pairs against the book.

Alternatively If you prefer not to use translation, ask students to notice the patterns. Concept check any areas of difficulty and elicit a few more examples. If time, write the examples on the board and tick them if correct. If the sentences are wrong, ask the students to correct them or correct them yourself.

GRAMMAR

Present tenses in future time clauses

Aim

To focus on the use of the present simple with time clauses about the future.

Step 1 Write the examples on the board and ask students which tense is used in each clause and what time this refers to. Highlight the use of the present simple after *when, after, before, until, as soon as,* even though this refers to the future.

Step 2 Ask students to look at the sentences in A and choose the correct alternative. Check in pairs then check with the whole group.

Answers

1 I'm
2 are you going to do
3 arrive
4 I'm going to move
5 you
6 you get
7 I'll (pay)
8 I
9 We'll support
10 I'll call

Direct students to the grammar reference on page 154 if they still seem unsure.

Step 3 Ask students to look at the sentences in B and complete them with their own ideas. Monitor and correct as they write. Then put them in pairs to compare what they have written. Conduct feedback by asking a partner to tell the class one interesting thing their partner told them.

 **15B** see Teacher's notes p. 127.

VOCABULARY Dealing with banks

Aim

To introduce and practise collocations associated with the topic of banks.

Step 1 Lead in briefly by asking students what they think about banks, what different things banks do, etc. Then ask students to look at the pairs of phrases in A and complete them with the correct verb from the box. Check in pairs then with the whole group.

Answers

1 open	5 transfer
2 take out	6 pay
3 make	7 cancel
4 change	8 charge

Step 2 Tell students they are going to test each other. Put them in AB pairs. Bs should close their books while As read out the verbs from the list in exercise A and Bs try to remember the two collocations.

Step 3 Put students in pairs / threes and ask them to discuss the questions in exercise C. Conduct brief feedback.

SPEAKING

Aim

To give fluency practice and round off the unit.

Step 1 Ask students to look at the scenarios in A and choose two of the situations to role-play. They should decide who is playing which role and take a few minutes to prepare what they are going to say. Tell weaker students to look at the audioscript on page 177 to help them with ideas.

Step 2 When they are ready, ask students to have the conversations. Monitor and note down errors for a correction slot at the end.

Optional activity Ask a strong pair to role-play their conversation for the class.

16 DATES AND HISTORY

UNIT OVERVIEW
The main aims of this unit are to learn how to talk about **major historical events, to ask and answer linked questions** and to **describe parties** and **special days in your life**. The main grammar aims are **verb patterns with *-ing* and *to-* infinitives**, and **nouns / *-ing* forms following prepositions**.

SPEAKING

Aim
To lead in to the topic / unit and give fluency practice.

Step 1 Ask students to look at the items in A. Put them in small groups and ask them to discuss the questions. Get them to try to help each other with meaning and tell them to look at the *Vocabulary Builder* on page 62 if they are not sure. Conduct brief feedback on which kind of party they think is the worst to go to, why?

VOCABULARY Describing parties

Aim
To introduce words and phrases about parties and lead in to *Listening*.

Step 1 Lead in by asking students about what kind of parties they like. Have they been to all kinds of parties from the box in *Speaking*? Then ask them to look at the words in bold in A and translate them into their own language. Tell them to check answers in the *Vocabulary Builder*. Then check answers as a class.

Tip In a monolingual class put students in pairs to check their translations with each other. In a multilingual class ask students to check meaning together after they have completed their translations.

Alternatively If you don't want them to use translation, ask students to try to think of a definition or example for each one. Ask them to check in the *Vocabulary Builder* on page 62 for ideas.

Answers
warm = friendly
background = music playing quietly, but not the main thing that you hear
converted = changed into something different
cold and distant = not friendly
buffet = meal where people serve themselves
cleared = emptied
venue = place where event is happening
ruined = spoilt
bowls = dishes to put food in
impressive = very good

Step 2 Ask students to look at the questions in B and match each one with one of the sentences in A. Put students in pairs to check their answers and think of other possible answers for each question. Check with the whole group.

Answers
1 8, 10 2 3, 7 3 5, 9 4 2, 6 5 1, 4

Step 3 Ask students to look at the questions in B and to think of one more way of answering them. They could do this is pairs, or individually and then check in pairs. Check their ideas as a class.

LISTENING

Aim
To give practice in listening for specific information and detail.

Step 1 Tell students they are going to hear three conversations about parties. Ask them to look at the questions in A and answer them as they listen. Play the recording. Check in pairs then check with the whole group.

Answers

Conversation 1: 1 a wedding
2 a friend's
3 in a castle
4 fantastic

Conversation 2: 1 a housewarming
2 a friend's
3 in her flat, a converted church
4 good at first

Conversation 3: 1 a dinner party
2 her / his own
3 in her flat
4 it was lovely

16.1

Conversation 1

A: Did you have a nice weekend?
B: Yes, it was great, actually.
A: Yeah? What did you do?
B: One of my oldest friends got married on Saturday, so I went to the wedding in the afternoon and then the reception later on. It was really good.
A: Oh yeah?
B: Yeah, they hired an old castle on the coast for it. It was an amazing venue. And they had a big buffet there, with really good food, and a DJ and everything.
A: That sounds great. What was the music like?
B: Excellent. I was expecting typical wedding reception music, but this DJ played lots of modern things as well. The dance floor was full all evening.

Conversation 2

C: Did you do anything last night?
D: Yeah, I did, actually. I went to a friend's house-warming. She's just moved into this new place. It's an amazing flat – in a converted church. It's a really impressive place.
C: Oh wow! So what was the party like? Was it good?
D: It was great to begin with, yeah. All the other guests were lovely. Everyone was really warm and friendly and very easy to talk to, but then my ex arrived with his new girlfriend.
C: Oh no!
D: Yes, and to make things worse, she was absolutely gorgeous! All the guys there couldn't stop looking at her.
C: Oh, you poor thing! That's awful.
D: I know. It ruined the night for me, to be honest. I didn't stay much longer after that.

Conversation 3

E: So what did you do last night? Anything interesting?
F: Yeah, I had a little dinner party.
E: Oh really? What was the occasion?
F: There wasn't one. I just felt like inviting some friends round and cooking for them.
E: Nice. So how did it go? Was it good?
F: Yeah, it was lovely. It was nice to see people and chat.
E: How many people came?
F: Twelve.
E: Wow! That's a lot of cooking.
F: I know! It took me ages to get everything ready.
E: Did you cook everything yourself?
E: Yeah.
F: You must be a good cook.
E: I don't know about that! I just follow recipes.
F: So what did you do?
E: Well, for starters, I did grilled aubergines covered in yoghurt and served with a slightly spicy sauce and then ...

Step 2 Ask students to look at the adjectives in B and decide which conversation each one applies to. Ask them to compare their ideas in pairs then play the recording again for them to check. Check with the whole group.

Answers

spicy – 3 (the sauce)
easy to talk to – 2 (the other guests)
typical – 1 (the wedding)
modern – 1 (the music)
gorgeous – 2 (her ex-boyfriend's new girlfriend)
grilled – 3 (the aubergines)
lovely – 3 (the dinner party); 2 (the other guests)
impressive – 2 (the flat)
full – 1 (the dance floor)

Step 3 Put students in pairs or threes to discuss the questions in C. Conduct brief feedback at the end.

NATIVE SPEAKER ENGLISH *round*

Read out the examples in the box and check students understand this use of *round* = to my house, to someone else's house. Check they understand it is fairly informal. Elicit a few more examples from them.

DEVELOPING CONVERSATIONS
Linked questions

Aim
To show how we often follow one question with another.

Step 1 Read out the box, checking as you read. Then ask students to match a question from 1–8 with one from a–h in A. Do the first example with them to demonstrate. Check in pairs then check with the whole group.

Answers

1 e	3 c	5 b	7 g
2 f	4 a	6 h	8 d

Step 2 Put students in pairs and ask them to write positive and negative answers for each pair of linked questions in A, as in the example. Monitor and correct as they write.

Step 3 Ask students to write linked questions about the topics in C to ask other students. Again, monitor and correct as they write.

Step 4 Get students to ask their pairs of linked questions to other students in the group. They could ask each other across the class or you could conduct this as a 'mingle': get students to stand up and walk around and ask as many students as they can their different questions. Monitor and check everyone always has someone to talk to – they can talk in threes if necessary. Conduct brief feedback at the end.

CONVERSATION PRACTICE

Aim
To give freer practice of the target language.

Step 1 Tell students they are going to have a similar conversation to the ones in *Listening* about three parties / celebrations, real or invented, that they have been to in the last five years. Ask them individually to look at the questions in A and think about what they are going to say. They could make some notes and look back at the language used in the unit for ideas.

Step 2 Put students in pairs and ask them to have conversations beginning with, *So, what did you do last night? Anything interesting?* Model with a strong student then in open pairs, before continuing in closed pairs. Monitor and note down errors in target language for a correction slot at the end.

pp. 112–113

Next class Make photocopies of **16A** p. 158.
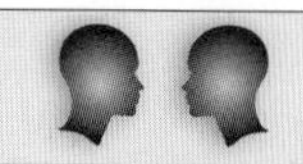

VOCABULARY Historical events

Aim
To introduce and practise words associated with historical events.

Step 1 Lead in by asking students what they think about some important historical events in their country. Then ask students to look at the Fact File and complete the sentences with the correct form of the words from the box. Check in pairs then check with the whole group.

Answers
1 was founded
2 invaded
3 became
4 ended
5 were defeated
6 ruled
7 gained
8 was crowned
9 join

Step 2 Ask students to look at the definitions in B and find the correct word in the Fact File in A to match them with. Check in pairs then check with the whole group.

Answers
1 civil war
2 occupation
3 execution
4 battle
5 monarch
6 empire

READING

Aim
To give practice in reading for gist and specific information.

Step 1 Tell students they are going to read an article from a series called *Around the world in 300 words*. Ask them what they think the article will be about.

Step 2 Ask students to read the first paragraph and then put them in pairs to discuss the questions in A. Ask them to discuss what they know about Kazakhstan. Conduct brief feedback.

Step 3 Ask students to look at the questions in B and try to answer them as they read the rest of the article. Check in small groups then check with the whole group.

Answers
1 since the Stone Age
2 the people used to be nomads
3 in 1991
4 oil and gas
5 student's own answers
6 student's own answers

Grammar

Prepositions and nouns / *-ing* forms

Aim
To focus on the use of *-ing* forms after prepositions.

Step 1 Read out the explanation in the box, checking as you read. Then ask students to match the verbs with the correct endings. Check in pairs then check with the whole group. Concept check by asking for other examples of each one, e.g. *lead to / result in problems, war; depend on the weather, the time of year; date from the Middle Ages, the nineties; be accused of murder, robbery; be opposed to the government, an idea, a policy; be caused by a person, an organisation; be involved in a campaign, a club; ban smoking, a film; vote for a party, a person.*

Answers

1 d	6 g
2 e	7 j
3 b	8 i
4 a	9 h
5 c	10 f

Direct students to the grammar reference on page 155 if they still seem unsure.

Step 2 Ask students to write five true sentences about events and people in history, using some of the verbs and prepositions in A. Monitor and correct as they write.

Optional activity You could then get students to turn their sentences into questions with *what, who, when*, etc. and get them to quiz each other in pairs or across the class.

16A see Teacher's notes p. 127.

Pronunciation Dates

Aim
To help students with the pronunciation of dates.

Step 1 Lead in by asking students to tell you some famous dates in history and what they are famous for. Ask them to say today's date and their dates of birth. Read out the box, modelling and drilling the dates.

Step 2 Ask them to listen to the recording and write down the dates they hear. Play the recording. Then ask students to check by saying the dates to each other. Check with the whole group. Drill for pronunciation.

16.2
1 From the 8th to the 15th century
2 From the 14th to the 16th century
3 The twelfth of April 1961
4 The twenty-third of April 1616
5 The twenty-fourth of December
6 July the fourth 1776
7 September the second 1945
8 November the ninth

Step 3 Put students in pairs and ask them to discuss which date from *Listening* corresponds to the events in B. Check with the whole group.

Alternatively If your students have access to the Internet, ask them to go and find the answers as fast as they can, then come back and report them to the class.

Answers

1 7	5 4
2 1	6 3
3 5	7 8
4 6	8 2

Speaking

Aim
To extend the topic and give fluency practice.

Step 1 Put students in small groups and ask them to look at A and choose one of the items. Ask them to discuss the questions in B. Groups could then quiz each other across the class to check the answers.

Step 2 Tell students they are going to write *Around the world in 300 words* for their own country. Ask them to read C and give them time to think about what they could include in different categories and why, and make a few notes.

Tip In a monolingual group they could work in pairs or small groups. In a multilingual group, they could work individually or in same-nationality pairs. Ask groups to present their ideas to the rest of the class at the end.

Optional activity Ask students to discuss these in class and then work further on these as homework to bring and present to the class for the next lesson.

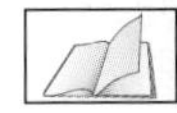
pp. 114–115

Next class Make photocopies of **16B** p. 159.
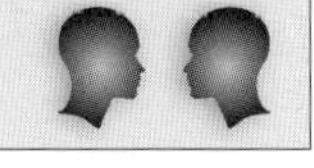

Speaking

Aim
To give personalised practice and lead in to *Listening*.

Step 1 Put students in small groups and ask them to tell each other about the prompts in A. Check they understand *national* = country wide, and *global* = world wide. Conduct brief feedback.

Note If your students don't celebrate their birthdays, ask them to talk about another special day for them.

Listening

Aim
To give practice in listening for specific information.

Step 1 Tell students they are going to listen to five people talking about special days. Ask them to take notes on the special day each one mentions and why it was special. Then play the recording. Check in pairs then check with the whole group.

Answers
1 election of Barack Obama – very important for him as a black person
2 day she visited her grandmother's village – she felt connected to her roots
3 death of Diana – loved her
4 when he climbed Mount Kinabalu – incredibly beautiful and memorable
5 day she had an operation – life has been much better since

16.3
1 I grew up in Mississippi in the 1960s and lived through some very hard times. As a black man, I was treated like a second-class citizen: there were places I was never allowed to sit, cafes and restaurants I couldn't enter and so on, so the fact that Barack Obama, a man of colour, managed to become President of the United States was truly remarkable. I'll remember the day he was elected for as long as I live.

2 My great-grandmother on my mum's side was Ukrainian. We never met as she died before I was born, but a few years ago my mum and I decided to go on a trip to the village that she came from. We spent a night in the house she'd been born in, which was very moving. The people were very welcoming and I felt a real connection with the place. It was incredible – a day I'll never forget.

3 August the Thirty-First will always be a very special day for me as it's the anniversary of the day that Princess Diana died. Her death in 1997 was a real tragedy and I still feel her loss today. Diana loved helping people and she touched the lives of millions of people all over the world. One of my biggest regrets is that I wasn't able to go to London for her funeral. I wanted to go, but I just couldn't afford to buy a ticket from Brazil.

4 When I was 23 or 24, I spent six months travelling round South-East Asia. It was an amazing time in my life and I had lots of great experiences, but perhaps the day I remember best was when I climbed Mount Kinabalu in Malaysia, one of the highest mountains in the region. We started climbing at midnight, with a local guide, and we reached the peak just as the sun was coming up. It was incredibly beautiful.

5 March the 24th is a very special day for me as it's the anniversary of the day I had a special operation on my stomach to stop me gaining weight. Five years ago, I weighed over 150 kilos and wore size 50 trousers. Today I'm 75 kilos and wear size 34! I go the gym every day now, I no longer have diabetes and I've even found a partner! Thanks to my surgeon, I've been given a second chance in life and I'll always be grateful for that!

Step 2 Ask students to look at the sentences in B and try to remember the three words which are missing from each one. Put them in pairs to compare their ideas then play the recording again for them to check.

Answers

1a second-class citizen	1b as I live
2a my Mum's side	2b a real connection
3a the anniversary of	3b a real tragedy
4a in the region	4b reached the peak
5a me gaining weight	5b a second chance

Step 3 Ask students to look at the questions in D and think about how they would answer them. Then put them in small groups to discuss their ideas. Conduct brief feedback at the end.

Language patterns

Aim
To draw students' attention to patterns with *just as*.

Step 1 Ask students to look at the sentences in the box and notice the similarities (*just as* + past simple or continuous to talk about two things which happened at the same time in the past). Ask students to translate these sentences into their own language. In monolingual classes ask students to compare their translations. In multilingual classes ask students to work in pairs and tell each other if the sentences were easy to translate and whether they were able to translate them word for word.

Step 2 Ask students to cover the English translations and translate the sentences back into English using their translations. Then ask them to compare their translations in pairs against the book.

Alternatively If you prefer not to use translation, ask students to notice the patterns. Concept check any areas of difficulty and elicit a few more examples. If time, write their examples on the board and tick them if correct. If the sentences are wrong, ask the students to correct them or correct them yourself.

Grammar

Verb patterns (*-ing* and *to-* infinitives)

Aim
To focus on *-ing* forms and *to-* infinitives following certain verbs.

Step 1 Read out the explanation in the box. Tell students that some verbs can be followed by either the *to-* infinitive or the *-ing* form. With some verbs, e.g. *start, begin*, this does not change the meaning much. With others, e.g. *stop, remember, try*, the meaning is quite different. See page 155 of the grammar reference for help with this. Then ask students to look at the sentences from *Listening* and complete them by using the correct form of the verbs in the box. Check in pairs then ask students to check by looking at the audioscript on page 178.

Answers
1 to sit
2 to become
3 to go
4 helping
5 travelling
6 gaining

Step 2 Ask students to look at the sentences in C and choose the correct form. Check in pairs then check with the whole group. Direct students to the grammar reference on page 155 if they still seem unsure.

Answers
1 seeing
2 to take
3 to pass
4 feeling
5 eating
6 to become
7 to marry
8 sharing
9 watching, to watch
10 going, to go

Step 3 Ask students to look at the items in D and think about how they would answer them. Then put them in pairs or threes to discuss their ideas. Conduct brief feedback.

Speaking

Aim
To give fluency practice, personalise the topic and round off the unit.

Step 1 As a class ask students to look at the picture – what do they think is happening and why might the day be special for the man in it? Then ask them think about two special days for them. Tell them to look at the questions in A and make a few notes about their two special days.

Step 2 When they are ready, put students in small groups to share their experiences. Encourage their partners to ask questions. Ask each group to decide whose experience was the most special and why.

Step 3 Ask one student from each group could to report to the class on the most special experience in their group.

16B see Teacher's notes p. 127.

04 REVIEW

LEARNER TRAINING

Aim
To encourage students to think about their writing and different ways they might improve it.

Step 1 Ask students how they feel about writing in their own language and in English, what difficulties they have, what kinds of things they write, etc.

Step 2 Read out the information and ask students what they think of the two methods: have they tried both? Which do they find more useful?

Step 3 Put students in small groups and ask them to discuss which of the strategies they have tried and whether they think they are a good idea. Ask each group to come up with one more strategy to help with their writing. Get them to report back to the rest of the class at the end.

GAME, CONVERSATION PRACTICE & ACT OR DRAW

For aims and suggested procedures see Review 01, pp. 32–33.

QUIZ

Answers
1. *Star Wars, Bladerunner, The Matrix* – or more contemporary films – all have **amazing special effects**.
2. An **exhibition** is a show (often temporary), a **gallery** is a place where art is shown.
3. **Censorship** could be of a film or TV, or of books or newspapers.
4. Two examples of **corruption** are if someone gives a job to a friend or relative, even when there is a better applicant; or when the votes in an election are deliberately miscounted.
5. People **take out mortgages** because they want to buy a house but don't have the money themselves.
6. People become **refugees** because of war, political problems or poverty.
7. You need a **towel** to dry yourself.
8. **Archaeologists** dig to find ancient remains.
9. During **a recession**, people lose their jobs or houses.
10. People **take out loans** to buy something or have a holiday.
11. Your holiday, wedding, car, house or belongings could be **covered by insurance**.
12. There might be **an election** because the government has been in power for a certain length of time, or because the government has become very unpopular.
13. The weather, bad food or a terrible hotel could **ruin** your holiday.
14. **Invading** means going into a country aggressively; **occupying** means staying there.
15. If people are **nomadic** they don't live in any fixed place; they move around.

COLLOCATIONS

For aims and suggested procedure see Review 01, pp. 32–33.

PRONUNCIATION Phonetic symbols

Aim
To help students understand phonetic script and encourage them to use it

Step 1 Write a few words whose sound / spelling are very different and ask students what is difficult about these words. Or you could write *ough* on the board and ask students how many ways they think this combination of letters can be pronounced. Elicit some words with these letters pronounced in different ways: *through, cough, tough* etc.

Step 2 Ask students to look at the phonetic transcription of words 1–10 and to match them with the actual words a–j. Check in pairs then play the recording for them to check. Ask them to repeat after each one. Check they understand all the words.

R4.1

1 region	6 shame
2 weird	7 shares
3 execution	8 diabetes
4 voice	9 charity
5 monarch	10 publish

Answers

1 g	6 a
2 h	7 i
3 f	8 d
4 j	9 e
5 c	10 b

Step 3 Ask students to write the words shown in phonetic script in C. Play the recording for them to check. Ask them to repeat after each one.

R4.2
1 rehearse
2 technique
3 wealth
4 forecast
5 iron
6 duvet
7 vegetarian
8 execution
9 civil war
10 vacuum cleaner

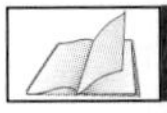

pp. 118–119

LISTENING

For aims and suggested procedure for the rest of the review see Review 01, pp. 32–35. The audio is R4.3.

Exercise A answers
a - b 2 c 3 d 4 e 1

Exercise B answers
a 3 b 2 c 4 d - e 1

GRAMMAR

Exercise A answers
1 graduate
2 used to play / played
3 'm (currently) looking for
4 have (you two) known
5 hear
6 've been learning

Exercise B answers
1 for
2 must
3 of
4 tired
5 where
6 time

Exercise C answers
1 got bored of
2 have known each other
3 for twenty years
4 which comes from India
5 mustn't forget
6 in the last few months
7 are opposed to
8 'm really worried about

LANGUAGE PATTERNS

Answers
1 just
2 at
3 managed
4 such
5 with
6 manage

PREPOSITIONS

Answers
1 over
2 in
3 through
4 over
5 by
6 under
7 in
8 by
9 in
10 from

FORMING WORDS

Answers
1 elected
2 welcoming
3 popularity
4 reception
5 occupation
6 designer
7 connection
8 explosions
9 Unemployment
10 predictable

ADJECTIVES

Answers
1 vintage
2 violent
3 social
4 silly
5 high
6 distinct
7 dairy
8 strong

NOUNS

Answers
1 condition
2 rival
3 significance
4 attention
5 scheme
6 interest
7 diet
8 border

Note Direct students to units 13–16 in the *Vocabulary Builder* if they need more help with this.

VERBS

Answers
1c emerged
2a directed
3b stars
4b repair
5a convince
6c invest
7c made
8b completed
9a generated
10c voted

AN INTRODUCTION TO WRITING IN *OUTCOMES*

In this section we will look at two broad reasons for writing in a foreign language: to practise and play, and for the real world. We explain what we mean by them and how they may differ in teaching, tasks and feedback.

Practice and play The first reason for writing in a foreign language is simply to practise new language, experiment and learn more English. Writing may have significant benefits for students learning English. In contrast to speaking, students have time to plan what they want to say; they can look words up in a dictionary, they can check and re-write grammar and they may be more able to notice how English works. That might then give benefits in terms of their overall competence in English.

Writing for the purpose of practice and play does not depend on any particular genre or standard organisation in writing; it could be short sentences, paragraphs, dialogues, etc.; it could be about anything the student wants or it could be a theme the teacher chooses; it could be random connections of sentences – true or imagined. Some grammar and vocabulary tasks in the Student's book are of this nature, with students having to complete sentences using their own ideas. Below are some more tasks. The ideas focus on revising language, but it doesn't have to be so. Here are some ideas your students could try:

- Write a diary about your day, trying to include new words or structures that you've learnt.
- Write five to ten lines of English every day about anything you like.
- Write every day / week about a story in the news you saw or read about.
- Write a poem or story using a new word you've learnt.
- Write a conversation based on one you had with someone during the class.
- Write an imagined conversation with someone you know based on a topic you've studied.
- Write an imagined conversation that takes place in a particular place.

As these kinds of writing tasks are unconnected to any particular genre, they require no 'teaching' or preparation, and can be set at any time. In terms of feedback, you may want to simply write a personal response to what the student wrote such as, *This really made me laugh* or *That's interesting*. Alternatively, you could engage in a dialogue with the student by asking them genuine questions, which they answer in writing. You may want to correct aspects of the key structure or words that they practised, or use common errors from different students as a way to re-teach language in class. However, we feel correction should be kept to a minimum with these kinds of texts. The aim isn't assessment: it is to encourage students, to engage with them and get them to play with language.

For the real world The second broad reason for writing is that students need to write a specific kind of text for an assessment or for a 'real life' task such as sending an email. These texts are generic in some way. They often have specific vocabulary (including large chunks or expressions) or grammar connected with them. They also have rules about the way they are presented, how they are paragraphed and ordered, and other aspects of discourse. The problem for foreign learners of English is that these rules of discourse might be different in their languages. Unlike speaking, where listeners might accept errors because they can see other things to help interpret the message, with writing a reader may misunderstand a message or even be offended when the rules or conventions of a genre are broken. For this reason, students need careful preparation for writing such texts, and feedback should be more thorough.

The writing units in the Student's book aim to provide this careful preparation. They are based on genres commonly tested in international exams such as KET or PET, or on functional writing tasks we may perform at work or when studying in an English-speaking context.

WHAT'S IN *OUTCOMES* WRITING UNITS?

Each double-page spread teaches a different style of writing. You can follow them in any order or do them after every two units in the main Student's book. The units contain:

Speaking The units aim to be interactive. Speaking activities provide a warmer, relate to the topic, discuss the text types or may be part of planning for writing.

Writing The writing sections present model texts. While there may be some basic comprehension questions around these, the main focus is noticing useful language for the genre and how the texts are organised.

Key words This section focuses on words / expressions which link sentences and clauses and give texts coherence. They follow a similar pattern to grammar exercises, with a short explanation or guided questions and controlled practice.

Vocabulary and grammar There are often short grammar or vocabulary sections if there is a close relation to the text type. Note there's *no* link to the grammar reference or *Vocabulary Builder*.

Practice This is a task for students to write a similar kind of text to the one they looked at in **Writing** and try to incorporate some of the other language they have learnt in the unit. This section can be set as homework or be done in class. Doing the practice in class can be interactive, particularly if using a 'process writing' approach.

Process writing

Process writing approaches focus on the fact that good writers often go through several stages to produce a good piece of writing. They may:

- brainstorm ideas
- write a plan
- write a draft
- discuss their draft with someone
- write a second draft
- put it through a spell-checker
- have corrections made by someone
- write the final draft.

Obviously, we don't always go through all these stages when we write, but in the case of our students, having different stages and allowing for more than one draft gives more opportunity for teaching and learning. In fact, brainstorming and planning stages are often included in **Practice** or at some other stage of the lesson. However, there is no reason why any of the stages above shouldn't be done in pairs in class. Another way you might want to incorporate a process approach is to give the **Practice** task for homework *before* they do the actual writing lesson. They then re-write their work in light of what they learn.

Marking and feedback

There are a number of options available to teachers to mark and give feedback on students' writing.

Using symbols You can mark essays using symbols above the inappropriate word or grammar. Here are some examples:

- t = wrong tense
- wf = wrong word form (e.g. noun not adjective)
- col = wrong collocation (e.g. the noun is the right meaning but doesn't go with the verb)
- voc = you have the wrong word (it makes no sense here)
- prep = you need a different preposition
- pl = plural is wrong or should be plural
- sp = wrong spelling
- wo = the word order is wrong
- art = the article is wrong or absent

The idea of doing this is to make students notice their errors and try to find answers. You could do this as a pair activity in class. It may help them to become more aware of their common errors and edit their own work more carefully. The difficulty is that mistakes don't fit neatly into categories and students may still get the language wrong. You should mark the text again.

Re-formulation You may simply want to cross out and rewrite things that are 'wrong' in the text. This may have the advantage of teaching students the correct language (though note they may still be unclear *why* it was wrong). It may also be time-consuming for you and demoralising for students if they see lots of crossing out.

In this case – and indeed with all cases of teacher feedback – you need to strike a balance. At Pre-Intermediate, you shouldn't expect complete accuracy. Students should be able to deal with a basic set of text types, and be aware of informal and formal registers. Students should also be able to structure basic writing texts and use language appropriate to such texts.

Content and structure When you mark the texts you could ignore 'grammar' and individual vocabulary mistakes and focus only on whether the writing answers the question and is organised well. You simply write comments on the writing or at the end. This is often quicker for you, the teacher.

Marking this way trains students to appreciate the importance of these aspects of writing over basic 'accuracy'. Readers in fact will often ignore mistakes if the overall structure of the text is clear and the content is relevant, logical and / or interesting.

However, students will want to know if their writing is correct unless you clearly warn them beforehand that you'll only deal with content and structure.

Peer correction Students can also give feedback. Get them to read each other's writing and evaluate the texts and / or suggest changes. To do this they really need a 'mark scheme', this could be a list of statements they tick or adapt such as:

- *I enjoyed this.*
- *I wanted to know more about...*
- *I didn't understand the bit about...*
- *You used some words / grammar I didn't know how to use.*

Another way is to give them marking criteria from an established source such as the KET or PET exam. Check they're not too difficult for your students.

The advantage of peer correction is that it's interactive and based on genuine readers' responses. It's also easy on the teacher! However, it is not so good for dealing with language – apart from general statements – as students may not trust each other's judgement – often with good reason! However, it is a useful stage and may save you time by reducing mistakes or inconsistencies before you come to mark the texts.

Writing and portfolios

Whichever way you choose to correct the students' texts, we suggest you get students to re-write them. This would guarantee that the students focus on their errors and produce an improved text which they could then keep in a portfolio. Portfolios of work are recommended by the CEF and can provide evidence of the students' progress and level.

WRITING LESSONS 1–8

UNIT AIMS

There are eight writing units in total. The aims of these units are to give additional writing practice and to introduce students to the kind of texts they might need or want to write in real life. It is suggested that you use these units towards the end of every two units of the *Student's Book* as extra material, especially when you feel your students would benefit from the change of focus that writing activities provide. It is also recommended that you follow the steps suggested in the *Student's Book*, although of course other variations are possible. You could either set the final writing task (*Practice*) in class and get students to mark / correct each other's work, or you could set it as a test or for homework.

01 PERSONAL PROFILE

VOCABULARY Describing people

Answers

Hair	Height	Body shape
long	tall	well-built
blonde	medium-height	thin
straight	short	slim
short		overweight
medium-length		
curly		

GRAMMAR Adjectives

A Answers

1 His hair is very long.
2 Is he OK? He looks sad.
3 She's got long, blonde hair.
4 correct
5 correct
6 correct
7 He's got big, blue eyes.
8 I've got brown eyes.

KEY WORDS FOR WRITING

but, and, also, too

A Answers

1 but
2 and
3 and, but
4 and, also
5 but, too (or also)

02 EXPRESSING OPINIONS

VOCABULARY Talking about jobs

A Answers

1 tiring
2 well-paid
3 brilliant
4 boring
5 satisfying
6 technical
7 lonely
8 part-time

WRITING

C Answers

1 Firstly, I have to
2 Secondly, there's
3 what's more, it's tiring
4 Thirdly, my bosses
5 finally,

KEY WORDS FOR WRITING Sequencers

B Suggested answers

1 working on engines and cars
2 helping people to keep their cars running well
3 meeting lots of different people
4 the hours are great
5 it's never a boring job

03 DESCRIBING PLACES

VOCABULARY Describing places

A Answers

1 b
2 a
3 e
4 d
5 f
6 c

B Answers

1 modern
2 humid
3 lively
4 polluted
5 noisy
6 green

WRITING

A Answers

a 3 b 4 c 2 d 1

KEY WORDS FOR WRITING *because, so*

A Answers

1 so
2 because
3 so
4 because
5 because
6 because

B Answers

1 It's very quiet and green, so I love living here.
2 The area is really polluted, because we're surrounded by lots of factories
3 This city is always very lively, so I love living here.
4 When I travel I usually visit museums and old churches, because I love history.
5 We think country life is better for children, so we're going to move.
6 I love it here, because this city's my home.

GRAMMAR Modifiers

A Answers

1 really / very
2 really
3 very / really
4 a bit
5 really
6 really / very

B Answers

1 really
2 very / really / a bit
3 very / really / a bit
4 very / really / a bit
5 very / really / a bit

04 PLANS AND SCHEDULES

WRITING

A Answers

1 is
2 meet
3 starts
4 go
5 gives
6 continue
7 begin
8 present
9 feedback
10 break

GRAMMAR Present simple for timetables

A Answers

look forward to seeing you, the meeting is at the Clarion Hotel, all managers meet at 9.30, starts with coffee, we go to the conference room, each national manager gives, continue until lunchtime, topic is, lunch is from, we divide, begin our brainstorming, groups present, feedback on presentations, break for coffee, final session begins, Liv Applund answers, concludes, you have

B Answer

C

C Answers

1 is
2 leaves
3 don't land
4 does (your train) arrive
5 break
6 lasts
7 don't start
8 does (the meeting) end

KEY WORDS FOR WRITING Time expressions

A Answers

1 until
2 then / after that
3 until
4 until, then / after that
5 until
6 then
7 until
8 then / after that

05 ANECDOTES

WRITING

Answers
Good things: met nice people, invited out to dinner, good chat with Scott, second dish nice

Bad things: restaurant crowded – two hour wait, awful food, music very loud, overcharged

KEY WORDS FOR WRITING
When, *while* and *during*

A Answers
1 during
2 while
3 when

B Answers
1 during
2 when
3 during
4 while
5 when
6 when

GRAMMAR Pronouns

A Answers
1 It = dinner
2 He = Scott
3 it = the restaurant
4 it = his life
5 mine = my dish
6 one = dish
7 they = the waiting staff
8 one = the dish

B Answers
1 it
2 it
3 it
4 she
5 them
6 them
7 her
8 It
9 It
10 them
11 us

VOCABULARY Adverbs of attitude

A Answers
1 obviously
2 unfortunately
3 luckily
4 amazingly
5 Sadly
6 Stupidly

06 POSTCARDS

WRITING

A Answer
A cruise

C Answers
1 Sara likes it, Bruce doesn't like it.
2 They agree about the food and the weather.

VOCABULARY Postcard expressions

A Answers
1 Wish you were here.
2 Hope you're all well.
3 Can't wait to tell you about it!
4 Here we are in Panama.
5 Looking forward to seeing you soon.
6 Greetings from Greece!
7 Writing this in a cafe.
8 Having a great time here in London. / In London. Having a great time here.

KEY WORDS FOR WRITING
although and *despite*

A Answers
1 despite
2 although
3 although
4 despite

B Answers
1 despite the rain
2 Although it was crowded
3 studying although we were really tired
4 despite it being sunny
5 despite having a headache

07 COMPLAINTS

WRITING

A Answers
faulty MP4 player; replacement never arrived; many calls to call centre; still no replacement

B Answers
1 c
2 f
3 e
4 a
5 g
6 d
7 b

C Answers
1 further
2 after-sales
3 faulty, replacement
4 enquire
5 request
6 Consumer

KEY WORDS FOR WRITING

but and *however*

A Answers
1 but
2 However
3 however
4 but

08 INVITATIONS

WRITING Invitations

B Answers
1 less formal
2 formal
3 less formal
4 less formal
5 formal

VOCABULARY

Formal and informal language

A Answers

1 F	11 LF
2 F	12 F
3 LF	13 F
4 LF	14 LF
5 LF	15 F
6 LF	16 LF
7 LF	17 LF
8 LF	18 F
9 F	19 F
10 F	20 F

B Answers
Start: 2, 3, 6, 19
End: 9, 10, 11, 13, 15, 16, 18

KEY WORDS FOR WRITING

if, *when* and *unless*

A Answers

1 d	4 f
2 e	5 a
3 b	6 c

B Answers
1 when
2 If
3 if
4 unless
5 when
6 unless

TEACHER'S NOTES

1A Who is it?

Aim
To consolidate vocabulary related to people and use the present simple.

Before class
Make enough copies for students to work in groups of three. Give each student an A, B or C card.

In class
A To introduce the activity begin by saying *This person works in a hospital and looks after people. Who is it?* (Nurse.) Tell students they can ask questions. Put students in groups of three and tell them they are going to take turns explaining the words on their card to each other.
B Tell them to use the present simple to explain, and tell the students guessing they can ask questions to help them guess the person e.g. *Does this person work in...? Where does this person work / live?*
C Extend the activity by getting a volunteer to sit in front of the board. Write a different word (e.g. *aunt*) on the board and tell the other students to give the volunteer clues to guess the word (make sure the student sitting doesn't turn round to look at the word).

1B Are they the same?

Aim
To give further practice using expessions of similarities and contrasts.

Before class
Make one copy for each pair of students.

In class
A To introduce the activity put a large blown-up copy of the handout on the board. Get students to tell you what they can see, or pass the photocopy round the class for everyone to see.
B Tell students they are going to look at the pictures in pairs and you want them to find similarities and differences.
C Divide the class into pairs and give them a copy of the activity.
D Tell them they have five minutes to write phrases about the pictures, but they must use the structures *None of them... / All of them... / Two of them... / No-one... / Both...* .
E If time, put students into groups of four to compare sentences. Otherwise just check their ideas as a class.

2A Something I want

Aim
To provide further practice of the past simple.

Before class
Make one copy for each student.

In class
A Introduce the activity briefly by asking students if they did any shopping at the weekend and what they bought.
B Give out the photocopy and tell students to write an answer for each item.
C When they are ready put them in pairs and tell them to ask each other questions to find out the information. Write an example on the board if necessary, e.g. *What did you lose? Where did you lose it?*
D To extend the activity get some open class feedback and find out how many students had the same or similar answers.

2B Crossword

Aim
To recycle vocabulary and give further practice of passives / comparatives.

Before class
Make one copy for each pair of students.

In class
A Tell students they're going to do a crossword in pairs. Explain that they have to find the words using the clues and the words can go across or down.
B Hand out the photocopy and tell them to do the crossword in pairs.
C Get fast finishers to help each other.
D Extend the activity by getting students to write two definitions of a vocabulary word from the unit and giving them to their partner to guess.

Answers

Across	Down
3 smart	1 similar
4 crowd	2 worse
5 accused	6 discount
9 boots	7 laptop
10 supermarket	8 better

3A Have you ever...?

Aim

To provide further practice of the present perfect simple.

Before class

Make one copy for each student.

In class

A Introduce the activity by asking the class the first question from the handout, *Have you ever eaten something really disgusting?* Encourage them to expand on the information.

B Hand out the photocopy. Tell them they have to stand up and ask people questions until they find someone who answers *yes*. They write the person's name next to the phrase.

C Tell them to move round asking different students until they have found someone for each question.

D Extend the activity by getting students to form groups of three to compare their answers.

3B Excuses! excuses!

Aim

To provide further practice of *too / enough* + offers, requests, suggestions and permission.

Before class

Make enough copies of set A for half the class and enough copies of set B for the other half.

In class

A To introduce the activity make a request or suggestion and ask students to give you excuses not to do it using *too* or *enough*, e.g. *Would someone lend me some money?* Student: *Sorry, I can't, I'm too poor; Sorry, I don't have enough money even to buy a sandwich; etc.*

B Tell students they are going to practise giving excuses, and they will have 30 seconds to give as many excuses as possible to the questions they are asked. Hand out the photocopy. Put students in groups of four. Allocate roles to each student. Pair 1: Student A asks pair 2 questions using a question starter and a phrase in the box, Student B times the answers and writes down how many excuses Pair 2 make in the time limit (30 seconds). Pair 2: Both try to say as many excuses as possible to each question.

C After five minutes ask groups to change roles. At the end see who has the most excuses.

D Ask students to vote on the best excuse overall.

4A Snakes and ladders

Aim

To provide further practice of present tenses, and plans and wishes for the future.

Before class

Make one copy of the game for every two / three students. You also need enough dice for each group. If you don't have dice, use slips of paper with numbers 1–6 in an envelope for students to pick from.

In class

A Explain to students that they are going to play a game of snakes and ladders. They need a different counter each – a coin, ring, paper clip, etc.

B They should take turns to throw the die and move that number of squares from the START square. If they land on a ladder, they go up; on a snake they go down. If they land on a blank square, they stay there until their next turn. If they land on a square with a sentence, they should decide if the sentence is correct or not. If it's not correct they should correct it. Their partner(s) should decide if they are right.

C You should monitor and help if they don't agree. If they get it right, they move forward two squares. If not, they move back two squares. The students all take turns throwing the die and working through the board until one student reaches the FINISH square. The first player to reach FINISH wins.

D Monitor as they play to check they are identifying the incorrect sentences.

Answers

Incorrect sentences:

7 I am doing a training course this week.
9 I hope / I'm hoping to get a new contract next week.
11 I'd like to work here full-time.
16 She is going to work abroad soon.
18 I'm planning to stay here for another two years.
21 What are you doing?

4B How good is your memory?

Aim

To provide further practice of the past simple and past continuous.

Before class

Make enough copies of picture A for half the class and enough copies of picture B for the other half.

In class

A Ask students what they can remember about Annie and the office she works in. (*Reading*, page 30.)

B Tell students they're going to do a memory test. They will show a picture to their partner for one minute, then take it away and test their partner's memory by asking questions, e.g. *What was Rick doing when the boss walked in?*

C Divide students into As and Bs and give out the corresponding pictures. Check their understanding by asking a volunteer to explain the activity.

D When they're ready, ask As to start by giving their picture to B, timing them for a minute, then taking the picture away and asking questions. Then they swap.

E Monitor and help out as necessary.

5A Weekend plans

Aim

To provide further practice of language for talking about the future: *might, be going to* + verb, present continuous.

Before class

Make one copy for each student.

In class

A Introduce the activity by telling students three things you have planned for the weekend, or might be doing. Use the three structures: *might, be going to* + verb, present continuous.

B Hand out the photocopy. Tell students to work individually, writing an activity for each of the six prompts. Then, tell them to think of questions to ask each other, e.g. *What are you going to do on Saturday?*

C When they are ready put them in pairs to talk about their plans.

D Extend the activity by forming groups of four. Tell them to find out how many of them are doing the same things. Who has the most interesting plans?

5B Do you know the answer?

Aim

To extend the use of superlatives.

Before class

Make enough copies of set A for half the class and enough copies of set B for the other half.

In class

A To introduce the activity write a question on the board using a superlative, e.g. *Which country has the largest hotel in the world?* Malaysia, Hawaii, Germany? Tell them to guess if they don't know (Malaysia).

B Put students into A pairs and B pairs. Then put an A pair with a B pair. The pairs take it in turns to ask each other quiz questions: Pair A asks Pair B questions, then they swap. (The correct answers have a star next to them.)

C Give out the sets of questions. Write the rules for scoring on the board = 2 points if answered correctly, 1 point if pair asks for clues.

D Extend the activity by getting pairs to write two more quiz questions to ask each other.

6A Cultural know-how

Aim

To provide further practice of language related to talking about things.

Before class

Make one copy for each student.

In class

A Tell students they are going to guess things about other countries and decide if the phrases are true or false.

B Give out the handout and tell them to complete it individually.

C When they are ready put them in pairs to discuss their answers and form conclusions together.

D Encourage them to use question forms, e.g. *Do you think you can...? Do you think that...?*

E Go over the answers in open class and extend the activity by asking them about their own customs / rules, etc.

Answers

1 true	3 true	5 false	7 false
2 true	4 true	6 false	8 true

6B Offers and promises!

Aim

To provide further practice of *will / won't*.

Before class

Make one copy for each pair of students.

In class

A Introduce the activity by writing something you need or a problem you have on the board, e.g. *I have too many books to carry*. Elicit possible ways to offer help or make a suggestion, e.g. *I'll help you / Why don't you leave some on the desk for later?*

B Put students in pairs and give out the worksheets. Tell them to match the problems with one of the suggestions or offers.

C When they have finished, get them to compare answers in groups of four.

D Extend the activity by getting pairs to prepare two more phrases to pass to the other pair. Get them to write a response using *will / won't* then pass their answers back.

Answers

1 D 2 E 3 A 4 H 5 F 6 B 7 C 8 G

7A What's my problem?

Aim
To provide further practice of ways to give advice.

Before class
Make one copy for each group of four. Cut out the cards and put a full set into an envelope for each group.

In class
A Introduce the activity by eliciting three different ways to give advice (*should / ought to; why don't you...?*) Tell students they're going to guess what their problem is, by listening to the advice they're given to solve it. Model with this situation: *You are afraid of sleeping in the dark.* Clues: *Why don't you sleep with the light on? Why don't you go to bed when it's still light?*
B Put students into groups of four. Tell one student to sit in front of the other three. Tell the groups of three to take a card with a problem and give advice to the 'chair person' on how to solve the problem. Remind them to use the structures. The 'chair person' can't leave the chair until they find out what their problem is. When the student guesses the problem they swap roles and repeat.

7B What and where?

Aim
To give further practice of imperatives.

Before class
Make enough copies of set A for half the class and enough copies of set B for the other half.

In class
A Introduce the activity by miming something. Students guess what the sentence is and where it might be said, e.g. *Don't speak, people are reading!* (in the library).
B Put students into AB pairs and hand out the photocopies. Tell students individually to match the sentences to where they take place. Then in pairs they take turns miming the sentences. Student A mimes, Student B guesses what the instruction is, and where it takes place. Then swap.
C If time, get them to write some more situations in pairs and put them with another group to mime / guess.

Answers
Student A
At the optician's: Put one hand over your left eye and read the letters.
Learning to drive: Turn the key and press slowly down on the accelerator.
At the doctor's: Don't take more than four in 24 hours.
At the dentist's: Open your mouth wide and show me where it hurts.
Student B
At home: Clean your teeth before you go to bed.
At the gym: Jump up and down for one minute.
At the hospital: Sit and wait over there until the nurse calls you.
In class: Open your book and turn to page ten.

8A Articles casino

Aim
To revise the use of articles.

Before class
Make one copy for each group of three.

In class
A Begin the activity by explaining the meaning of *place a bet*. Tell students they have to bet on each sentence by deciding if they think it's correct or not.
B Put students in groups of three. Hand out the photocopies, then go through the instructions. Give them 100 points to start.
C Tell them to read the first sentence, decide if it's right or wrong then place a bet on it. Once you see they have understood the game tell them to do the same with the rest of the sentences.
D Go through each answer one at a time and get each group to either subtract or add points.
E The winning group is the one with the most points.

Answers (wrong sentences)
1 Travel makes wise people better and stupid people worse.
3 I hate jazz music!
4 I can't drink the coffee they sell in England. It's disgusting.
7 Love is the most important thing in life.

8B Guess where and what

Aim
To give further practice of quantifiers and revise vocabulary related to transport.

Before class
Make enough copies of set A for half the class and enough copies of set B for the other half.

In class
A Introduce by asking students questions about their travel habits, e.g. *How do you get to class?*
B Put students into AB pairs. Give out the photocopies. Tell student's individually to match the definitions to a category. Monitor to check their answers.
C When they are ready tell them to take turns testing their partners – Student A reads a definition and Student B guesses what it refers to. Then swap.

Answers

A		B	
1 e	4 a	1 a	4 e
2 c	5 d	2 c	5 b
3 b		3 d	

9A Animal encounters

Aim
To give further practice of the past perfect simple.

Before class
Make enough copies of part A for half the class and enough copies of part B for the other half.

In class
A Introduce the activity by writing this sentence starter on the board: *When I got home I was mad because the cat ...* Ask students to complete it using the past perfect. E.g ... *had broken my favourite vase.*
B Tell students they are going to pretend they have had animal encounters and invent endings using the sentence starters. Put them in pairs and give out the photocopies. Tell them they must use the past perfect to complete the sentences.
C Students do this individually, then they take turns miming their sentences to their partner. Tell students to write down their partner's mimed sentences when they guess them correctly. When they have finished they compare to check they're the same.

9B An Indian folk tale

Aim
To give further practice of reported speech.

Before class
Make enough copies of set A for half the class and enough copies of set B for the other half.

In class
A Tell students they are going to read an animal folk story.
B Put students in groups of four then split them into AB pairs. Tell them As have the first half of the story and Bs have the second half. They have to read the story and tell the other pair what happened. Give out the photocopies and ask them to read their part of the story. Give them time in their pairs to prepare their summaries of the story. Then As tell their story to pair B, and vice versa.
C When they have finished ask them if they can remember two things the tiger told the wise old man, one thing the jackal asked, and one thing the wise old man said to the tiger. Tell them to write them down. Check this as a class.

Answers
The tiger told the wise old man it was going to eat him. / That everyone had told it (the tiger) that he was a wise old man.
The jackal asked if the wise old man could explain again.
The wise old man said it had promised not to eat him. / The wise old man said it wasn't fair.

10A Boarding school

Aim
To practise using the first conditional.

Before class
Make enough copies so you can divide the roles up evenly in pairs. If you have an odd number, use role card 1 as parents instead of a parent.

In class
A To introduce the activity write *Boarding school* on the board. Ask students to tell you what kind of school it is. (A school where students also live during the week.)
B Put students in pairs. Give out the role cards and ask each student to read their role silently. Check they understand.
C Tell each student with role card 1 to begin by forming questions with the phrases on their card using *What happens if* ... and for students with role card 2 to form answers with *If* ... Put these structures on the board.
D Monitor that pairs are using the first conditional accurately.
E When they have finished, ask if they were happy about the answers the Head Teacher provided.

10B Pictionary

Aim
To provide further practice of *had to / could*.

Before class
Make one copy for each group of students. Cut them up and put them in envelopes for each group.

In class
A Tell students they're going to get phrases and they have to draw them and guess the sentence. Tell them each sentence has *had to / could* in it and they must get that right to win the point
B Put students in pairs / threes and hand out the envelopes.
C Tell students to take turns to pick a phrase out of the envelope and then draw it until their partner(s) guess the sentence. They get one point for each correct sentence. Then swap.

11A What would you do if...?

Aim
To provide further practise of the second conditional.

Before class
Photocopy and cut up a set of situations for each small group of students.

In class

A Get the students into pairs / threes. Put one set of cut-up situations face down between each group and tell them they are going to play a guessing game. Explain that each piece of paper has an imaginary situation that happens in a hotel on it. One student reads the situation then, without telling their partner(s) what the situation is, they give clues to their partner(s) who must guess the situation.

B Model the activity with this situation – *If you were served snake, what would you do?* Use these as clues for the students to guess:
I'd ask the waiter if it was alive or dead.
I wouldn't eat it.
If it was alive, I would let it slide off my plate.

C Tell one student in each group to start. When someone has correctly guessed the situation they have a turn. The game continues until all the situations have been talked about.

11B You used to...

Aim

To give further practice of the structure *used to.*

Before class

Make one copy for each student.

In class

A Introduce the activity by writing *used to / never used to / usually* on the board. Then write activities, e.g. *camping holidays, cricket, football.* Ask students to guess things about you, e.g. *You used to like camping holidays* (no), *You used to like playing football* (yes), *You never used to play cricket* (yes), etc.

B Give out the photocopies. Tell students they have to fill in the bubbles, and their partner will guess which bubble goes with which word / phrase. Tell them not to fill in the bubbles in the same order as the instructions. They should write single words / phrases rather than sentences.

C When they have finished, put students in pairs. They should guess which bubble goes with which topic by making complete sentences (as in the model).

D Conduct brief feedback by asking about things they heard they found surprising, strange, etc.

12A Short conversations

Aim

To give further practice of the present perfect with *just, still, already* and *yet.*

Before class

Make one copy of set A and set B for each pair. Cut up the sets and put them separate envelopes.

In class

A Tell students they are going to look at two short dialogues (A and B) and put them in order.

B Put students in pairs and give out the photocopies. Show them how the dialogues are separated into sets A and B.

C When they have finished, get them to identify the situations.

D Extend the activity by getting students to role-play the dialogues.

Answers

A Situation: Making plans with a friend

Hi Sue. Do you still need some help, or have you finished painting?
No, I haven't even started yet! And we're supposed to be going out for a drink later.
Shall I come round and help?
That would be great. Can you bring an extra paintbrush?
Of course. That's not a problem.
Great. We can get it done in no time and still go for a drink later!

B Situation: Talking to the telephone company

Hello, I'm calling because I'm still having problems with my phone.
I'm really sorry but we haven't had time to solve the problem yet.
Well, I've already phoned three times to tell you!
We'll deal with it immediately.
When?
Oh, actually, the technician has just left to go to your house.

12B Who said that?

Aim

To consolidate language changes in reported speech.

Before class

Make enough copies so each pair has one.

In class

A Introduce the activity by writing on the board: *He said he had a dream.* What was the quote? *I have a dream.* Ask students who said that – a Martin Luther King or b Nelson Mandela (a).

B Put students in pairs. Give out the photocopies. Tell them to write down what the original quote was and to choose who they think said it.

C Do open class feedback. If time, ask students to decide which quote they like the best and why.

Answers

1 a John Lennon 'Work is life and without it there is nothing but insecurity.'
2 c Albert Einstein 'A person who has never made a mistake has never tried anything new.'
3 c William Shakespeare 'The object of art is to give life a shape.'
4 a Mahatma Ghandi 'If you don't ask you don't get.'
5 b Terminator 'I will be back.'
6 b Ernest Hemmingway 'It is better to have loved and lost than never to have loved at all.'

13A Agree or disagree?

Aim

To provide further practice of adjectives ending with *-ed / -ing*.

Before class

Make one copy for each student.

In class

A Introduce the activity by asking students what kinds of films they like, recycling the vocabulary from the unit.

B Give out the photocopy and tell them to decide if they agree or disagree with the statements.

C When they're ready, put them in groups of three. Tell them to discuss their answers and encourage them to expand on why.

D Expand the activity by playing a game – guess the film. Tell them to write three sentences about a film and take turns reading out their examples for the other students in their groups to guess.

13B How long...?

Aim

To contrast the present perfect and present perfect continuous (+ verbs that don't take the continuous).

Before class

Make one set of cards for each group.

In class

A Introduce the activity by giving out the question cards. Ask volunteers to ask you questions for each so you can establish the kind of questions you want them to use. For example:

Q How long have you been in Madrid?

A I've been in Madrid for two months.

Q How long have you been studying English?

A I've been studying English for one year.

B Put them in threes. Students A and B take turns asking each other questions. Tell them they can make questions and answers up, but they just have to be grammatically correct. Student C writes down the questions and answers and allocates points: 1 point for a correct question and 1 point for a correct answer. Get students to exchange roles.

C Extend the activity by doing an open class feedback on the questions they asked.

14A What do you call...?

Aim

To provide further practice of relative clauses and to revise vocabulary from the unit.

Before class

Make enough copies so each group of three has a set.

In class

A Introduce the activity doing some definitions of your own for them to guess (e.g. *a court:* it's the place where you play a game such as tennis or basketball; *a kettle:* it's the thing which you use to boil water with; *a witness:* it's the person who sees a crime).

B Put them in groups of three and give a set of cards to each group. Tell them to take turns turning over a card and defining the object, place or person for the others to guess.

C Monitor closely to see if they are using the correct relative clauses or if they need help understanding their word.

14B Learning to do the right thing!

Aim

To provide further practice of *must* and *mustn't*.

Before class

Make enough copies so half the class have Family 1 and half have Family 2.

In class

A Introduce the activity by asking students if they know any neighbours who don't recycle rubbish or buy lots of junk food. What do they think about this?

B Divide the class into pairs. Give out the corresponding information.

C Tell them to read the information then write some sentences about the families using *must* and *mustn't*, e.g. This *family must eat more fruit; They mustn't keep on buying coke. / This family must be very lazy. They mustn't leave the TV on all night.*

D Extend the activity by getting the pairs to form groups of four. Get them to read out the information to the other pair and the ideas they had to help each family. Encourage groups to think of more things to extend the ideas.

15A Talking about you

Aim
To provide further practice of time phrases with tenses.

Before class
Make enough copies so you can divide the class into pairs and each student has the corresponding questions.

In class
A Introduce the activity by asking students if they can remember three things they did in the last few hours before class. Write tenses on the board, e.g. the present continuous / the present perfect simple / the future / *used to*. Elicit appropriate time phrases for each one, e.g. *currently / since last year / in two weeks' time / in the past.*
B Divide the class into pairs. Give out the corresponding information.
C Tell them to answer the questions individually. When they are ready, tell them to take turns asking and telling each other. Student A asks question one, Student B answers, then Student A tells B their own answer, then vice versa with the following question until they have completed all of them.
D Extend the activity by getting As to sit in pairs together and Bs to do the same. Get them comparing and telling each other their answers.

15B Categories

Aim
To provide further practice of present tenses in future time clauses.

Before class
Make enough copies of the card sets so you can have one set per group of five. Cut them up and place them in piles on your desk.

In class
A Introduce the activity by writing a category on the board (e.g. money problems) and put the five clauses on the board in large letters: *when, as soon as, before, after, until.*
B Elicit some phrases using *will / won't / can / be going to* or an imperative, e.g. ***When** I can save I won't have any money problems. I will earn more money to solve my problems **as soon as** possible. I'm going to stop spending **before** I start having money problems.*
C Divide the class into groups of five. Put their sets of cards on the table in front of you.
D Nominate a runner in each group. The runner comes to the teacher's desk and reads the category on the card. Only let them turn over and read one card at a time. The runner returns to the group to tell them what the category is. The group must invent five sentences, each one using a different time clause. The first group to finish shouts 'stop'. Continue until all groups have done all categories. Remind them they must use the five time clauses + a future meaning.

16A Noughts and crosses

Aim
To provide further practice of prepositions and *nouns / -ing*.

Before class
Make enough copies of the game for groups to play in threes.

In class
A Tell students they're going to play 'Noughts and Crosses'. Draw the grid on the board and explain the rules, i.e. each player need to get three answers in a line, which can be vertical, horizontal or diagonal. One student is X symbol and one student is O symbol, or let them choose their own.
B Write in one of the boxes *be accussed* + preposition + noun and ask students to tell you a possible phrase using that structure (e.g. *people were accused of crimes they didn't commit.*)
C Divide the class into groups of three. Nominate one as the game master (responsible for checking and making decisions about correct sentences). Give out a copy of the grid. Tell the game master he / she can help with clues if necessary.
D Tell the pairs they can use their books to help them, but not copy sentences from it.
E Monitor closely to help out with sentence queries. If time, extend the activity by asking for example sentences to write in the grid on the board as a way to consolidate.

16B Memorable experiences

Aim
To provide further practice of verb patterns *-ing* and *to*-infinitive.

Before class
Make one copy of either story 1 or story 2 for each pair of students. Cut the photocopy in half and stick them on the walls. Give each story and each pair a number so students B are clear about what they have to look at and read.

In class
A Tell students they're going to read a story either about passing a driving test or about flying to Hong Kong.
B Put students in AB pairs, tell them their numbers and allocate roles. Student A is the writer and student B is the reader.
C Tell student B to find their numbered story on the wall, read and remember the sentences, then go back to student A and dictate it. They don't have to remember the whole story, just the general idea. Tell students A to listen and write what they hear.
D When they have finished, give each pair their story and get them to compare it with what they have written.
E Put an A pair and a B pair together and tell them to tell their stories to each other from memory.

1 A Who is it?

Student A

- uncle
- waiter
- flatmate
- actress

Student B

- neighbour
- lawyer
- housewife
- best friend

Student C

- businessman
- colleague
- teenager
- cousin

1B Are they the same?

None of them... / All of them... / Two of them... / No-one... / Both...

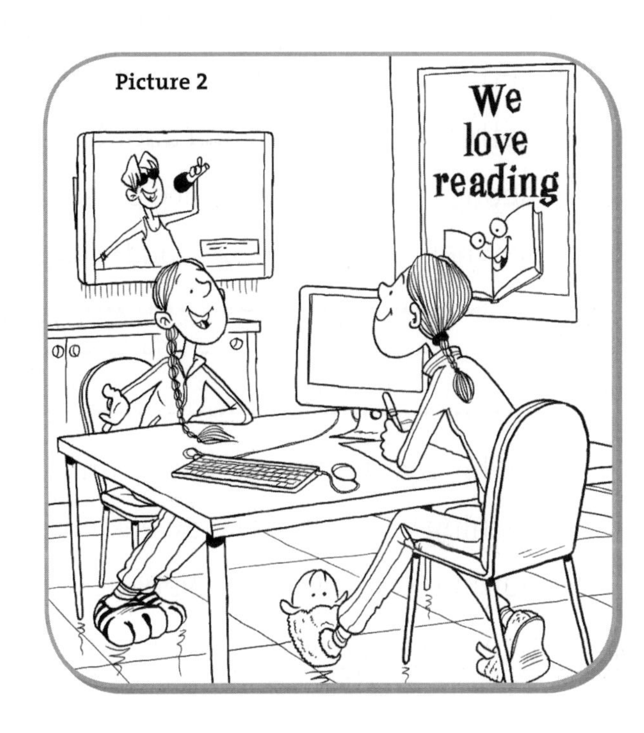

None of them... / All of them... / Two of them... / No-one... / Both...

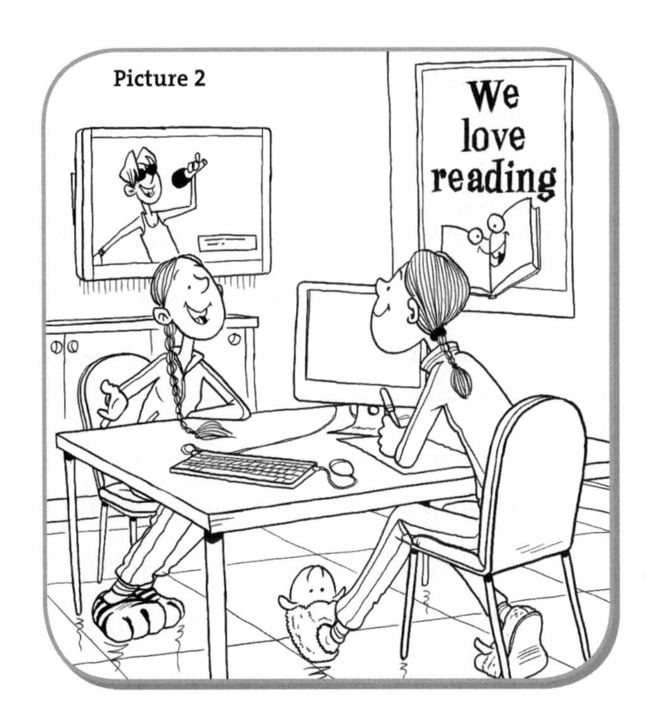

2A Something I want

Something you lost and never found again ______________________

Something you bought last week / month ______________________

Something you complained about in a shop ______________________

Someone who gave you a nice present ______________________

Somewhere you went that you thought was boring ______________________

Something you lost and never found again ______________________

Something you bought last week / month ______________________

Something you complained about in a shop ______________________

Someone who gave you a nice present ______________________

Somewhere you went that you thought was boring ______________________

Something you lost and never found again ______________________

Something you bought last week / month ______________________

Something you complained about in a shop ______________________

Someone who gave you a nice present ______________________

Somewhere you went that you thought was boring ______________________

Something you lost and never found again ______________________

Something you bought last week / month ______________________

Something you complained about in a shop ______________________

Someone who gave you a nice present ______________________

Somewhere you went that you thought was boring ______________________

Complete the crossword.

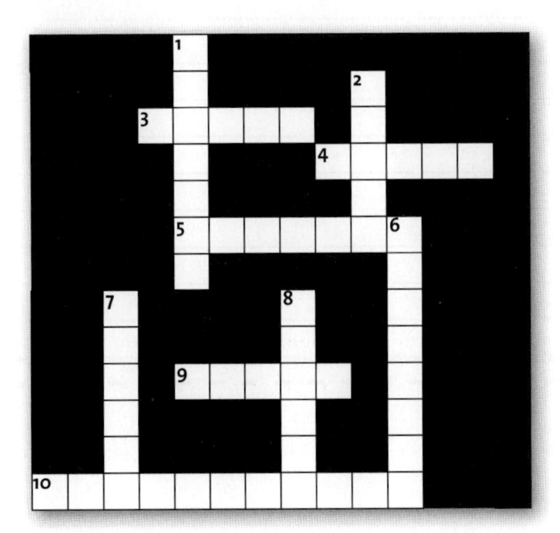

Across ⇨

3 If you go for an interview you need to look ____.
4 a large group of people
5 Primark was one of the low cost chains ____ of exploitation.
9 You wear these on your feet, more in winter. They are usually made of leather.
10 Food is sold in this kind of large shop.

Down ⇩

1 When something is not exactly the same, but nearly.
2 The comparative of bad.
6 Sometimes offered in shops on the original price.
7 It's smaller than a PC and you can carry it around with you.
8 The comparative of good.

Complete the crossword.

Across ⇨

3 If you go for an interview you need to look ____.
4 a large group of people
5 Primark was one of the low cost chains ____ of exploitation.
9 You wear these on your feet, more in winter. They are usually made of leather.
10 Food is sold in this kind of large shop.

Down ⇩

1 When something is not exactly the same, but nearly.
2 The comparative of bad.
6 Sometimes offered in shops on the original price.
7 It's smaller than a PC and you can carry it around with you.
8 The comparative of good.

Complete the crossword.

Across ⇨

3 If you go for an interview you need to look ____.
4 a large group of people
5 Primark was one of the low cost chains ____ of exploitation.
9 You wear these on your feet, more in winter. They are usually made of leather.
10 Food is sold in this kind of large shop.

Down ⇩

1 When something is not exactly the same, but nearly.
2 The comparative of bad.
6 Sometimes offered in shops on the original price.
7 It's smaller than a PC and you can carry it around with you.
8 The comparative of good.

Complete the crossword.

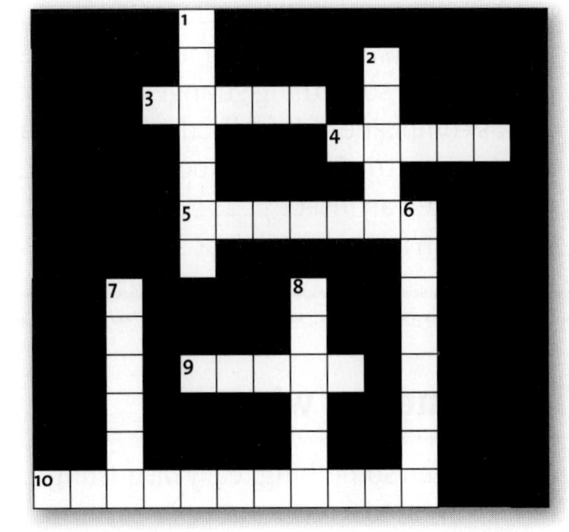

Across ⇨

3 If you go for an interview you need to look ____.
4 a large group of people
5 Primark was one of the low cost chains ____ of exploitation.
9 You wear these on your feet, more in winter. They are usually made of leather.
10 Food is sold in this kind of large shop.

Down ⇩

1 When something is not exactly the same, but nearly.
2 The comparative of bad.
6 Sometimes offered in shops on the original price.
7 It's smaller than a PC and you can carry it around with you.
8 The comparative of good.

Find someone who...

1 has eaten something really disgusting ______
2 has invented a recipe ______
3 has cooked for more than 10 people ______
4 has found something strange in their food ______
5 has complained about food in a restaurant ______
6 has never tried Mexican food ______
7 has eaten an insect ______
8 has won a cookery contest ______

Find someone who...

1 has eaten something really disgusting ______
2 has invented a recipe ______
3 has cooked for more than 10 people ______
4 has found something strange in their food ______
5 has complained about food in a restaurant ______
6 has never tried Mexican food ______
7 has eaten an insect ______
8 has won a cookery contest ______

Find someone who...

1 has eaten something really disgusting ______
2 has invented a recipe ______
3 has cooked for more than 10 people ______
4 has found something strange in their food ______
5 has complained about food in a restaurant ______
6 has never tried Mexican food ______
7 has eaten an insect ______
8 has won a cookery contest ______

Find someone who...

1 has eaten something really disgusting ______
2 has invented a recipe ______
3 has cooked for more than 10 people ______
4 has found something strange in their food ______
5 has complained about food in a restaurant ______
6 has never tried Mexican food ______
7 has eaten an insect ______
8 has won a cookery contest ______

3B Excuses! excuses!

Pair 1

Would you like to...? Could you...? Could we...? Shall we...?

open the door	lend me some money
grab a coffee after class	visit a museum on Saturday
have some soup	eat some Mexican food
go out tonight	cook a meal

Pair 2

Would you like to...? Could you...? Could we...? Shall we...?

get me a drink	eat a cake
walk home after class	go dancing tonight
drink some whisky	help me with my homework
pay the bill	buy some chocolate

Pair 1

Would you like to...? Could you...? Could we...? Shall we...?

open the door	lend me some money
grab a coffee after class	visit a museum on Saturday
have some soup	eat some Mexican food
go out tonight	cook a meal

Pair 2

Would you like to...? Could you...? Could we...? Shall we...?

get me a drink	eat a cake
walk home after class	go dancing tonight
drink some whisky	help me with my homework
pay the bill	buy some chocolate

4A Snakes and ladders

21 What are you do?	**22** My sister is attending a conference tomorrow.	**23** I'd like to have my own business one day.	**24**	**25 FINISH**
20 I usually work at weekends.	**19**	**18** I'm planning stay here for another two years.	**17**	**16** She going to work abroad soon.
11 I'd like working here full-time.	**12**	**13**	**14** I'm studying music at the moment.	**15**
10	**9** I'm hope to get a new contract next week.	**8**	**7** I am do a training course this week.	
1 START	**2**	**3** They're going to tell us to leave.	**4**	**5** My dad is retiring tomorrow.

21 What are you do?	**22** My sister is attending a conference tomorrow.	**23** I'd like to have my own business one day.	**24**	**25 FINISH**
20 I usually work at weekends.	**19**	**18** I'm planning stay here for another two years.	**17**	**16** She going to work abroad soon.
11 I'd like working here full-time.	**12**	**13**	**14** I'm studying music at the moment.	**15**
10	**9** I'm hope to get a new contract next week.	**8**	**7** I am do a training course this week.	
1 START	**2**	**3** They're going to tell us to leave.	**4**	**5** My dad is retiring tomorrow.

4B How good is your memory?

5A Weekend plans

Saturday	Sunday
Something you might do ______	Something you might do ______
Something you will definitely do ______	Something you will definitely do ______
Someone you're going to see ______	Someone you're going to see ______

Saturday	Sunday
Something you might do ______	Something you might do ______
Something you will definitely do ______	Something you will definitely do ______
Someone you're going to see ______	Someone you're going to see ______

Saturday	Sunday
Something you might do ______	Something you might do ______
Something you will definitely do ______	Something you will definitely do ______
Someone you're going to see ______	Someone you're going to see ______

5B Do you know the answer?

Pair A

1 **Who do some experts consider the best athlete of all time?**

a Steffi Graf
b Tiger Woods
c Michael Jordon*

2 **Which is the richest football club in the world?**

a Manchester United
b Real Madrid*
c Boca Juniors

3 **Who was nominated as the worst actress in the Razzie awards in 2009?**

a Paris Hilton*
b Jessica Alba
c Cameron Diaz

4 **Which sport do experts say is the most dangerous in the UK?**

a Horse riding
b Fishing
c Swimming*

5 **Which is the noisiest country in Europe?**

a Spain*
b Scotland
c Holland

6 **Which is the most commonly spoken language in the world?**

a Mandarin Chinese*
b English
c Hindustani

Pair B

1 **Which film received the highest number of oscars of all time?**

a Ben-hur
b The Lord of the Rings
c Titanic*

2 **Which planet is nearest to the sun?**

a Jupiter
b Mercury*
c Neptune

3 **What is probably the most common leisure activity in the UK?**

a Listening to the radio
b Watching TV*
c Playing team sports

4 **What is the most popular sport in New Zealand?**

a Rugby*
b Baseball
c Hockey

5 **Where is the highest point in the world?**

a In the Andes
b In the Rockies
c In the Himalayas*

6 **How old is the oldest message in a bottle ever found?**

a 150 years old
b 60 years old
c 92 years old*

6A Cultural know-how

China USA Indonesia Turkey

Germany Great Britain Egypt

Statement	
1 If you to Egypt you have to buy a visa when you arrive at the airport.	True or False?
2 In Turkey if you're a woman, you have to cover your arms and legs if you want to visit a mosque.	True or False?
3 In Indonesia you don't always have to have an invitation to go to a wedding.	True or False?
4 In Germany you can travel at any speed on the motorway because there isn't a speed limit.	True or False?
5 In the USA you don't have to have a green card to work in the country.	True or False?
6 In Great Britain you have to show your passport to cross over from England to Scotland.	True or False?
7 If you go to China you can walk around all the Great Wall of China in a day.	True or False?
8 In Singapore you can't chew chewing gum in the street.	True or False?

China USA Indonesia Turkey

Germany Great Britain Egypt

Statement	
1 If you to Egypt you have to buy a visa when you arrive at the airport.	True or False?
2 In Turkey if you're a woman, you have to cover your arms and legs if you want to visit a mosque.	True or False?
3 In Indonesia you don't always have to have an invitation to go to a wedding.	True or False?
4 In Germany you can travel at any speed on the motorway because there isn't a speed limit.	True or False?
5 In the USA you don't have to have a green card to work in the country.	True or False?
6 In Great Britain you have to show your passport to cross over from England to Scotland.	True or False?
7 If you go to China you can walk around all the Great Wall of China in a day.	True or False?
8 In Singapore you can't chew chewing gum in the street.	True or False?

China USA Indonesia Turkey

Germany Great Britain Egypt

Statement	
1 If you to Egypt you have to buy a visa when you arrive at the airport.	True or False?
2 In Turkey if you're a woman, you have to cover your arms and legs if you want to visit a mosque.	True or False?
3 In Indonesia you don't always have to have an invitation to go to a wedding.	True or False?
4 In Germany you can travel at any speed on the motorway because there isn't a speed limit.	True or False?
5 In the USA you don't have to have a green card to work in the country.	True or False?
6 In Great Britain you have to show your passport to cross over from England to Scotland.	True or False?
7 If you go to China you can walk around all the Great Wall of China in a day.	True or False?
8 In Singapore you can't chew chewing gum in the street.	True or False?

China USA Indonesia Turkey

Germany Great Britain Egypt

Statement	
1 If you to Egypt you have to buy a visa when you arrive at the airport.	True or False?
2 In Turkey if you're a woman, you have to cover your arms and legs if you want to visit a mosque.	True or False?
3 In Indonesia you don't always have to have an invitation to go to a wedding.	True or False?
4 In Germany you can travel at any speed on the motorway because there isn't a speed limit.	True or False?
5 In the USA you don't have to have a green card to work in the country.	True or False?
6 In Great Britain you have to show your passport to cross over from England to Scotland.	True or False?
7 If you go to China you can walk around all the Great Wall of China in a day.	True or False?
8 In Singapore you can't chew chewing gum in the street.	True or False?

6B Offers and promises!

1 I get lonely in the evenings.	**A** I'll just go and see if there are any aspirin.
2 I miss my parents a lot.	**B** I'll turn the TV off, if you want.
3 I've got a terrible migraine!	**C** I'll go in a couple of minutes, I promise!
4 I really need you to help me first thing in the morning.	**D** I'll drop in later to keep you company.
5 The house is so dirty!	**E** I'll drive you down to visit them next week, ok?
6 This film is really boring!	**F** I'll help you to clean it up a bit, if you like.
7 You didn't remember to go and buy the groceries!	**G** I'll lend you some, ok?
8 Oh, no! I don't have any money with me!	**H** Don't worry, I won't forget! Tomorrow at 9 in the morning!

1 I get lonely in the evenings.	**A** I'll just go and see if there are any aspirin.
2 I miss my parents a lot.	**B** I'll turn the TV off, if you want.
3 I've got a terrible migraine!	**C** I'll go in a couple of minutes, I promise!
4 I really need you to help me first thing in the morning.	**D** I'll drop in later to keep you company.
5 The house is so dirty!	**E** I'll drive you down to visit them next week, ok?
6 This film is really boring!	**F** I'll help you to clean it up a bit, if you like.
7 You didn't remember to go and buy the groceries!	**G** I'll lend you some, ok?
8 Oh, no! I don't have any money with me!	**H** Don't worry, I won't forget! Tomorrow at 9 in the morning!

7A What's my problem?

You are having trouble getting out of bed in the morning.

You get a rash on your face when you wear woolly clothes.

You get insomnia when you sleep in a different bed.

You've moved to a new area and you're lonely because you don't know anyone.

You get an upset stomach every time your mum cooks pasta.

You lose your voice every time you sing.

You can't stop sneezing every time you kiss your boyfriend / girlfriend.

You can't stop eating biscuits when you're at work.

You are having trouble getting out of bed in the morning.

You get a rash on your face when you wear woolly clothes.

You get insomnia when you sleep in a different bed.

You've moved to a new area and you're lonely because you don't know anyone.

You get an upset stomach every time your mum cooks pasta.

You lose your voice every time you sing.

You can't stop sneezing every time you kiss your boyfriend / girlfriend.

You can't stop eating biscuits when you're at work.

Student A

At the optician's ▪ Learning to drive ▪ At the doctor's ▪ At the dentist's

Don't take more than four in 24 hours.

Open your mouth wide and show me where it hurts.

Put one hand over your left eye and read the letters.

Turn the key and press slowly down on the accelerator.

Student B

At home ▪ At the gym ▪ At the hospital ▪ In class

Jump up and down for one minute.

Sit and wait over there until the nurse calls you.

Open your book and turn to page ten.

Clean your teeth before you go to bed.

Articles Casino

Read each sentence. Decide if the articles are correct, then place your bet. You have 100 points to start. If you're right, add your bet to your total. If you're wrong, subtract the bet from your total. You get 20 extra points if you can correct the wrong sentences. **Remember!** You must bet on every sentence.

1 THE TRAVEL MAKES WISE PEOPLE BETTER AND STUPID PEOPLE WORSE.
Bet_____

2 WE BOUGHT A SMALL HOUSE NEAR THE BEACH .
Bet_____

3 I HATE THE JAZZ MUSIC!
Bet_____

4 I CAN'T DRINK COFFEE THEY SELL IN ENGLAND. IT'S DISGUSTING!
Bet_____

5 WHEN WE WENT ON HOLIDAY LAST YEAR WE VISITED THE BLACK FOREST.
Bet_____

6 IS THIS THE RIGHT WAY TO THE HOTEL?
Bet_____

7 THE LOVE IS THE MOST IMPORTANT THING IN LIFE.
Bet_____

Articles Casino

Read each sentence. Decide if the articles are correct, then place your bet. You have 100 points to start. If you're right, add your bet to your total. If you're wrong, subtract the bet from your total. You get 20 extra points if you can correct the wrong sentences. **Remember!** You must bet on every sentence.

1 THE TRAVEL MAKES WISE PEOPLE BETTER AND STUPID PEOPLE WORSE.
Bet_____

2 WE BOUGHT A SMALL HOUSE NEAR THE BEACH .
Bet_____

3 I HATE THE JAZZ MUSIC!
Bet_____

4 I CAN'T DRINK COFFEE THEY SELL IN ENGLAND. IT'S DISGUSTING!
Bet_____

5 WHEN WE WENT ON HOLIDAY LAST YEAR WE VISITED THE BLACK FOREST.
Bet_____

6 IS THIS THE RIGHT WAY TO THE HOTEL?
Bet_____

7 THE LOVE IS THE MOST IMPORTANT THING IN LIFE.
Bet_____

Articles Casino

Read each sentence. Decide if the articles are correct, then place your bet. You have 100 points to start. If you're right, add your bet to your total. If you're wrong, subtract the bet from your total. You get 20 extra points if you can correct the wrong sentences. **Remember!** You must bet on every sentence.

1 THE TRAVEL MAKES WISE PEOPLE BETTER AND STUPID PEOPLE WORSE.
Bet_____

2 WE BOUGHT A SMALL HOUSE NEAR THE BEACH .
Bet_____

3 I HATE THE JAZZ MUSIC!
Bet_____

4 I CAN'T DRINK COFFEE THEY SELL IN ENGLAND. IT'S DISGUSTING!
Bet_____

5 WHEN WE WENT ON HOLIDAY LAST YEAR WE VISITED THE BLACK FOREST.
Bet_____

6 IS THIS THE RIGHT WAY TO THE HOTEL?
Bet_____

7 THE LOVE IS THE MOST IMPORTANT THING IN LIFE.
Bet_____

Articles Casino

Read each sentence. Decide if the articles are correct, then place your bet. You have 100 points to start. If you're right, add your bet to your total. If you're wrong, subtract the bet from your total. You get 20 extra points if you can correct the wrong sentences. **Remember!** You must bet on every sentence.

1 THE TRAVEL MAKES WISE PEOPLE BETTER AND STUPID PEOPLE WORSE.
Bet_____

2 WE BOUGHT A SMALL HOUSE NEAR THE BEACH .
Bet_____

3 I HATE THE JAZZ MUSIC!
Bet_____

4 I CAN'T DRINK COFFEE THEY SELL IN ENGLAND. IT'S DISGUSTING!
Bet_____

5 WHEN WE WENT ON HOLIDAY LAST YEAR WE VISITED THE BLACK FOREST.
Bet_____

6 IS THIS THE RIGHT WAY TO THE HOTEL?
Bet_____

7 THE LOVE IS THE MOST IMPORTANT THING IN LIFE.
Bet_____

8B GUESS WHAT AND WHERE!

Student A

a THE UNDERGROUND b MOTORWAY c NO PARKING ZONE d THE NEWS e DEMONSTRATION

1. The problem with taking part in one of these is that it's likely to cause lots of traffic problems in the city centre and make many people irritable.
2. If you leave your car in one of these areas, you'll get a fine.
3. I usually go on this when I travel long distances by car because it's faster and there are fewer problems with traffic.
4. There are many different lines all over the city and it's faster than a bus but sometimes there aren't many seats because it gets crowded.
5. There's so much bad news on it that I've stopped watching it!

Student B

a WEBSITE b CYCLE LANES c FLIGHT DELAYS d POLLUTION e PUBLIC TRANSPORT

1. I looked on it to find out if there were any delays but there was so little information there I decided to phone the transport office instead.
2. It isn't much fun when you have to wait at the airport because of these.
3. Sometimes there is so much of this in the city centre that it's hard to breath.
4. I don't use it much because I take the car when I have to travel anywhere.
5. Lots of people use them these days. It's a good way to travel safely on your bike through the city centre.

9A Animal encounters

Student A

1. When I got home my dog was going crazy because ...
2. I was scared because the gorilla ...
3. I was really shocked because the horse ...
4. The cat destroyed all the curtains in the house because ...

Student B

1. When I looked at the pigeon it was lying on the ground because ...
2. I felt a bit nervous because the snake ...
3. I had to wait in the car because a dangerous bull ...
4. The vet came to take my parrot away because ...

Student A

1. When I got home my dog was going crazy because ...
2. I was scared because the gorilla ...
3. I was really shocked because the horse ...
4. The cat destroyed all the curtains in the house because ...

Student B

1. When I looked at the pigeon it was lying on the ground because ...
2. I felt a bit nervous because the snake ...
3. I had to wait in the car because a dangerous bull ...
4. The vet came to take my parrot away because ...

9B An Indian folk tale

Set A

The tiger, the wise old man and the jackal
– an Indian folk story. Part 1

One day a wise old man was walking in the forest when he heard a strange noise. He saw a tiger trapped in a cage. 'Please free me from this cage.' 'No,' the wise old man replied. 'If I set you free, you will attack and eat me.'

'I promise I won't,' said the tiger. The wise old man didn't believe the tiger, but he opened the door for the tiger anyway. The tiger decided to eat the wise old man.

'Everyone told me you were a wise man but how could you believe the word of a tiger? Now I'm going to eat you.' 'But that's not fair,' said the wise old man.

'It is fair. I am a tiger and tigers eat people,' replied the tiger. 'But you promised,' said the wise old man.

'Of course. I said that so you would help me. But I'm still going to eat you,' said the tiger.

'Well, if you're going to eat me, please give me one last thing before I die,' replied the wise old man. 'Let me walk through the forest. I will go and ask the first three things that I meet what they think. If they believe you've been unfair, you will let me go. But if they say you have been fair, you can eat me.'

'Very well,' said the tiger, 'but everyone will agree with me.'

Set B

The tiger, the wise old man and the jackal
– an Indian folk story. Part 2

The wise old man walked into the forest. First he came to a tree and he explained his problem. 'Fair!' replied the tree. 'I offer shade to everyone, but still people cut off my branches and feed me to their fires. The tiger is right.'

Next he met a buffalo. Again he explained. 'I give people all the milk I can. But when I can't give any more, they will kill me and eat me. The tiger is right!' said the buffalo.

Finally, he saw a jackal and he began to explain his story. But the jackal said, 'I'm sorry, but I don't understand. Could you explain it again, please?'

Again the wise old man explained, but still the jackal didn't understand. 'Come with me,' he said. 'The tiger can help you to understand.'

'Please explain our situation to the jackal' said the wise old man to the tiger. So the tiger explained, but the jackal shook his head. 'Let me see, the wise old man was in the cage and...' said the jackal.

'No, I was in the cage,' replied the tiger angrily.

'Ah, yes I was in the cage,' replied the jackal. 'No, that's not right, oh this is very difficult,' he continued.

Now the tiger was angry. 'Look. I was in the cage.' And he walked into the cage for the jackal to see.

'Ah, now I understand,' said the jackal smiling. And very quickly he closed the door of the cage.

Set A

The tiger, the wise old man and the jackal
– an Indian folk story. Part 1

One day a wise old man was walking in the forest when he heard a strange noise. He saw a tiger trapped in a cage. 'Please free me from this cage.' 'No,' the wise old man replied. 'If I set you free, you will attack and eat me.'

'I promise I won't,' said the tiger. The wise old man didn't believe the tiger, but he opened the door for the tiger anyway. The tiger decided to eat the wise old man.

'Everyone told me you were a wise man but how could you believe the word of a tiger? Now I'm going to eat you.' 'But that's not fair,' said the wise old man.

'It is fair. I am a tiger and tigers eat people,' replied the tiger. 'But you promised,' said the wise old man.

'Of course. I said that so you would help me. But I'm still going to eat you,' said the tiger.

'Well, if you're going to eat me, please give me one last thing before I die,' replied the wise old man. 'Let me walk through the forest. I will go and ask the first three things that I meet what they think. If they believe you've been unfair, you will let me go. But if they say you have been fair, you can eat me.'

'Very well,' said the tiger, 'but everyone will agree with me.'

Set B

The tiger, the wise old man and the jackal
– an Indian folk story. Part 2

The wise old man walked into the forest. First he came to a tree and he explained his problem. 'Fair!' replied the tree. 'I offer shade to everyone, but still people cut off my branches and feed me to their fires. The tiger is right.'

Next he met a buffalo. Again he explained. 'I give people all the milk I can. But when I can't give any more, they will kill me and eat me. The tiger is right!' said the buffalo.

Finally, he saw a jackal and he began to explain his story. But the jackal said, 'I'm sorry, but I don't understand. Could you explain it again, please?'

Again the wise old man explained, but still the jackal didn't understand. 'Come with me,' he said. 'The tiger can help you to understand.'

'Please explain our situation to the jackal' said the wise old man to the tiger. So the tiger explained, but the jackal shook his head. 'Let me see, the wise old man was in the cage and...' said the jackal.

'No, I was in the cage,' replied the tiger angrily.

'Ah, yes I was in the cage,' replied the jackal. 'No, that's not right, oh this is very difficult,' he continued.

Now the tiger was angry. 'Look. I was in the cage.' And he walked into the cage for the jackal to see.

'Ah, now I understand,' said the jackal smiling. And very quickly he closed the door of the cage.

10A Boarding school

Role card 1

You want your child to get the best education possible, so you've decided to send them to a private boarding school. You're going to meet the Head Teacher of the school. Before you pay a lot of money, you want to know more about the school's educational policy and other details. You have made a list of the areas you want to know more about:

- your child is doing badly, is there extra help?
- you have financial problems and can't pay one month
- your child has problems with other children – will the parents be contacted?
- your child is naughty
- you can't collect your child one weekend – can your child stay at the school?
- your child doesn't like the food there

Role card 2

You are the Head Teacher of an expensive boarding school. A parent is coming to visit you to ask some questions about the school. You have made a list of possible things the parent might want to know about in preparation for the interview.

- child doing badly – extra tuition available, but at an extra cost!
- financial problems, there is a possibility of delaying the payment for two months.
- problems with other children; parents contacted immediately; possibility of moving to another class
- naughty children; get extra homework and parents contacted if it continues
- children can stay weekends, but parents must contact the school three days in advance
- varied menus for children who don't like the usual menu

Role card 1

You want your child to get the best education possible, so you've decided to send them to a private boarding school. You're going to meet the Head Teacher of the school. Before you pay a lot of money, you want to know more about the school's educational policy and other details. You have made a list of the areas you want to know more about:

- your child is doing badly, is there extra help?
- you have financial problems and can't pay one month
- your child has problems with other children – will the parents be contacted?
- your child is naughty
- you can't collect your child one weekend – can your child stay at the school?
- your child doesn't like the food there

Role card 2

You are the Head Teacher of an expensive boarding school. A parent is coming to visit you to ask some questions about the school. You have made a list of possible things the parent might want to know about in preparation for the interview.

- child doing badly – extra tuition available, but at an extra cost!
- financial problems, there is a possibility of delaying the payment for two months.
- problems with other children; parents contacted immediately; possibility of moving to another class
- naughty children; get extra homework and parents contacted if it continues
- children can stay weekends, but parents must contact the school three days in advance
- varied menus for children who don't like the usual menu

10B Pictionary – photocopiable

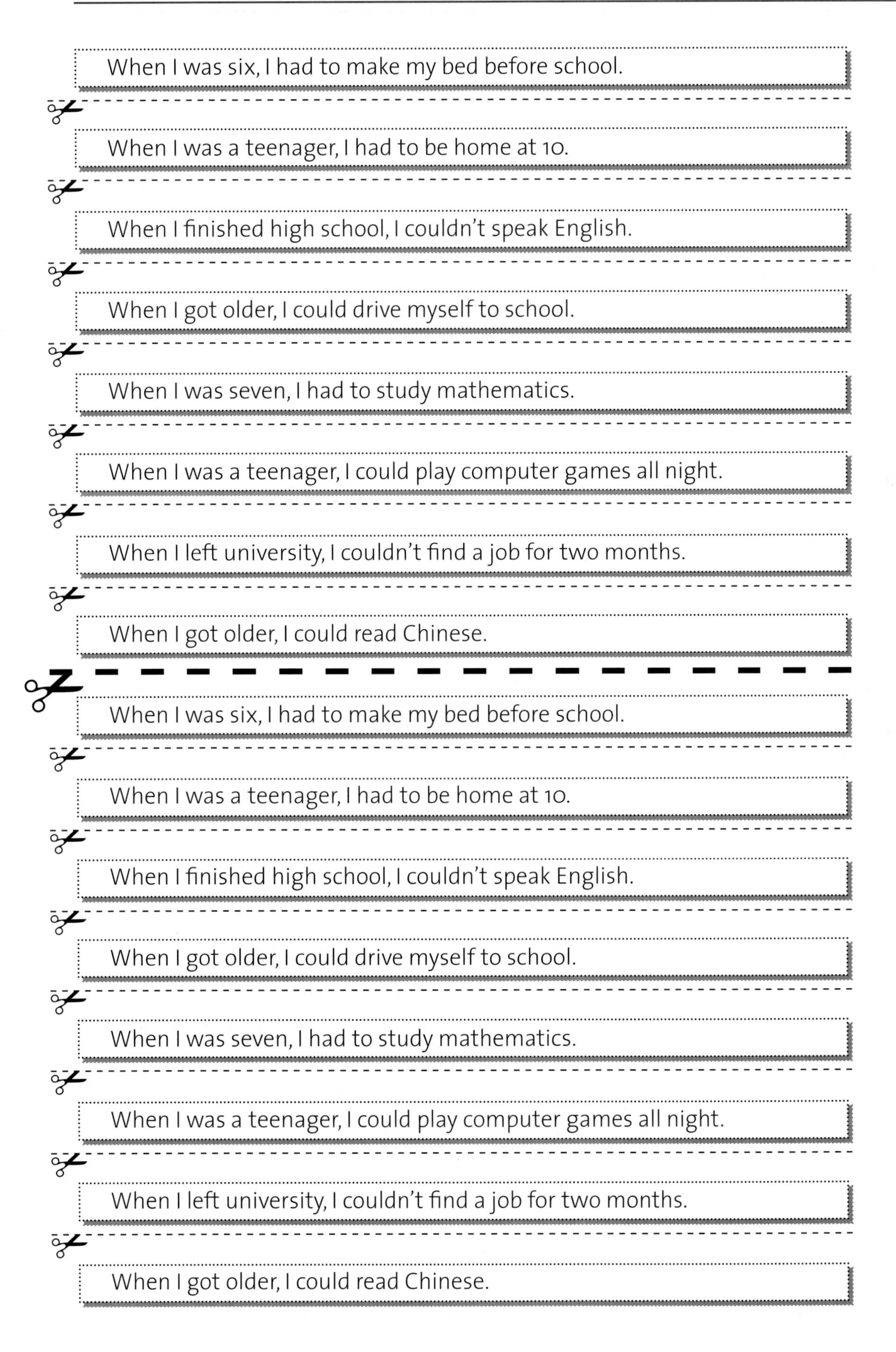

When I was six, I had to make my bed before school.

When I was a teenager, I had to be home at 10.

When I finished high school, I couldn't speak English.

When I got older, I could drive myself to school.

When I was seven, I had to study mathematics.

When I was a teenager, I could play computer games all night.

When I left university, I couldn't find a job for two months.

When I got older, I could read Chinese.

When I was six, I had to make my bed before school.

When I was a teenager, I had to be home at 10.

When I finished high school, I couldn't speak English.

When I got older, I could drive myself to school.

When I was seven, I had to study mathematics.

When I was a teenager, I could play computer games all night.

When I left university, I couldn't find a job for two months.

When I got older, I could read Chinese.

11A What would you do if?

1 What would you do if you arrived at the hotel and somebody was sleeping in your room?

2 What would you do if you found a rat in your bed?

3 What would you do if the hotel forgot your wake-up call and you missed your flight?

4 What would you do if you got home then realised the hotel had overcharged you by 150%?

5 What would you do if the person in the next room snored very loudly all night?

1 What would you do if you arrived at the hotel and somebody was sleeping in your room?

2 What would you do if you found a rat in your bed?

3 What would you do if the hotel forgot your wake-up call and you missed your flight?

4 What would you do if you got home then realised the hotel had overcharged you by 150%?

5 What would you do if the person in the next room snored very loudly all night?

1 What would you do if you arrived at the hotel and somebody was sleeping in your room?

2 What would you do if you found a rat in your bed?

3 What would you do if the hotel forgot your wake-up call and you missed your flight?

4 What would you do if you got home then realised the hotel had overcharged you by 150%?

5 What would you do if the person in the next room snored very loudly all night?

1 What would you do if you arrived at the hotel and somebody was sleeping in your room?

2 What would you do if you found a rat in your bed?

3 What would you do if the hotel forgot your wake-up call and you missed your flight?

4 What would you do if you got home then realised the hotel had overcharged you by 150%?

5 What would you do if the person in the next room snored very loudly all night?

11B You used to...?

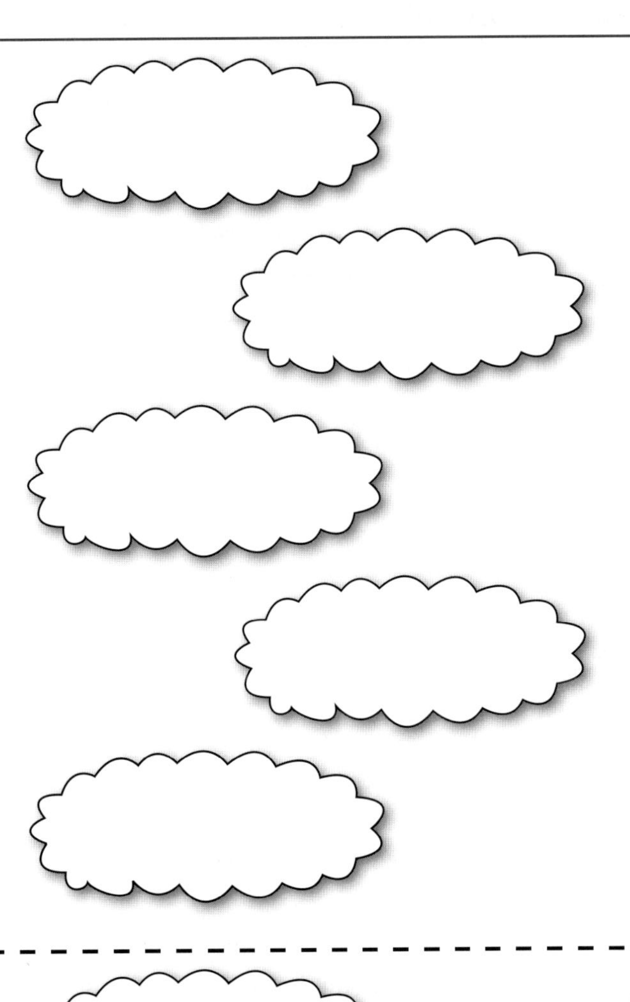

Likes
You used to...

Dislikes
You used to...

Hobbies
You used to...

Places or Holidays
You never used to go...

Activities
You usually...

- -

Likes
You used to...

Dislikes
You used to...

Hobbies
You used to...

Places or Holidays
You never used to go...

Activities
You usually...

12A Short conversations

Hi Sue. Do you still need some help, or have you finished painting? **A**

No, I haven't even started yet! And we're supposed to be going out for a drink later. **A**

Shall I come round and help? **A**

That would be great. Can you bring an extra paintbrush? **A**

Of course. That's not a problem. **A**

Great, we can get it done in no time and still go for a drink later! **A**

Hello, I'm calling because I'm still having problems with my phone. **B**

I'm really sorry but we haven't had time to solve the problem yet. **B**

Well, I've already phoned three times to tell you! **B**

We'll deal with it immediately. **B**

When? **B**

Oh, actually, the technician has just left to go to your house. **B**

12B Who said that?

Who said ...?

1 **Work was life and without it there was nothing but insecurity.**
a John Lennon b Paul McCartney c Ringo Starr
What was the quote?

2 **A person who never made a mistake had never tried anything new.**
a Napoleon Bonaparte b Winston Churchill c Albert Einstein
What was the quote?

3 **The object of art was to give life a shape.**
a Pablo Picasso b Francis Ford Coppola c William Shakespeare
What was the quote?

4 **If you didn't ask you didn't get.**
a Mahatma Ghandi b Nelson Mandela c Mother Teresa
What was the quote?

5 **He would be back.**
a Rambo b Terminator c Freddy Kruger
What was the quote?

6 **It was better to have loved and lost than never to have loved at all.**
a Van Gogh b Ernest Hemmingway c Mark Twin
What was the quote?

Who said ...?

1 **Work was life and without it there was nothing but insecurity.**
a John Lennon b Paul McCartney c Ringo Starr
What was the quote?

2 **A person who never made a mistake had never tried anything new.**
a Napoleon Bonaparte b Winston Churchill c Albert Einstein
What was the quote?

3 **The object of art was to give life a shape.**
a Pablo Picasso b Francis Ford Coppola c William Shakespeare
What was the quote?

4 **If you didn't ask you didn't get.**
a Mahatma Ghandi b Nelson Mandela c Mother Teresa
What was the quote?

5 **He would be back.**
a Rambo b Terminator c Freddy Kruger
What was the quote?

6 **It was better to have loved and lost than never to have loved at all.**
a Van Gogh b Ernest Hemmingway c Mark Twin
What was the quote?

Who said ...?

1 **Work was life and without it there was nothing but insecurity.**
a John Lennon b Paul McCartney c Ringo Starr
What was the quote?

2 **A person who never made a mistake had never tried anything new.**
a Napoleon Bonaparte b Winston Churchill c Albert Einstein
What was the quote?

3 **The object of art was to give life a shape.**
a Pablo Picasso b Francis Ford Coppola c William Shakespeare
What was the quote?

4 **If you didn't ask you didn't get.**
a Mahatma Ghandi b Nelson Mandela c Mother Teresa
What was the quote?

5 **He would be back.**
a Rambo b Terminator c Freddy Kruger
What was the quote?

6 **It was better to have loved and lost than never to have loved at all.**
a Van Gogh b Ernest Hemmingway c Mark Twin
What was the quote?

Who said ...?

1 **Work was life and without it there was nothing but insecurity.**
a John Lennon b Paul McCartney c Ringo Starr
What was the quote?

2 **A person who never made a mistake had never tried anything new.**
a Napoleon Bonaparte b Winston Churchill c Albert Einstein
What was the quote?

3 **The object of art was to give life a shape.**
a Pablo Picasso b Francis Ford Coppola c William Shakespeare
What was the quote?

4 **If you didn't ask you didn't get.**
a Mahatma Ghandi b Nelson Mandela c Mother Teresa
What was the quote?

5 **He would be back.**
a Rambo b Terminator c Freddy Kruger
What was the quote?

6 **It was better to have loved and lost than never to have loved at all.**
a Van Gogh b Ernest Hemmingway c Mark Twin
What was the quote?

13A Agree or disagree?

I'm really interested in learning more about martial arts.	Agree / Disagree
I think romantic books are a bit boring.	Agree / Disagree
People who tell you the end of a film before you finish watching it are very annoying.	Agree / Disagree
I get bored watching long documentaries about history.	Agree / Disagree
I get scared when I see films that have a lot of blood in them and horrible murders.	Agree / Disagree
I feel excited when I see someone famous.	Agree / Disagree
Staying up really late watching a good film is fun, but tiring!	Agree / Disagree
I'm tired of seeing the same actors in nearly all the films.	Agree / Disagree
I love exciting and fast-moving stories.	Agree / Disagree

I'm really interested in learning more about martial arts.	Agree / Disagree
I think romantic books are a bit boring.	Agree / Disagree
People who tell you the end of a film before you finish watching it are very annoying.	Agree / Disagree
I get bored watching long documentaries about history.	Agree / Disagree
I get scared when I see films that have a lot of blood in them and horrible murders.	Agree / Disagree
I feel excited when I see someone famous.	Agree / Disagree
Staying up really late watching a good film is fun, but tiring!	Agree / Disagree
I'm tired of seeing the same actors in nearly all the films.	Agree / Disagree
I love exciting and fast-moving stories.	Agree / Disagree

I'm really interested in learning more about martial arts.	Agree / Disagree
I think romantic books are a bit boring.	Agree / Disagree
People who tell you the end of a film before you finish watching it are very annoying.	Agree / Disagree
I get bored watching long documentaries about history.	Agree / Disagree
I get scared when I see films that have a lot of blood in them and horrible murders.	Agree / Disagree
I feel excited when I see someone famous.	Agree / Disagree
Staying up really late watching a good film is fun, but tiring!	Agree / Disagree
I'm tired of seeing the same actors in nearly all the films.	Agree / Disagree
I love exciting and fast-moving stories.	Agree / Disagree

I'm really interested in learning more about martial arts.	Agree / Disagree
I think romantic books are a bit boring.	Agree / Disagree
People who tell you the end of a film before you finish watching it are very annoying.	Agree / Disagree
I get bored watching long documentaries about history.	Agree / Disagree
I get scared when I see films that have a lot of blood in them and horrible murders.	Agree / Disagree
I feel excited when I see someone famous.	Agree / Disagree
Staying up really late watching a good film is fun, but tiring!	Agree / Disagree
I'm tired of seeing the same actors in nearly all the films.	Agree / Disagree
I love exciting and fast-moving stories.	Agree / Disagree

13B How long...?

Question 1

How long have you been ...?

Question 1

How long have you been ...?

Question 2

How long have you been ... (+ *ing*)?

Question 2

How long have you been ... (+ *ing*)?

Question 3

How long have you known ...?

Question 3

How long have you known ...?

Question 4

How long have you had ...?

Question 4

How long have you had ...?

14A What do you call...?

a mop	a torch
a stapler	an iron
a neighbour	a babysitter
a conductor	a library
a football pitch	a building site
a mosque	a gallery

a mop	a torch
a stapler	an iron
a neighbour	a babysitter
a conductor	a library
a football pitch	a building site
a mosque	a gallery

Pair A

Family 1

This family all love junk food, but their doctor has told them they must change their eating habits. What must / mustn't they do if they want to become healthy?

These are the kinds of things they eat and drink:

- 200 cans of coke a week
- 2 dozen eggs every four days
- a large cake every day for dessert
- chips at least once a day
- several bars of chocolate every night while watching TV
- bacon, eggs and sausages for breakfast
- junk food every weekend so they don't have to cook

Pair B

Family 2

This family need to stop causing damage to the environment. The neighbourhood recycling group have told them they must change their habits. What must / mustn't they do to stop damaging the environment?

These are the things they do:

- never separate rubbish
- buy large trays of fruit with plastic wrapping
- pick up new plastic bags every time they go to the supermarket
- have the air conditioning on all day when it's hot
- leave the TV on all night
- like having all the lights on so they don't have to keep switching them on
- always buy water in small plastic bottles

15A Talking about you

Student A

1 What's one thing that you currently enjoy doing?
2 Can you remember how much time you've spent studying English at home this month?
3 Can you think of something you need to buy in a few days' time?
4 Can you think of two things that you used to love doing when you were younger but don't do now?

Student B

1 Can you tell me of one thing in your life you're thinking about changing?
2 Can you remember when you were on holiday last year and what you did?
3 Can you think of something you're going to do to spend less money in the next few weeks?
4 Can you remember two ways you used to save money when you were younger?

Student A

1 What's one thing that you currently enjoy doing?
2 Can you remember how much time you've spent studying English at home this month?
3 Can you think of something you need to buy in a few days' time?
4 Can you think of two things that you used to love doing when you were younger but don't do now?

Student B

1 Can you tell me of one thing in your life you're thinking about changing?
2 Can you remember when you were on holiday last year and what you did?
3 Can you think of something you're going to do to spend less money in the next few weeks?
4 Can you remember two ways you used to save money when you were younger?

15B Categories

SAVE MONEY

BETTER QUALITY OF LIFE

GET A BETTER JOB

SPEND MONEY

GET A MORTGAGE

GET RICH

depend + preposition + noun	*be involved* + preposition + noun	*live* + preposition + noun
lead + preposition + noun	*be accused* + preposition + noun	*vote* + preposition + noun
be caused + preposition + noun	*be opposed* + preposition + noun	*result* + preposition + noun

depend + preposition + noun	*be involved* + preposition + noun	*live* + preposition + noun
lead + preposition + noun	*be accused* + preposition + noun	*vote* + preposition + noun
be caused + preposition + noun	*be opposed* + preposition + noun	*result* + preposition + noun

Story 1

I'll never forget trying to pass my driving test. I got so nervous each time I had to take it I used to start shaking and crying before even getting into the car. I always managed to do something wrong! The first time I took it I crashed the car into a traffic light! The driving instructor offered to take me home. I don't think he wanted to see me ever again!

I eventually passed after taking it nine times!

The day I passed it was the happiest of my life. I started crying again, but this time from happiness!

Story 2

I'll always remember flying to Hong Kong. I also remember feeling a bit worried about flying such a long distance. When I got to the airport I waited to give my ticket to the check-in person. He offered to change my ticket for a first class one! I'll never forget getting on the plane and the flight attendant asking me if I wanted to drink champagne, wine or juice. I was so nervous I said 'all of them please'!

I couldn't stop smiling on the plane, drinking champagne and eating chocolate in the middle of the sky!

GRAMMAR REFERENCE

01 FAMILY AND FRIENDS

QUESTION FORMATION

Exercise 1

1A Where does she work?
2A Do you like football?
3A Sorry, what did you say?
4A Did he have a nice time?
5A What is he studying?
6A Are you looking for something?
7A Have you been to the States?
8A How long have they been married?

Exercise 2

1 A How old is your gran?
2 A What kinds of things do you do at the weekend?
3 A What film did you see in the end?
4 A How long have you lived here?
5 A What questions did they ask in the exam?
6 A What is the best way to get there?
7 A How far do you have to travel to get to work?
8 A How many students are there in your class?

Exercise 3

1 What are you talking about?
2 Have you seen that new Kate Winslet film?
3 Where did you get your book?
4 Who did you go with?
5 What are you listening to on your iPod?

THE PRESENT SIMPLE

Exercise 1

1 Is your sister married?
2 correct
3 correct
4 Why do you still live at home?
5 My brother and I always go to watch football on Saturdays.
6 My sister's quite shy. She doesn't have many friends.
7 correct
8 My brother works for my father's company.
9 I eat fast food once or twice a week.
10 correct

SIMILARITIES AND CONTRASTS

Exercise 1

1 all
2 both
3 Neither
4 both
5 whereas
6 any
7 any, all
8 either

02 SHOPS

THE PAST SIMPLE

Exercise 1

1 I went there yesterday.
2 Sorry. What did you say? Can you repeat it?
3 I wanted to buy a coat, but I didn't see anything nice.
4 I love your earrings. Where did you get them?
5 They lived in France when they were kids.
6 I have to admit, I cried at the end of the film.
7 She told me not to say anything, so I didn't.
8 He complained and I did too, but it didn't make any difference.
9 I broke a glass and cut my finger.
10 It started to rain five minutes after we left the house.
11 Why weren't you in class yesterday?
12 Where did you go last night?

COMPARATIVES

Exercise 1

1 quicker
2 more pleasant
3 less busy / not so busy
4 wiser, earlier, not as heavy
5 more fluent, not as good as
6 not as strict as, later
7 more intelligent than, more determined, harder

PASSIVES

Exercise 1

1 blown
2 broken
3 brought
4 built
5 bought
6 caught
7 found
8 given
9 hit
10 kept
11 left
12 lent
13 paid
14 put
15 run
16 seen
17 sold
18 shown
19 stolen
20 taken
21 taught
22 thrown
23 woken
24 written

Exercise 2

1 I was told I couldn't take my bag into the shop.
2 He was caught stealing some perfume.
3 I am sent junk emails all the time.
4 The building was knocked down over two years ago.
5 It is usually made with lamb, but it can be made with beef.
6 My house was broken into last night.
7 A new tax on luxury goods was introduced last year.
8 A huge shopping centre has been built nearby.

Exercise 3

1a taught
1b was taught
2a left
2b was left
3a were shown
3b showed
4a was woken up
4b woke up
5a gave
5b was given

Exercise 4

1 correct
2 How did the accident happen?
3 A dog suddenly appeared in front of me.
4 Fortunately, none of us was badly hurt.
5 correct
6 Those batteries didn't last very long.

03 EAT

THE PRESENT PERFECT SIMPLE

Exercise 1

A

1 Have you been here before?
2 Have you ever eaten snake?
3 Have you tried that new restaurant round the corner?
4 Has Dave spoken to you about tonight yet?
5 Have you two been introduced?
6 How long has she lived there?

B

1 c
2 a
3 f
4 d
5 b
6 e

Exercise 2

1B I've never been
2A Did you go out
3A Have you had
3B I made
4A did you go
4B We've been
4A we had

Exercise 3

1a lost
1b has lost
2a Did you visit....?
2b Have you visited
3a I've never tried
3b did not try them on
4a Have you ever seen
4b Did you see

TOO / NOT ENOUGH

Exercise 1

1 too
2 very
3 enough
4 many
5 very, much
6 much
7 too
8 to

OFFERS, REQUESTS, PERMISSION, SUGGESTIONS

would, could, shall

Exercise 1

1 Would you like more of anything?
2 Could I close the window?
3 Shall we go for a Thai meal?
4 Could you pour me some water?
5 Could we wait till our friend arrives?
6 Would you like me to hang your coat up?
7 Shall I pay with my card?
8 Would you mind turning down the air conditioning?

04 JOBS

PRESENT CONTINUOUS AND PRESENT SIMPLE

Exercise 1

1a are doing
1b do
2a run
2b am running
3a try
3b is trying
4a am waiting
4b wait

PLANS AND WISHES FOR THE FUTURE

Exercise 1

1 What are you hoping to learn on this course?
2 Next year, we are planning to open a factory in China.
3 I really wouldn't like to work night shifts!
4 Where are you thinking of moving to?
5 Who is going to organise the launch party?
6 We are hoping to develop a new anti-cancer drug.
7 What kind of work would you like to do in the future?
8 He is thinking of applying to do some voluntary work.
9 I'm not planning to start work immediately. I'm hoping to go travelling for a while first.
10 When are you going to realise that your boss is never going to change?

Exercise 2

1 d
2 b
3 a
4 e
5 c

THE PAST CONTINUOUS AND PAST SIMPLE

Exercise 1

1 wasn't feeling
2 were they thinking
3 were you living
4 wasn't enjoying
5 were having
6 weren't offering
7 was snowing
8 was presenting

Exercise 2

1 1 went
2 offered
3 decided
4 was having
5 walked
6 sat down

2 1 did
2 was writing
3 was starting
4 went
5 made
6 put
7 started
8 rang
9 jumped
10 spilt / spilled

3 1 met
2 were both working
3 liked
4 went
5 were sitting
6 met
7 knew
8 took

05 RELAX

MIGHT, THE PRESENT CONTINUOUS, *BE GOING TO* + VERB

Exercise 1

1 are you doing, are meeting, to see
2 having, having, hire
3 are playing, to play
4 to watch, to get

SUPERLATIVES

Exercise 1

1 I think it's the worst film I've ever seen.
2 It's freezing outside so wear your thickest coat.
3 My mum's probably the most generous person I know.
4 We're busiest in the afternoons, so ring in the morning.
5 Ironing is my least favourite job.
6 That must be the saddest thing I've ever heard!
7 Honestly, it's the most disgusting thing you'll ever see.
8 Deano's has the widest selection of clothes in town.

Exercise 2

1 He's the nicest person I've ever met.
2 It's the most exciting race I've ever taken part in.
3 That computer is the most reliable we've ever had.
4 This is the most complicated game I've ever played.
5 It's the funniest book I've read in a long time.
6 That's the smartest I've ever seen you look.

06 HOME

HAVE TO, DON'T HAVE TO / CAN

Exercise 1

1 We have to tell ...
2 My sister can stay ...
3 My friend Juan has to find ...
4 You don't have to do it ...
5 ... I can drive you home.
6 ... but I can't afford it.

Exercise 2

1 c 2 d 3 e 4 a 5 b 6 f

WILL / WON'T

Exercise 1

1 won't
2 'll
3 won't
4 'll, won't
5 'll, won't
6 won't
7 won't
8 'll

Exercise 2

1 is coming
2 won't bite
3A What're you doing
3B I'm just going to go
4 is getting
5 I'll help
6B I'm going , I'll post

07 MIND AND BODY

GIVING ADVICE

Exercise 1

1 You shouldn't eat so much!
2 You should watch less TV!
3 You really should go and see a doctor about it. You shouldn't just ignore it.
4 I guess I should take it back to the shop and complain!
5 The government should do more ...
6 ... you should really shouldn't miss the cathedral there.

Exercise 2

1 Why don't you go on a diet?
2 You should put some cream on that rash.
3 What do you think we ought to do?
4 Why don't you phone and make an appointment?
5 Selling pirate DVDs ought to be stopped.
6 Maybe you should drink less coffee.

IMPERATIVES

Exercise 1

1 Don't panic. Stay calm.
2 Don't whisper. Speak up. We can't hear you.
3 Be careful. Don't slip.
4 Don't just sit there. Do something.
5 Take your time. Don't rush.

6 Be quiet. Don't make so much noise.
7 Get up. Don't be so lazy.
8 Don't wait for me. Go ahead. I'll catch you up.

Exercise 2
1 Could you pour me some water, please?
2 You should try talking to someone about it.
3 Could you bring me the bill, please?
4 Could you help me carry these bags to the car?
5 You shouldn't drive if you're taking that medication.
6 You shouldn't call him now. It's too late.

08 GETTING THERE

ARTICLES
a, *an* and *the*

Exercise 1
1 We hired a boat and sailed down the River Nile.
2 I usually come to school by train.
3 Our friends have a lovely cottage in the Black Forest.
4 I'm meeting a friend of mine later.
5 One day I'd love to try and climb Mount Everest.
6 My father is a pilot, so he's away from home a lot.
7 Happiness is more important than money.
8 I don't like eggs. I don't know why. I just don't.

Exercise 2
1 The food in Laos was quite strange. Most days, we had spicy noodles for breakfast – sometimes with an egg on top.
2 I'm from Quito – the capital of Ecuador.
3 Life always seems better when the sun is out!
4 The hotel we were in had a great view of the sea.
5 Did the police find the guy who stole your luggage?

QUANTIFIERS AND UNCOUNTABLE NOUNS
1 much
2 little
3 many
4 much
5 much, few
6 lot
7 Hardly

09 SCIENCE AND NATURE

THE PAST PERFECT SIMPLE

Exercise 1
1 'd seen
2 'd forgotten
3 'd left
4 'd been, had never met
5 hadn't been told the class had been cancelled
6 had done, had cheated

Exercise 2
1 After they'd had one date, he asked her to marry him.
2 I rang you as soon as I had heard the news.
3 I had never been on a plane until I went to Japan.
4 They had had an argument before I arrived, so there was a bad atmosphere. It was quite uncomfortable.
5 I was fed up after I found out I hadn't got the job.

REPORTING SPEECH 1

Exercise 1
1 said
2 told, said
3 say
4 were asked
5 were told
6 asked, was told
7 was asked, told
8 said
9 were asked

Exercise 2
1 I told him to stop, but he ignored me.
2 correct
3 My science teacher said we only use 10% of our brains!
4 correct
5 My teacher told me not to text in class.
6 I asked my dad if I could go to the party, but he said no.
7 correct
8 He asked me to help him with his Chemistry homework.

10 EDUCATION

FIRST CONDITIONALS

Exercise 1
1 d 2 b 3 e 4 f 5 c 6 h 7 a 8 g

Exercise 2
1 If I go to England, my English will get better.
2 You won't do well at the interview tomorrow if you don't dress well for it.
3 correct
4 If I find the website address, I'll send it to you later.
5 correct
6 If I don't go to university, my parents will be really upset.

HAD TO / DIDN'T HAVE TO / COULD / COULDN'T

Exercise 1
1 could
2 had to
3 didn't have to, have to
4 couldn't, had to, can

Exercise 2
1 We couldn't come yesterday, because of the train strike.
2 correct
3 We didn't have to do exercise 4 – we only needed to do exercise 3.
4 The question was so difficult, I couldn't answer it.
5 When I was at school, we always had to stand up when the teacher came into the classroom.
6 correct
7 He had to re-take the test twice before he passed.

11 PLACES TO STAY

SECOND CONDITIONALS

Exercise 1

1 c / a 2 e 3 a 4 f 5 d 6 b

Exercise 2

1 was
2 I'd, wasn't
3 were, wouldn't, I'd
4 It'd, was
5 would, wasn't
6 were, could

USED TO

Exercise 1

1 When I was a kid, we usually went to the mountains during the summer.
2 I used to work as a researcher for a drug company.
3 correct
4 I never used to have lunch at school. I always had lunch at home.
5 correct
6 On Fridays, we used to watch a DVD at home together.
7 Last week, I had to study for my exams.
8 correct

12 PHONE

JUST, ALREADY, YET AND *STILL*

Exercise 1

1 Have you spoken to the bank yet?
2 I haven't had time yet. I'll do it tomorrow.
3 She's only just graduated.
4 She's still trying to decide what to do with her life.
5 I'm afraid he isn't back yet.
6 Don't worry. I've already sorted everything out.
7 She's just handed the work to me this second. I'll put it in the post now.
8 He's already made $1 million, and he's only 26!

REPORTING SPEECH 2

Exercise 1

1 was in hospital
2 said he was working in an ice-cream factory
3 had had a baby
4 would tell
5 I wanted to work for them
6 my career goals were
7 if I had had any other interviews
8 if there was anything else I'd like to ask them

13 FILM AND ENTERTAINMENT

-ED/-ING ADJECTIVES

Exercise 1

1 confusing
2 excited
3 boring
4 annoyed
5 disappointing
6 amazed
7 amazing
8 bored
9 shocking
10 worried

Exercise 2

1 annoying me
2 doesn't interest me
3 really shocked me
4 worries me
5 surprised me

THE PRESENT PERFECT CONTINUOUS AND PRESENT PERFECT SIMPLE

Exercise 1

1 I've been learning Chinese since I was eight.
2 I've been going to the gym every day for the last two months / I've been to the gym every day for the last few months.
3 They've been together for quite a long time.
4 The Conservatives have been in power since the last election.
4 He's been living there since last year.
5 I've been trying to find a job for months.

14 THINGS

RELATIVE CLAUSES

Exercise 1

1 who
2 which
3 where
4 who
5 which
6 where

Exercise 2

1 Sertab Erener is a Turkish singer who won the Eurovision Song Contest in 2003.
2 Storaplan is a very trendy area where there are lots of nice shops and restaurants.
3 Sue Briggs was an English teacher who persuaded me to go to university.
4 A campsite is a place where you stay when you go camping.
5 Shostakovitch was a Russian composer who wrote some amazing pieces of music.
6 Istanbul is a city where Europe and Asia meet.
7 What do you call those machines which do your washing-up for you?
8 I need to buy one of those things which you wear round your waist and keep your money in.

MUST/MUSTN'T

Exercise 1

1 must	3 mustn't	5 must	7 must
2 must	4 must	6 mustn't	8 must

Exercise 2

1 People have to pay for throwing rubbish away.
2 You're not allowed to leave rubbish bags on the street.
3 I mustn't forget to call him.
4 You must be very excited about going away.

15 THE ECONOMY AND MONEY

TIME PHRASES AND TENSE

Exercise 1

1 over the last five years; since last year; in the last six months
2 at the moment
3 last month; three months ago; the other week; when I was
4 in two years; in three months' time

Exercise 2

1 The prime minister has lost popularity in the last year.
2 I used to spend a lot more money in the past.
3 I got a loan from the bank the other month.
4 The recession is getting worse at the moment.
5 They are going to invest more money in schools over the next five years.
6 He lost his job three years ago.

PRESENT TENSES IN FUTURE TIME CLAUSES

Exercise 1

1 before	4 After	7 As soon as
2 when	5 until	8 when
3 until	6 before	9 as soon as

Exercise 2

1 We'll obviously discuss the deal with everyone before we make a final decision.
2 correct
3 We can have something to eat when we get home.
4 After you register, you'll be able to access your account online.
5 correct
6 correct
7 Inflation will continue to rise until the government does something about it.
8 I won't believe in UFOs until I see one with my own eyes.

16 DATES AND HISTORY

PREPOSITIONS AND NOUNS / *-ING* FORMS

Exercise 1

1 After invading Kazakhstan, many of the Mongols settled in the region.
2 Before seeing the film, I knew nothing about the history of slavery.
3 By bringing the two sides together for peace talks, the king basically ended the civil war.
4 Because of rising unemployment, there's a lot of competition for jobs.
5 Despite having a good education system, health care is poor.

VERB PATTERNS

Exercise 1

1 I like watching tennis, but I prefer playing / to play it.
2 I've decided not to go to university.
3 correct
4 Would you mind going to the shop for me?
5 I don't really enjoy shopping for clothes.
6 I spent six months travelling round Africa.
7 correct
8 correct
9 correct
10 Sorry I'm late. I stopped to have lunch on the way.
11 Can you please stop making so much noise?
12 correct